MARY COLWELL

BEAK, TOOTH AND CLAW

WHY WE MUST LIVE WITH PREDATORS

WILLIAM
COLLINS

William Collins
An imprint of HarperCollins*Publishers*
1 London Bridge Street
London SE1 9GF

WilliamCollinsBooks.com

HarperCollins*Publishers*
1st Floor, Watermarque Building, Ringsend Road
Dublin 4, Ireland

First published in Great Britain by William Collins in 2021
This William Collins paperback edition published in 2022

2023 2025 2024 2022
2 4 6 8 10 9 7 5 3 1

Set in Berling LT Std
Printed and bound in the UK using 100%
renewable electricity at CPI Group (UK) Ltd

MIX
Paper from
responsible sources
FSC™ C007454

This book is produced from independently certified FSC™ paper
to ensure responsible forest management.

For more information visit: www.harpercollins.co.uk/green

MARY COLWELL is a producer and writer and author of two books, *John Muir – The Scotsman who saved America's Wild Places*, published by Lion Hudson in 2014, and *Curlew Moon*, published by William Collins in 2018. In 2017 she was awarded the BTO Dilys Breese Medal for outstanding communication in science and in 2018 she won the National Gamekeepers Association Bellamy Award for nature conservation for her work on curlews. She has organised four national conferences on curlew conservation which have brought together a wide range of people from across the conservation spectrum. She is listed in the top 50 most influential conservationists in Britain by *BBC Wildlife* magazine. She has written for the *Guardian*, *BBC Wildlife* magazine, *Country Life* and many other publications. She makes nature documentaries for BBC Radio 3 and 4, and is a public speaker on the natural world and environmental issues.

Praise for *Beak, Tooth and Claw*

'A must read for all wildlife lovers'   DOMINIC DYER

'Provocative, thought provoking and life affirming. Mary Colwell enters a world steeped in blood, much of it on our hands. A masterpiece of conservation writing'   SIR TIM SMIT of the Eden Project

'This fascinating – and balanced – book wrestles with our confused, paradoxical relationship with predators ... and argues that our relationship with them needs to be evaluated within the context of its history'   *The Field* magazine

'This book made me question what I thought that I knew about species ranging from seals to wolves'   *BTO* magazine

'There are few more fraught topics than the status of Britain's larger predators ... It takes immense courage to be a voice of calm ... and once again Mary Colwell has stepped up to the mark. There is much to learn from this book'   BBC *Wildlife* magazine

'Colwell seeks to steer those who legally cull predators towards a more thoughtful stance, while urging others to understand why predators have to be managed'   BBC *Countryfile* magazine

'An engaging, balanced and wise book on a contested subject ... A lesson both in open-mindedness and in sweet reason'
JEREMY MYNOTT, author of *Birdscapes*

'A brave book ... that seeks out a fair-minded variety of opinions ... thoroughly researched, indexed and annotated ... this honest scrutiny of our relationship with middle-sized British predators is timely, informative and necessary'   JULIET BLAXFORD

Praise for *Curlew Moon* by Mary Colwell

'Mary's walk is no small feat, and her account is beautifully written, soundly researched and inspiring in terms of what each of us can contribute to saving Curlews. There is gritty realism too. Mary does not shy away from controversy and engages so positively with the intractable issues in the English uplands, where Curlews could so easily be the casualty of grouse versus predators'
BTO Book Review

'Colwell tackles her subject sensitively, with first-hand experience and fact-finding research. She is in the possession of a rare attribute in the world of nature conservation: an open mind'   *Elementum*

For Julian, because everyone
needs a lighthouse and an albatross.

Contents

Introduction

As ravenous wolves come swooping down on lambs
or kids to snatch them away from right amidst their flock
… so the Achaeans mauled the Trojans.[1]

The term predator is usually ascribed to large meat-eaters such as birds of prey, wolves and big cats, and is derived from *praedator*, the Latin for plunderer. Predation, a verb to describe hunting and killing for food, comes from *praedari*, to rob. The word 'predator', therefore, means a thief that steals life, and predation is the act of plundering and pillaging. These harsh definitions evoke immorality and ruthlessness and appear in ancient literature to portray violent human behaviour – a dominant force attacking and consuming the

weak and vulnerable. The Roman poet Ovid describes the rape of
the mythical goddess Philomela by her brother-in-law Tereus as an
act of predation:

> The captive has no chance
> To escape, and the raptor sits eyeing his prey …
> She [Philomela] trembled like a quivering lamb, who,
> After it has been wounded and then spat out
> By a grey wolf, cannot yet believe it is safe;
> Or like a dove whose feathers are smeared
> With its own blood and who still shudders with fear
> Of those greedy talons that pierced her skin.[2]

Writing in the pre-modern era, James Tyrrell, in his 1697 *History
of England*, uses a word which has predation as its root – *depredations* – to describe an English army setting out to repel a violent
Scottish invasion: 'The Yorkshire men, being resolved to put a stop
to these depredations … raised an army of about 10,000 men.'[3] In
modern vernacular, the term predator has been appropriated to
describe someone who hunts down a victim for sex or even murder.
Throughout time we have used the natural behaviour of wild creatures by analogy to impose moral judgement, and although we
think of our twenty-first-century selves as enlightened, rational and
scientific, the ancient idea that ruthless predators attack innocent
victims still has a hold on the popular imagination.

Contradictions swirl around predators. We may fear and often
revile them, but we also admire their beauty and strength. Beguiled
by their fur or their plumage, we have stripped these from their
bodies and fashioned them into coverings for our own skins, often
to convey status, wealth and sex appeal. For thousands of years we
have folded our dreams and our flaws into predator pelts, playing

with the image of ourselves. If we don't literally inhabit their skins, we take on their image. Big cats, eagles and bears, creatures we associate with dominance and courage, commonly adorn heraldic shields and advertising billboards. Predators the world over hold our stories.

Even the way we speak and convey ideas is bound to our concept of predators. They weave through our speech as metaphor and simile, casting light onto human nature – sly as a fox, eagle-eyed, a wolf in sheep's clothing, political hawks and doves, brave as a lion ... And yet, our primal fear of predators and the damage they can cause to both our bodies and our livelihoods can provoke such intense emotions that we drive them to extinction. They are too in-your-face, too disruptive, too damaging – simply too much like us – to be tolerated. Predators large and small are the most perse-cuted creatures on earth.[4] They always have been, and still are, gods or vermin, heroes or villains. There is nothing straightforward about how we use the terms predator and predation; they are redo-lent with meaning beyond the necessity of killing to eat.

The pure biological definition is much broader and simpler – predators kill other living creatures for all or part of their diet. This applies to vast swathes of life on earth, including some plants. Sharks, peregrines and wolves are predators, but so too are minnows, blue tits and dormice. But as the complex, emotional and cultural beings that we are, we have discarded the biological definition and formed our own human-centred categorisation, which holds on to vestiges of the past associations. In the modern mind's eye, it is still a laden term for animals with an array of sharp beaks, claws, talons and teeth; weaponry that can damage us phys-ically and metaphorically.

Predators are, therefore, what we want them to be, and that is very often far beyond reality. This book focuses on British meat-eaters; the ones living alongside us now, the long-gone, extinct creatures, and the predators that may reappear in the future. It is about our relationship with them, but because of our complex perceptions, it is as much about people as it is about the animals themselves.

It may feel as though the realm of predators and predation is remote from our modern, urban lives; that these bloody activities belong out there in the wilderness and shown in wildlife documentaries, but in reality, we are all surrounded by predators every day.

As I sit and write on a bright spring day in Bristol, a blue tit pecks aphids off roses to feed its chicks, and overhead swifts swoop and swerve, snapping insects from the air, not unlike sharks feasting on shoals in the ocean. Over Somerset's fields and copses, mewing buzzards soar on thermals to hunt rabbits, small birds and insects, while crows scan the landscape from their perches, searching for nests of chicks. Along the Bristol Channel, seals pursue fish, a bounty they share not only with us but with myriad screeching seabirds that plunge into the tidal race. As evening falls, the languid song of a blackbird is a wild-wood lament for a long-gone landscape of open forest. This black-coated chorister is also a prolific killer. On one birding forum an astonished gardener writes:

Whilst digging up my very neglected garden to grow veggies I am enjoying the company of a male blackbird. He appears within minutes of me starting to dig and approaches to within a metre or so. In one ten-minute session he consumed 3 medium sized worms, 2 big ones, 5 centipedes, 1 leather jacket, 1 grub species unknown and 1 spider. He also appeared to consume 6 insects that were too small for me to see. In two more visits this afternoon he seemed to eat similar amounts.

He is not taking food away and I have not seen any sign of a female so I am assuming he has not paired up yet. I am amazed at the quantity he can put away.[5]

When night falls, moonlit woodlands will see tawny owls land on branches, as silent as ghosts; listening, waiting for the small and scuttling creatures to feed their owlets. Tiny bones and teeth will appear in pellets scattered among the leaves. This witching hour sees bats replace the swifts as aerial hunters, and in the milky shadows, hedgehogs devour worms and foxes feast on rabbits and voles. All over the country, day and night, in the city, out in the fields, under the water and in the air, there is an orgy of predation, an 'odious scene of violence and tyranny', in the words of philosopher John Stuart Mill.[6]

Yet, despite the plethora of killing, blackbirds and blue tits are considered garden delights and we assign them a different category to sparrowhawks, which hunt and kill these small birds. Perhaps it is because common garden birds eat worms and insects, creatures we don't relate to, and their act of predation doesn't involve spilling blood, that we downgrade them to something much softer and less menacing than a full-blown, meat-eating predator. They are, though, officially in that category. So too are great tits, only slightly larger than their blue cousins. These tick-tocking, busy-body birds are opportunists that are as happy feeding off a bird table as on a carcass left by large predators. They have even been recorded eating the flesh of hanged people. Ornithologist John Barnes wrote of their 'murderous tendency' and described a group of pied flycatchers, 'found dead with smashed skulls in nest-boxes taken over by great tits'.[7] Their powerful bills can crack acorns and hazelnuts as well as the skulls of hibernating bats, where they splinter the bone and then eat the brains. Author Becky Crew dubbed them 'zombie tits'.[8] Even so, they are still one of the nation's favourite birds.

It is part of the predator paradox that we consider some creatures as predators but exclude others; and even this restricted category is filled with subtle subdivisions. There are courageous predators, such as lions and bears, on whose muscular shoulders we project our ideal of strength and dignity in battle. Aerial predators like eagles and hawks speak to our yearning for mastery of the skies and freedom from the shackles that bind us to the earth. We admire the endurance and teamwork of pack hunters like wild dogs, wolves and hyenas. Most fearsome of all are the alien, cold-blooded killers in the form of sharks and crocodiles, chilling in their seeming lack of emotion.

These are apex predators at the top of the food chain. They eat large prey and have big territories; they are the 'red-in-tooth-and-claw' creatures, the ones most likely to spring to mind when the word predator is mentioned. Beneath them are the smaller and more numerous meso (middle-sized) predators, which usually have a wider diet and are often regarded as a nuisance rather than with fear. The cunning fox and the fast and furious weasel, for example, are exasperating in their ability to evade our control. There are also those predators that occupy a shifting hinterland, a permeable place, where creatures come and go depending on who is looking at them. Badgers are lovable bumblers when they eat grubs, but we are thrown into cognitive dissonance when they overturn a hedgehog and devour the soft underbelly. Hedgehogs themselves are cute when curled in a ball, but they also devour the helpless nestlings of ground-nesting birds. These are the confusing creatures, the ones that challenge our concept of 'adorable' and sit uneasily alongside wolves and eagles. The hunters we place on the outside of the bloodied 'predator' box are creatures such as songbirds, waders and small mammals because they target prey that we dislike or have no relationship with. We cannot understand our reaction to hunters without acknowledging our attitude to the hunted.

We know this scenario. A wildlife documentary shows a lioness crouched in long grass. She is hungry and locked-on to a young antelope that has strayed from its mother. It walks with delicate poise through shimmering heat. The lioness inches forwards. Time slows down and the moments stretch. The calf is naive and unaware of its imminent, violent death, and we will it to flee. Then, without warning, a burst of energy, confusion and the sound of fear sees the calf die with its throat in the grip of canines that are ten times longer than our own. It is helpless in the face of such overpowering aggression. As life ebbs from its body we are flooded with complex emotions. Most of us will never have direct contact with antelope in the wild, yet there is an understanding of the terror and pain that is woven through this narrative; we have entered the drama.

The word empathy combines the Greek word for feeling, *patheia*, with the prefix *en*, giving a sense of within. *Enpatheia*: literally, to be in-feeling with something or someone, to be inside what they are experiencing. The word empathy only appeared in common usage in the early twentieth century, but it gives additional depth to the term sympathy, which is a more surface recognition of suffering. Sympathy acknowledges distress, empathy shares it. Empathy is not abstract or conceptual, it is focused on an individual; we place ourselves in the position of the one who is suffering and imagine their pain. Empathy for prey is the other side of the fear of predation, and it is deeply human.

As humanity evolved as hunter gatherers, first in Africa and then across the world, it was safer to live in small groups with strong social bonds. The ever-present threat of attack from other tribes or dangerous wildlife required social cohesion cemented by caring and sharing. Empathy emerged out of this sociability, the ability to connect deeply with another's feelings. It is highly developed in human beings, but it is also found in varying degrees in primates, elephants, cetaceans and rodents. Without empathy we too easily disregard suffering, causing relationships and communities to fall apart.

The Dutch primatologist Frans de Waal believes empathy is so important he places it at the heart of mammalian societies:

> This capacity likely evolved because it served our ancestors' survival in two ways. First, like every mammal, we need to be sensitive to the needs of our offspring. Second, our species depends on cooperation, which means that we do better if we are surrounded by healthy, capable group mates. Taking care of them is just a matter of enlightened self-interest.[9]

To reach across a boundary and vicariously feel another's anguish, which then translates into a desire to help, is a powerful driver. Humanity can do it so well that it can spill outside the human sphere and be extended to other species; especially if those species are appealing. A mother bear protecting her young from an aggressive male, a deer being run down by wolves, baby turtles being picked off by gulls; these are the kinds of situations found in nature that stimulate our empathetic brains. We, too, feel overwhelmingly protective of our children, battle against the odds, understand the feeling of being chased. The struggles in nature reflect the struggles in our own lives. Natural history documentaries play on it and Disney films make their millions by manipulating our feelings of empathy towards other species. But it only works if we see the predator as a danger to ourselves and if we can relate to the plight of the prey.

When a song thrush eats a snail, there are no tears for the alien-looking mollusc that would otherwise ruin our garden plants. The act of predation itself involves no obvious pain; there is no heart-racing hunt or agonising death, and it certainly helps that the thrush has a heavenly song. This act of predation seems scarcely worthy of the description. However, if a sparrowhawk swoops into the garden and grasps the thrush in its dagger-like talons, we can feel hostility towards the hawk and a desire to help the songbird.

In personal correspondence Frans de Waal wrote, 'we consider predators those animals which eat animals we care about. Krill doesn't interest us, so a humpback whale is no predator, but an orca is, because it may eat the whale.'

We humans, then, are contrary creatures. We have evolved in a dangerous world, assailed by both actual and imagined pain. Our coping mechanisms leave us scanning the skies and peering across the horizon searching for danger. We are spooked by a slight shift in the shadows; a noise in the night, a looming shape in the mist, and we turn to each other for safety. We are empathetic, we feel for our family, friends and neighbours, as well as for the wider world. Yet, we are predators too, capable of callous killing and appropriation, especially of creatures that are deemed a threat.

Britain once had an impressive array of apex meat-eaters, but we had removed native bears and lynx by early medieval times, and wolves by the end of the sixteenth century. We had virtually exterminated birds of prey and wildcats by the time Queen Victoria had left the throne. There are many mesopredators that still live alongside us, and they continue to test the limits of our tolerance. This is where the potent battles in conservation are to be found today, in the unstable interface between people and the foxes, corvids, seals, badgers and raptors of Britain. They raise vital questions, not only for conservationists but for society as a whole. Should we control predator numbers? If not, what are the consequences? If so, how many should we kill and over what area and timescale? Who does the controlling and who pays for it? Whose opinions matter? The answers to these questions are varied and complex, and they depend as much on social factors as they do on conservation science. Logic may dictate one course of action, but there is so much more to our decision-making than what makes sense in an equation.

Woven throughout human history are dreams and aspirations, heritage and respect for ancestral toil. Different communities imprint their mark on landscapes and those communities build strong bonds and establish cultures that deepen over time. They become part of a place and its landscape. It is impossible to look at Britain, be that countryside, village or city, and not to see the mark of generations of people and their relationships in the warp and weft of the tapestry. When face to face with a fox predating lambs or a hen harrier taking grouse chicks, our reponse may not lie in a simple assessment of a problem and its rational solution, but in the realm of fuzzy logic. This concept was invented by Berkeley mathematician, Lofti Zadeh. In summary it states that when the number of elements to be considered increases, definitive statements lose meaning and precision, and the harder it becomes to provide simple solutions. Most predator–prey issues can't be reduced to A + B = C; they are much more complex than that.

David Macdonald, professor of zoology and conservation at the University of Oxford, is firmly of the belief that today, conservation sits alongside social science, politics and, increasingly, ethics, when it comes to finding solutions to the problems of predators in a human-dominated world. In the twenty-first century we have reached a place where a more holistic view of the natural world and our role within it has to be considered. In an interview I did with him for this book, he said:

'We are no longer in the era where "the only good one is a dead one", you can't get away with that, or indeed "the only good one is a live one", you can't get away with that either. As the complexity of the problems has become clearer, and the gridlock between positions based on natural science and social science has become clearer, and the fact that there is no right answer and no silver bullet to any of these issues, I think people find themselves having to acknowledge that different views of the landscape lead people to have different conclusions. Accepting that is the case, then we have to take a philosophical position on what is the right thing to do – what should we do.'

This view was echoed in a Scottish report on predation, 'Understanding Predation', published in 2017, by a partnership of organisations – the British Trust for Ornithology, University of Aberdeen, Centre for Ecology and Hydrology and the University of Stirling. Focusing mainly on birds, but with findings applicable more widely, it states:

Predation is a natural process. Yet it often causes controversy and divides opinion, with the scientific understanding of different predator–prey interactions not being recognised by those who work on the land, whose local understanding derives from what they see on a daily basis, and vice versa. To identify better solutions to longstanding problems, it is clear that we must first bring together the differing views about predation. A polarised and adversarial approach to our understanding of predation only serves to perpetuate the problems.[10]

Predation is a philosophical issue. It involves not just a practical assessment of the act itself and its consequences, but demands ethical and moral judgement. Predation is so powerful a concept that it goes to the heart of who we think we are and how we believe we should relate to each other and the natural world. It even infiltrates religion. In the West, where Christianity has held sway over cultures and ideas for 2,000 years, predators and the act of predation have played a defining role in Christian concepts of good and evil. Wolves, snakes, foxes, scorpions and lions sit alongside lambs, deer and doves as essential symbols for the presence of evil and good in the world, their traits projected onto human behaviour. But the fact that predation exists at all, the necessity of killing to eat, has proved challenging to theologians. Christianity has struggled with the biological necessity for killing to survive on a planet that has been brought into being by a good and loving god. Jefferson McMahan, professor of philosophy at Oxford University, believes that our understanding of predation has fundamentally challenged how we view the forces behind the universe; questions he explores in his essay 'The Moral Problem of Predation':

> Virtually everywhere that there is animal life, predators are stalking, chasing, capturing, killing, and devouring their prey. The means of killing are various: dismemberment, asphyxiation, disembowelment, poison, and so on ... The unceasing, incalculable suffering of animals caused by predation is also an important though largely neglected element in the traditional theological 'problem of evil' – that is, the problem of reconciling the idea that there is a benevolent, omnipotent deity with the existence of suffering and other evils.[11]

Writer and Christian theologian Nick Mayhew-Smith also pondered this dichotomy. In his book, *The Naked Hermit*,[12] he explores how the founding fathers of Christianity, saints Augustine, Basil and Bede, came to terms with the existence of predation. St Augustine, writing in the fourth century CE, thought it served a useful purpose by reminding people of the terrible disharmony introduced into the world through original sin, when Adam and Eve fell from grace in the Garden of Eden. Pain and bloodshed are consequences of the havoc we have wrought upon the earth and we should view it with humility. On the other hand, St Basil, also writing in the fourth century, and St Bede in the seventh took a more positive view, focusing on the contentedness and lack of aggression in the world before the Fall, when the whole of creation was friendly and vegetarian, a state to which we will return in the fullness of time. According to this doctrine, Mayhew-Smith tells us:

> … there was such harmony in the cosmos that even lions and wolves did not hunt for prey but were originally vegetarians, something implied in Genesis 1:30. 'Nor did the wolf search out and ambush around the sheepfold … but all things in harmony fed upon the green plants and fruits of the trees,' writes Bede in his commentary on this happy state of affairs.[13]

The desire for a world without killing is reflected in the writings of the prophet Isaiah, who lived through tumultuous times in Jerusalem in the eighth century BCE. His prophecies express a yearning for a non-violent, vegetarian state of holiness, where the world is without any form of violent death for people or animals; a return to the tranquillity of the Garden of Eden.

The wolf also shall dwell with the lamb, and the leopard shall
lie down with the kid; and the calf and the young lion and the
fatling together; and the little child shall lead them. And the
cow and the bear shall feed; their young ones shall lie down
together; and the lion shall eat straw like the ox.[14]

For Christianity, the necessity of killing to eat has become a sign of
humanity's sinfulness, and the absence of predation is a pure,
God-like state. Surely, then, argues McMahan, this is something we
should strive for. His essay takes the idea to its logical conclusion.
If it is morally good to reduce pain and suffering on earth, then it
follows that a vegan world for both people and animals is not only
desirable but something we should actively promote. In this pain-
less existence, predators and predation are eliminated; there is no
more agony inflicted on suffering prey. He uses the example of the
Siberian tiger, a big cat that is on the verge of extinction. If we
allow it to die out, he argues, then the pain it would have caused
to its future prey is also removed from the world. Allowing the
extinction of predators could be seen as an act of goodness by
removing the burden of future pain from the planet. Furthermore,
he suggests, biological engineering could also be explored to
remove an animal's desire to kill, by manipulating its genes. The
only logical conclusion to desiring a world without killing is to
remove the act of predation from the workings of ecosystems:

Ecological science, like other sciences, is not stagnant. What
may now seem forever impossible may yield to the advance of
science in a surprisingly short time ... we will almost certainly
be able eventually to eliminate predation while preserving the
stability and harmony of ecosystems. It will eventually become
possible to gradually convert ecosystems that are now

stabilized by predation into ones resembling those island ecosystems, some quite large, that flourished for many millennia without any animals with a developed capacity for consciousness being preyed upon by others. We should therefore begin to think now about whether we ought to exercise the ability to intervene against predation in an effective and discriminating way once we have developed it. If we conclude that we should, that may give us reason now to try to hasten our acquisition of that ability.[15]

McMahan is not ecologically naive; he is aware that large numbers of herbivores, unchecked by predation, can degrade a habitat so much they will die from starvation, which is also not a desirable situation. He therefore argues that allowing predators to disappear must only be considered where that scenario could be avoided, as in the case of the Siberian tiger, where its numbers are now so low through human persecution that its total disappearance will have negligible effect.

It is an intriguing but disturbing vision of a soft-play planet, where pain and fear are eliminated. From a western Christian perspective, it will be a return to a holy state, a world without killing, where we will no longer have treacherous wolves, untrustworthy foxes, evil snakes and malevolent scorpions, those creatures that have traditionally borne the weight of our dubious behaviour; we will, though, still have a profusion of gentle lambs, pure doves and swift deer to help us express what we believe is good and pure about humanity. But a beige earth that lacks the potency of predation would surely lose an essential essence of what it is to be human and extinguish the sparks of our creativity.

A Lion Attacking a Horse, by the eighteenth-century artist George Stubbs, shows a white horse being predated by a dark lion.

The lion is already on the horse's back, tearing into its flesh. The horse's ears are flattened against its head and it twists around to stare at its killer, eyes wide and bulging. This overly dramatic style from the Sublime school of art strips back the veneer of sophistication to reveal our inner, primitive passions. The lion symbolises primeval ferocity, the white horse represents the finer qualities of purity and nobility. Sublimists believed that the feeling of dread experienced by contemplating paintings such as this is an acknowledgement of our atavistic appetites. Within all of us, our good natures can be overwhelmed and consumed by far baser desires. Predation and its connection to our inner nature fascinated Stubbs and he made at least twenty versions of lions attacking horses in different media, all of them designed to evoke 'pleasurable terror', the feelings that emerge as we face the reality of who we really are.

In the lighter world of children's literature and illustration, predators can be topsy-turvy, out of kilter and delightfully unpredictable. A tiger creates havoc in the home of a little girl in a delicious tale of reaching out to the wild in *The Tiger Who Came to Tea* by Judith Kerr. A kind-hearted black panther leads a young boy to safety and later into adulthood in the fantastical *Jungle Book*, by Rudyard Kipling. Honey-pot philosophy sees Pooh Bear walking hand in hand with Piglet (an image that could be used to illustrate Isaiah's vision of holiness) as they muse on the meaning of life and friendship in *Winnie the Pooh*, by A.A. Milne. For young children, predators and prey are not bound by biology but can enchant a magical world where the ferocious becomes fun and friendly. Children's literature allows us to play with danger. What we read to our children is a window onto what is truly important to us, and by that measure the metaphors provided by lions, tigers, foxes, panthers and bears are irreplaceable. From ice-age cave paintings to fine art, from fashion design to computer games, predators hold a key place in our powerful, inner stories.

'There is no reality without interpretation; just as there is no innocent eye, there is no innocent ear',[16] observed the art historian, Ernst Gombrich. No one sees the world dispassionately; not one of us looks at a blank canvas. Differing perceptions accumulate around us through the ages and throughout our lives. Landscapes and wildlife are infused with the hopes and dreams, the histories and cultures of people. As the years roll by, each generation adds another layer that is built on the past but refashioned by the present. This is true for garden birds and wildflowers, and is particularly so for meat-eaters. Foxes, crows, ravens, seals, badgers, birds of prey, wolves, lynx and wildcats, the cast of creatures in this book, are especially heavily burdened with perceptions, with important consequences. Predators have always lived or died depending on whichever human attitudes hold sway.

In 2016, I walked across Ireland, Wales and England to discover more about the plight of Britain's largest wading bird, the curlew. Along the way I discovered the range of attitudes toward predators and the deep conflicts that surround them. This book is a result of thinking about those issues and a desire to go deeper into the role of predators in Britain today. I hope my personal experiences of meeting the creatures themselves and exploring their histories will help shed some light on these conflicts, but nowhere did I find easy or obvious answers. This book is not a field guide to British predators, nor is it a biological text on the form and behaviour of different species. Rather, it is an attempt to give an overview of our varying attitudes and to find the true nature of the animals, and the humanity, in the midst of difficult situations.

'A story has no beginning or end: arbitrarily one chooses that moment of experience from which to look back or from which to look ahead.'[17] These shrewd words from Graham Greene are a reminder that it is easy to be so locked in the moment that we can forget that our particular time on earth is simply a segment of a long and ongoing saga. The human story of living with predators is already aeons old, and it is soaked in blood and passion. You and I are in the process of writing the next chapter. I hope it will be written with compassion and wisdom.

Setting the Scene

May 2000, Babati, northern Tanzania

It is a warm, dry night and we are filming traditional honey gatherers preparing to search for wild bees for a BBC documentary. During the day we had hauled generators into a clearing in scrubby forest to light a set of a few logs placed around an open fire, which now spits and crackles. It is not far off midnight. Within the circle of dancing flames and glaring lamps the atmosphere is intense and upbeat. The throb of the generators is an underscore to the chatter of local women who are tending large pots of steaming stew; we will be here for hours. The stars of the scene, the honey-hunters, are crouched on the logs and deep in discussion; the crew are busy with equipment. I curse myself; I need some notes I had made earlier in the day but they are in a jeep parked a hundred metres down a rough track. Without telling anyone, I take a torch and go to get them. Within seconds it is dark. The comforting arena of light is confined to the set and the moonlight is subdued by cloud. The hubbub quickly fades. I am alone, virtually sightless and breathing fast.

The African night is unsettling for a city-dwelling westerner and panic rises at any sound. The heat pulsates with the rasp of cicadas and the darkness beyond the trees is impenetrable. I feel vulnerable and wish someone had come with me. Even though there is no visible enemy, I am on alert, but the rough ground makes it dangerous to hurry. I don't know if it's my imagination, but I feel I am being watched. At the car I grab the notebook, slam the door and swing the torch round to find the track. The beam stops dead just metres away at two eyes. They are at waist height and glint in the torchlight, holding a steady gaze. Something deep and primordial wants me to run but fear keeps me rooted to the ground. For what seems like an age the world is motionless. Then, silently, the spotted hyena turns and pads away. I watch its drooping head and sloping back disappear into the bush.

Years have passed since that encounter, but my memory of it is clear and the anxiety lingers whenever I recall that night. Large carnivores inhabit our psyche, ghost-like and prowling. Our survival instincts were honed in sub-Saharan Africa, on that uncompromising continent of opportunity and danger. Ancestral fears of being vulnerable and preyed upon still swarm in the pit of the stomach.

The jaws of hyenas are terrifying bone crushers, ten times more powerful than our own, and our thin hide covering a puny structure makes us easy meat. Hyena attacks on humans are very rare, but that is cold comfort when face to face with one in the loneliness of the night. Bones of ancient humans from half a million years ago in Morocco show signs of hyena gnawing, and in a cave in France the teeth of a Neanderthal child have been found in an ancient den, their surface smoothed by the acid in the predator's stomach. Wariness, though, is deservedly mutual. Many archaeological sites reveal butchering areas where the scored and scratched bones of hyenas were de-fleshed using flint knives. We killed them, and they ate us; in a way it was a raw and honest natural contract.

Super-sized and twice as heavy as those in Africa today, hyenas were part of the wondrous, outsized fauna that roamed European landscapes for much of the Pleistocene, otherwise known as the Ice Age. For the past two and a half million years the wobbling of the earth on its axis has caused intermittent periods of cold and warm; heat and ice have toyed with each other in a climatic tug of war, with warmth winning for the present. Beating to this rhythm, tracking the air temperature, life came and went in great swathes of migrations. Alongside the hyenas, predators such as scimitar-toothed cats, the size of modern lions with sharply serrated upper canines that reached down to the bottom of the lower jaw, and cave lions, the largest lions ever to have sunk their claws into flesh, preyed on an array of giant herbivores – woolly mammoths and rhinoceros, giant elk, aurochs, bison. And when we arrived in Europe, us too.

Modern humans – *Homo sapiens* – joined the shifting throngs over 40,000 years ago. We became part of the dance of the ice ages. We had lived alongside carnivores in Africa, and now we were neighbours in Britain. Archaeology has shown that we not only hunted for the same prey but also competed for the same shelter. At times we scared them away from good sites and guarded caves for ourselves, but at others we held an uneasy truce, occupying different caverns in the same system. It is hard to imagine this in Britain today, where our largest land predator is a badger.

Our modern, man-made environments have extinguished any active memories of living among dangerous wild creatures, but we still carry them in our depths. As night falls and something moves just out of sight, primal instincts stir. But then, it isn't really that long ago – a mere 30,000 years – since spotted hyenas were just one of a range of predators that lived alongside us in Britain. Recent research shows that our brains still prioritise the movement of people and animals, far more than man-made objects:[1] 'Better change detection for non-human animals than for vehicles reveals a monitoring system better tuned to ancestral than to modern priorities', as the paper concludes. Even though a fast-moving car is a greater threat to most of us than a tiger, recognising it as such is not how we have evolved. The first journey I made for this book was to try to reach back through time, to reconnect with that lost world where we battled with beasts.

On a bright winter day, I drove to the south coast of Devon, to the area known as the English Riviera, to visit Kent's Cavern, a naturally formed limestone cave high up on a valley wall. Pastel-pink houses with white fascias line the roads to Torquay; they looked pretty against the blue sky and distant sea. The small road leading to the cave comes suddenly and it is easy to miss the finger-post off a steep hill. Ancient hunters used this area as home: the cave would have commanded a good view of their prey funnelling along the valley floor – a conveyor belt of protein.

When Beatrix Potter visited Kent's Cavern in 1893, she had to walk along a muddy trail that wove its way through woodland to a wooden door flush against the rock. For a young girl with a vibrant imagination it was transformed into an enticing and magical front door to the cosy home of Mrs Tiggywinkle. Times have moved on. The track has gone, replaced by an access road and car park, and the door is enclosed by a 1930s entrance hall, café and shop.

Two centuries of excavations at Kent's Cavern have unearthed tens of thousands of animal bones buried in an accumulation of sediments that stretches back half a million years; a layer-cake of past life. In 1927, a small fragment of human upper jawbone came to light. It turned out to be at least 30,000 years old, the earliest remains of *Homo sapiens* in Britain. This tiny fragment is all that is left of a real person who lived alongside giant predators on our shores. I joined a public tour to discover more.

We gathered in an antechamber next to the Beatrix Potter door. Brightly lit cabinets displayed the skulls, teeth and bones of all kinds of ice-age life, including ancient humans. It was my first encounter with the hunters who lived here, but I found it uncomfortable that human bones were laid out in a row, clinical and cold. At some indefinable point in history human remains become an exhibit rather than an individual deemed worthy of a burial.

The guide led us through Mrs Tiggywinkle's door, locked it behind us, and we found ourselves in the first of an intricate system of caves and narrow tunnels that stretch back into the hillside. Thin shafts of light from ceiling lamps created bright pools on the floor; otherwise the darkness was deep and disorientating. The drip-dripping of water as it seeped through cracks echoed around the chamber. The air was dank and stale and infused with the acrid smell of wet rock. A disembodied voice boomed out a recorded history, telling us about the long occupation of this cave system. Eerie music and the sounds of snarling beasts added drama to the story of ancient hominins, now long extinct, who made their camps here. Both *Homo heidelbergensis* and Neanderthals left their hand axes buried in the dirt as glimpses of their practical lives, but of their thoughts and beliefs we know very little. Eventually, modern people arrived, anatomically identical to us, as evidenced by the jaw. They would have stood on this spot where we are gathered, dressed in skins and carrying spears, living or dying by their wits. We visitors were wearing fashionable coats and clutched our mobiles, otherwise there was little difference.

'We've reached the period when modern people, or *Homo sapiens*, are using the caves,' said the voice. 'Much as their forebears, they shelter here making tools, cooking and preparing for the next day's hunt. The cave is also home [the voice lowers and becomes more dramatic] to a pack of hyenas [sound of hyenas cackling]. Our small group of hunters are protected by the fire. However, thirty-one thousand years ago, a young member of the clan strays too far into the darkness [sound of loud snarls and yelping]. A small piece of human jawbone, found right next to where you are standing, gives us the evidence of this deadly combat.' We all looked around on the floor, half-expecting, half-dreading to see any other remains of death by hyena – a tiny femur or small bony hand poking up through the soil – but the floor was swept clean and worn smooth by the millions of feet that have trodden this tourist trail since 1880. Who knows whether this hapless, ice-age toddler was actually killed by hyenas or was scavenged after death, but it makes a good story in this atmospheric cave, and it gives an idea of the dangers that our ancestors faced and the forces that shaped our instincts.

In the darkness I tried to picture what it must have been like to have called this labyrinth of caves a home, to have looked out of the cave mouth to see a scimitar-toothed cat peering in, even worse a cave lion. It would have been a place where, according to Henry David Thoreau's observations of the virgin forest in America, 'there was clearly felt the presence of a force not bound to be kind to man.'[2]

Packs of wolves would once have dragged deer and horse kills to the entrance and left the chewed bones scattered over the floor, as did hyenas, but predators were not the only danger to us. No doubt many hunters were trampled by wild horses, charged by aurochs (wild cattle) and rhinos and crushed by mammoths. And sailing in the sky, looking down on the battles below, were large birds of prey – their bones too are in the cave deposits.

Eagle owls hunted birds and mammals and often nested in caves. Their soft, lonely hoots would have floated across the hard ground, a remarkably gentle sound for a bird whose wingspan is nearly two metres. Perhaps one of these was responsible for the bones found here of the ghost-like snowy owl, a feather-light killer with the demeanour of an angel. White-tailed and golden eagles, kites and rough-legged buzzards, as well as many smaller raptors, soared over the grasslands. Their remains are found with the bones of small birds, voles and lemmings. As unlikely as it seems, the English Riviera was once the site of so much flesh-ripping menagerie.

Downhill from the cave, where wetlands once merged with the sea, the harsh calls of brent and white-fronted geese, white storks, Bewick's swans, demoiselle cranes and shelduck would have filled the air. The poignant piping of many species of waders rising from the marshes added to the music of the skies. Out on the sea cliffs, vast, raucous colonies of cormorants, kittiwakes, gannets and razorbills were a seasonal bounty taken in the air or plucked from their nests. Bones of all these are found in ice-age caves. The sound of birds alone must have been overwhelming, but when mixed with the howls of wolves, the trumpeting of mammoths and the deep growls of bears, a surround-sound of fear and beauty must have suffused the daily lives of our ancestors. It is unimaginable today.

The last cavern is a transition between dripping, dark depths and the brightly lit tearoom. It is an exhibition area telling the stories of the first explorers who crawled through mud and rock to discover ever more astonishing bones. One of these was a young

Catholic priest from the west of Ireland, John MacEnery, who excavated the caves for a few years from 1825. Digging through the cave floor, he found evidence of humans, wolves, bears and mammoths in the same layer, incontrovertible proof that humans lived here in this extraordinary time. It was a flagrant challenge to the overriding theology of the first half of the nineteenth century, which dictated that humanity was a very recent and specially created addition to the earth, unconnected in any way to the mass of life that went before. We were considered to be just one step lower than the angels in the hierarchy that stretched from earthworms to God; favoured occupiers of a world made solely for our use and pleasure. It is hard for us to fathom how troubling this must have been to a young man beginning his life of holy orders. Faith and archaeology collided in MacEnery's heart. Lacking confidence in his own reasoning, he sent the bones to William Buckland, a pre-eminent theologian and palaeontologist, who outright rejected MacEnery's suggestion that people could have lived alongside now extinct creatures, and convinced him that the evidence before his eyes was an illusion. Buckland replied that he had been sent other examples, none of which stacked up as real proof, and he concluded:

Many of the caverns have been inhabited by savage tribes who, for convenience of occupation, have repeatedly disturbed portions of soil in which their predecessors may have been buried. Such disturbances will explain the occasional admixture of fragments of Human skeletons and the bones of modern quadrupeds with those of extinct species, introduced at more early periods and by natural cause.[3]

Despite the fact MacEnery had found flint knives, charcoal and animal bones beneath calcified layers that had not been disturbed, Buckland never accepted any evidence that humans coexisted with 'antediluvian' animals (those that had existed before Noah's flood). Accounts from friends reveal how MacEnery was torn between believing his own findings and being true to his faith and to the persuasion of the most eminent academic at the time. He lost heart with archaeology, turned his mind to heaven and locked away his paper, 'Cavern Researches'. He stopped visiting the cave; his ideas could find no audience in 'an apathetic and unbelieving world'.[4] Years later 'Cavern Researches' was rediscovered by accident and published in 1859, eighteen years after MacEnery's premature death at the age of forty-four. By then the progress of science and mounting evidence was beginning to rock the philosophy of Creationism to its foundations.

It was a thought-provoking end to my tour, a sad tale of head and heart in disarray when faced with the dizzying concept that humanity once lived with giant, extinct beasts in a world of ice. There has always been a complex interaction between what people want to believe, and our endeavours to understand the planet. Progress is strewn with casualties such as John MacEnery.

The caves shut away behind Mrs Tiggywinkle's door, I noticed the windows of the tea shop were adorned with cut-outs of cave-men shaking their spears at ferocious bears. Looking out onto the wooded hillside, the air still holds wisps of its ice-age past, and the spirits of these tough, sophisticated ancestors still seem to drift through the trees. If time travel were possible, I would visit them to find out about their loves and fears and listen to their songs, stories and laughter. I would learn much from their resilience in their strange, ferocious world. The local newspaper mused on their lives, too. 'Torquay has seen some fun times, but perhaps it's never been quite so wild as it was in the days when the locals used to chase mammoths down what is now the high street.'[5] But not everything in that long-gone world would have been unfamiliar.

When the large cats, hyenas and wolves had eaten their fill, and we humans had finished processing and cooking our own kills, the smell of the leftover blood and fat would have attracted those animals that receive far less attention in ice-age guidebooks, but whose bones are nonetheless buried alongside the charismatic giants. Keeping in the background, smaller hunters and scavengers like red foxes and badgers kept a safe distance, closely observing and judging behaviour, looking for signs that it was safe to move in and take the leftovers. They slipped in and out of the shadows, feasting on the spoils. Sometimes they miscalculated and we were waiting to capture them, because their bodies were useful to us too. The bones and skin of all creatures, large and small, hunter and hunted, were used by our ancestors for food, clothing, instruments and ornaments.

It would be wrong, though, to assume our hunter-gatherer relationship with wildlife was purely utilitarian. In *Why Look at Animals*, John Berger argues it is demeaning of complex societies to assume life was simply gritty survival. 'To suppose that animals first entered the human imagination as meat or leather or horn is to project a nineteenth-century attitude backwards across the millennia. Animals first entered the imagination as messengers and promises.'[6]

Deep inside cave systems in France and Spain, these messengers are painted on the walls, in creative gestures dating back some 30,000 years. Creatures we needed and feared, admired and worshipped are captured in a few deftly administered strokes in charcoal and ochre. They reveal a profound connection to lions, hyenas, deer, horses, mammoths and bison. The hint of a curve of the haunches, a contrasting coat pattern or the angle of a head to the body instantly identifies each animal. Removed from any depiction of landscape, they float on the rock walls as the sole focus for the eye, caught in the act of running, feeding or charging. There is nothing to distract the observer from their pure essence.

The artists worked in remote chambers away from natural light where they used the contours and irregularity of the walls to give added depth to the creatures' bodies. When lit by flickering torch-light, perhaps to the sounds of ceremony and incantation, the powerful beasts must have appeared to breathe the ice-age air and to move. These were cave-temples to the natural world, a meditation on the intimate relationship between people and the life around them. Small sculptures, talismans and spear-throwers have also been found, exquisitely carved in horn and bone. They include half-human half-animal figures, a hint that we believed the curtain separating us was gossamer thin, that humanity and nature were one.

The creatures on the cave walls shaped our ancestors' instincts, language, social structures, cultural life and spirituality. Both the predators that killed us and the prey we hunted dictated so much of our thought processes; but predators in particular beguiled us. Predators are, as Harvard biologist Edward Wilson says, part of who and what we are. 'We're transfixed by them, prone to weave stories and fables and chatter endlessly about them, because fascination creates preparedness, and preparedness, survival.' Even today, wild-life documentaries and magazines featuring large predators are by far the most popular. It is as though we cannot tear ourselves away from our past.

We are all still exquisitely sensitive to the shape and movement of animals,[7] to a slinking form, a combination of colours or the curve of a crouched back. We notice the distance between the eyes and extrapolate to estimate the size of the body. A flick of a tail, a slight shift on the edge of vision puts us on alert. All of these were vital signs used by ice-age hunters and they produced an immediate response. The art historian, Ernst Gombrich, wrote that it didn't matter if we overreacted, it was better to be vigilant and get it wrong than be complacent and dead.

> As our eyes scan the distant prospect, uncertainties about the size, shape, colour, and meaning of objects surely begin to matter … Sometimes in such a situation the process runs ahead and we believe we have received information that is not present. We all know that this happens particularly when our emotions are involved through anxiety or desire, which makes us keyed up, as the saying goes, for certain information and allows the slightest partial hint to trigger the relevant reaction. We will attack or run away at the slightest sensory suggestion of danger or the hoped-for prey.[8]

The difference between life and death relied on being able to detect both danger and food, often in confusing environments such as waving grass or dense trees. An in-depth knowledge of the behaviour and habits of animals was vital – we had to be alert and rely on hunches; these are what kept us alive. Layer upon layer of civilised life cannot erase deeper instincts. Our past as the hunter and the hunted rises up through the pavements of modern life, and certain triggers can immediately send us back in time to face our fears. Feature films have made their millions out of it. Predators inhabited us, and still do, despite the gloss of modernity.

We can only ever guess the reasons behind ice-age art, but the popular philosopher and author Alain de Botton once said about why he wrote books: 'Raw experience proves too overwhelming, dense, messy, confused or dark – and I have to download it.'[9] The cave paintings may be a prehistoric example of just such a downloading of life on the edge, an expression of fear, beauty and belief in a perilous world.

Kent's Cavern, and the many other ice-age caves throughout Europe, hold in their sediments and on their walls reminders that we once lived with jeopardy and we were fully alive in its presence. The outpouring of prehistoric creativity speaks to the potent connection between a thriving natural world, which includes peril, and our inner lives.

At the end of my visit to Kent's Cavern, I walked along the woodland trails that wind up through the trees that surround the caves. The trees were subdued in winter sleep, except for the introduced evergreen rhododendrons, their leaves as glossy as shiny plastic. We are so used to seeing exotic trees and plants, they barely register. From roses to magnolias to marigolds, the striking, fragrant, blousy world of gardens is now part of the wider countryside and brings new dimensions to the flora of Britain. A whole suite of non-native wildlife thrives here too. Rabbits were introduced from southern Europe, probably in the Iron Age. Black and brown rats, sheep, goats and sika deer came from Asia, grey squirrels and mink from North America. Brown hares came from northern Europe, fallow deer from Anatolia, muntjac from China and hens from India. Every year, over 40 million pheasants, originally from Asia, are released into the countryside for game shooting.[10] A recent study has estimated that today there are around 2,000 non-native species established in Britain, not to mention the 9 million domestic dogs, 11 million domestic cats and 1 million feral cats. What we think of as British natural history today is an exotic concoction from all over the world. There is nothing naturally British about a hillside of sheep, a copse containing sycamore trees, a plantation of Sitka spruce or a field of wheat with brown hares. If the world of the Palaeolithic hunter would seem alien to us, Palaeolithic hunters would be utterly bemused by the landscapes of today, a world made possible by another shift of the earth's axis: the world was warming once again.

In Britain and Europe, few of the astonishing creatures of the ice age survived into the Holocene, the present inter-glacial period that we now occupy. After the peak of the last ice advance hyenas didn't come back to Britain, and the scimitar cats, bears, woolly rhinos and cave lions also became extinct in the UK. They all fell foul of a warming climate, pressure from hunting by humans, the spread of woodland and competition from other species. Vast stretches of grassy plains and tundra upon which both predator and prey roamed were transformed into forests. Their world had come to an end, but ours was just taking off.

Over the following millennia, landscapes were taken into possession, tamed and subjugated. For the first time we believed we owned the earth. A sentence of just a few words belies a shift in the fortunes of humanity that is so enormous it is hard to grasp. The verb 'to own' shares the same root as 'to owe'. The land that we owed our lives to became owned. The warm, stable climate made a new way of life possible, one based on agriculture. We settled into domesticity, taking a coterie of animals with us. By 5000 BCE, wild sheep, goats and cows from Europe were transformed into livestock and corralled into pens, fenced off and guarded. No longer were we cohabitors with the wild creatures roaming across a shared wilderness, but managers of a limited palette of domesticated farmland conformers and based in one place. Anything that had a taste for the flesh of our beasts could not be tolerated and the wholesale slaughter of predators began.

The magic that is spun from a combination of fear and beauty faded from our lives, one species at a time. Lynx and brown bears were barely a memory by the time the last wild wolf in England probably met its end in the sixteenth century, and a hunter called Polson killed the last Scottish one in 1700. I doubt many wept over the body of this despised creature, its true nature distorted by hatred and superstition. A small grey headstone on the A9 near the village of Brora in the Highlands supposedly marks the spot where it fell. Wolf-less lands are lesser places because of their demise; there is a dull, aching void instead of completeness. But there was simply no place for wide-ranging, pack-living, untameable canine predators in farmed Britain. Nor for felines. Wildcats, Britain's only native cat, just about hang on today in remote parts of Scotland, but their genes are so mixed with those of domestic cats they are a shadow of their former hissing and spitting glory.

The slaughter in the air was no less. Red kites were driven to extinction in England and Scotland in the nineteenth century and the last white-tailed eagle was shot in 1918. Other birds of prey were reduced to tiny numbers by the early decades of the twentieth century through persecution and poisoning. And even though some species are now making a recovery, the killing is far from over.

During the last ten thousand years the assemblage of predators that we viewed with either fear or resentment, or both, was whittled away to virtually nothing, with wide-ranging consequences for these islands. The large top-of-the-chain apex predators were gone, leaving room for the smaller mesopredators to expand. In a process known as 'mesopredator release', the removal of the aggressive larger territorial predators allowed smaller predators to proliferate and assert a greater influence across the land. Taking advantage of the now empty territories and denning sites, their numbers began to vastly increase. Large predators eat large prey, but mesopredators often have a more varied diet, taking advantage of small birds, small mammals, reptiles and amphibians, and often supplementing their diet with carrion and vegetation. In many places, the burgeoning numbers of these smaller meat-eaters have driven some endangered species to extinction. Throughout the world, whole ecosystems have undergone tectonic shifts in response to the removal of larger carnivores.

The removal of apex predators changes their prey, too. While 'the landscape of fear' sounds like the title of a horror film, it is a phrase that has been used to describe an ecological concept, a scientific way of visualising how danger is spread around the land in response to the presence of large carnivores: 'The landscape of fear represents relative levels of predation risk as peaks and valleys that reflect the level of fear of predation a prey experiences in different parts of its area of use.'[11] A deer, therefore, will experience a peak of fear in an area with wolves and change its behaviour accordingly, becoming more vigilant. It is fearful not only in the presence of a wolf but also in the anticipation of being attacked, constantly impelled to move to less dangerous terrain. This in turn reduces the browsing and grazing pressure on vegetation in any one place – giving it breathing space to grow. Grass may flourish and trees are less damaged – ecosystems can regenerate if herbivores are kept to a manageable number. No such recovery is feasible if they are not.

There are consequences for landscapes when large predators are removed. The heart of the great American hunter-turned-environmentalist, Aldo Leopold, was changed forever by shooting a wolf in the early twentieth century. He and a band of fellow hunters spotted a female returning to her pups hidden in bushes as he sat on a mountainside. The pups greeted her in a writhing mass of fur and yelping. The hunters moved in and fired into the pack, firm in their conviction that fewer wolves meant more deer for their sport. The female went down and one pup with a wounded leg dragged itself into a pile of boulders. Leopold ran to his prize, but instead of experiencing triumph he saw 'a fierce green fire dying in her eyes', and he knew his act had been one of desecration. Ignorant and trigger-happy, he had not only blasted holes into this wolf's body, but he was also tearing to shreds the age-old workings of the landscape. As wolves were violently taken from their ranges a chain of unintended consequences was set in motion, which wrought their own devastation. Following his epiphany, Leopold wrote:

> Since then I have lived to see state after state extirpate its wolves. I have watched the face of many a newly wolfless mountain, and seen the south-facing slopes wrinkle with a maze of new deer trails. I have seen every edible bush and seedling browsed, first to anaemic desuetude, and then to death. I have seen every edible tree defoliated to the height of a saddlehorn ... In the end the starved bones of the hoped-for deer herd, dead of its own too-much, bleach with the bones of the dead sage, or molder under the high-lined junipers ... (the hunter has) not learned to think like a mountain. Hence, we have dustbowls and rivers washing the future into the sea.[12]

When wolves were reintroduced into Yellowstone National Park in the United States in 1995, elk more than doubled the length of time they spent looking out for wolf packs and the vegetation structure of the park shifted in response. Much of the former vegetation of the National Park and the habitat it sustained was restored, simply by putting back the wolves. This isn't always the case, though. As part of the predator paradox (which will be explored further in Chapter 8), returning large predators does not necessarily ensure the re-emergence of what was there before. In some cases, too much has happened in the intervening time between predator removal and return, and the landscape changes go beyond what can easily be restored.

When we remove an apex predator, we do much more than simply take a block off the top of the tower, we remove a supporting structure that keeps the whole edifice standing strong.

This fundamental transformation of the flora and fauna of Britain since the end of the last ice age, combined with the establishment of farming, has changed everything. In the twenty-first century we are, for the most part, sedentary consumers living off the proceeds of intensive agriculture and industry. The whole country is compartmentalised, regularised and managed for specific uses. The old hierarchy of predators has been top-sliced and eliminated. This has allowed smaller predators to proliferate, those adaptable species that fit into this human-dominated landscape. Professor Ian Newton, a renowned ornithologist, writes:

> The thing that has changed during our lives is the huge
> increase in foxes, badgers, buzzards and crows. This could be
> partly attributed to reduced game-keeper numbers compared
> with pre-war times, but it is, I think, chiefly a consequence of
> massively increased food-supplies for predators over the past
> 50 years, mainly in the form of pheasants dead and alive, and
> human food waste. The latter enables foxes and crows to thrive
> in abundance not only in the countryside, but also in towns and
> cities, from which they can disperse into the countryside.[13]

Our relationship with these middle-sized and small meat-eaters that are still living alongside us is not an easy one. The eternal tension between people and wildlife continues. It is against this backdrop that this book is set.

It is impossible to view predators today without some acknowledgement of our complex history together. The following chapters discuss UK animals only, and I use the common perception of predators, namely those creatures that can damage us or threaten what we want to protect. It is an arbitrary collection from a biological point of view (see more in Chapter 9), but fox, badger, birds of prey, seals, corvids, wildcats, lynx and wolves are the chosen few, mainly because of our intense relationship with them. I have not included adders, our only dangerous snake (of which there are very few left), or other, less emotive predators such as small birds, amphibians and insects. I do, however, consider what it might be like if lynx, wildcats and maybe even wolves return, animals currently under so much threat worldwide but that could conceivably, within the next fifty years, make a comeback.

*

I left Kent's Cavern with its tangle of dreams and imaginings and drove back to Bristol as winter darkness bled colour from the countryside and orange street lights spangled wet streets. Sprawled at the side of an A-road was the body of a red fox. I was acutely aware that I was at the wheel of the biggest and most indiscriminate killer of wildlife that has ever existed. It was dark when I parked near to my home in the centre of the city, just as a lithe and richly coloured young fox squeezed onto the pavement from under a gate, just a few metres ahead. Aware of me, it stood stock-still. Foxes are common in this metropolis of over half a million people, but even though I see them most days their beauty never fails to take my breath away. The street lights glinted off its coat; it looked knowing and assured. The smooth softness of its body was incongruous in the midst of straight-lined buildings and tarmac. This surely is an animal of the organic confusion of a woodland floor, not the world of hard edges and cold, damp concrete, yet it thrives among the gardens and back streets, the parks and the railway cuttings of a bustling British city. A siren wailed nearby but the fox was unconcerned; it was doing what it has always done throughout time, it was reading the situation, assessing the danger, and was poised and ready to act. A young man had also stopped and was standing next to me, taking photos with his phone. The fox was just a few strides away. We were the only two people on the street, connected by a moment of wildness and captivated by the beauty of this most successful of the ice-age survivors. Our breath and that of the fox hung in the winter air; then it turned and slipped into the shadows. 'Did that just happen?' said the man with a grin, before he too disappeared down a side street.

That small but life-enhancing encounter sat in stark contrast to my next trip, just a few weeks later, when I travelled to the rough farmland of northern England. Again, it was late, cold and dark and I was in the back of a pick-up truck staring across a field waiting for a fox. That night, though, the man standing next to me had a gun.

2

Fox

January 2019, northern England

The shooting of a fox – it seemed like something I should experience as research for this book, but now I am not so sure. We are
parked in a farmyard with a line of sight across a field to where
bait has been set – the putrefying guts of a deer. It is a cold and
dark January night with little starlight and a bitter wind. Trail
cameras have captured footage of a fox coming regularly to this
spot between 7 and 10 p.m., so now we wait. The back of the
truck is a viewing platform, the roof of the cab is a gun rest. I have
been given a hand-held spotting scope that detects heat from a
body, my keeper companion has a night-vision scope on his rifle.
Between us we can detect any living thing moving within a ninety-
metre radius.

The scope-view of the field is a blurred, surreal world of half shapes and imagined figures. The leafless trees are greyed-out and grainy, living but cold. Dotted among their bare-as-bone branches are red blobs, the heat signatures of numerous roosting birds glowing in the dark. The small ones make a Christmas-tree chain of lights through the woodland; just one is large, the scarlet smudge of a buzzard.

Scanning the field, part of me wills the fox not to appear. Even though I know the science and can recite the shocking facts about the decline of ground-nesting birds and the increase in the numbers of predators that eat them, I still don't want a fox to die. Conflicted doesn't come close to describing how I feel. Foxes are controlled here to protect lapwing, snipe and curlew, but this hard-edged, bloodied side of conservation is rarely discussed in public. It isn't the fault of the fox, it isn't a weakness of the highly vulnerable birds, it is just the way it is in Britain today. If a fox trots into this field tonight, it will be shot.

The sight of the gun is unsettling. I had never held one before one was handed to me earlier in the day, and I was taken aback by how heavy it was, and by the reality of its potential to kill. We had driven into a field with a grassy bank at the far end where a paper target had been placed ready for my first ever target practice. I settled the gun on a sandbag on the roof of the truck, aimed at the bullseye 50 metres away, and pulled the trigger. The shocking ricochet, the unnatural explosion of sound – they jolt the body and every sense; physical reminders of how violent it is to kill by shooting. So much energy concentrated into one bullet does horrific damage to soft-bodied mammals. What a terrible price to pay to protect some birds from extinction. We retrieved the target, which now had a hole to one side of the bullseye. If this had been a real fox, it would have been injured rather than killed outright, and it distressed me to think it would have crawled away to die in pain. My nerves were jangled. I folded the paper and put it in my pocket as the sun began its descent behind the hills. It was time to get ready for the real thing.

The European red fox *Vulpes vulpes* is found from the Arctic to India, Russia to North America. These animals can live alongside people or inhabit wildernesses, and virtually anything is food to them – carrion, live prey, human food waste, fish, fruit and game. They have survived the worst that the world can throw at them through the ages – dramatic shifts in climate, widespread changes to habitat and prey, the rise and rise of human persecution – yet they have come through to be skilled operators in modern, man-made landscapes. To see a fox is to behold one of the greatest all-rounders and survivors on the planet.

> The fox endures our chattering.
> Like the blathering of songbirds,
> our constant noise
> must menace him.
> So many roads and planes
> and poems
> where there was grass and wind.
> Nevermind.
> He thinks only of the wind change,
> the next hot meal,
> the vixen living near the river.
> Complaints don't serve his style.[1]

We start with the fox for two reasons. The first is that they are so familiar. They are common in cities and the countryside, and they inhabit our imagination. The fox trots through literature, children's stories, television programmes, photography, folklore, songs and nursery rhymes. These soft-footed, sleek-bodied predators are quietly curious about the world. As inquisitive as crows and less shy than badgers, foxes live among us, but not with us – wild beauties hiding in plain sight. Managing to be both confiding and aloof, they tempt us to come close and then melt away, leaving only their scats and a very strong smell; the 'sudden sharp hot stink of fox', as Ted Hughes calls it.[2] Foxes confound our desire for clear definitions; they look like a dog but act more like a nocturnal, prowling cat, but they are no domestic pet. Naturalist, photographer, filmmaker and one-time farmer, Rebecca Hosking, keeps orphaned foxes at home. 'You can never have a pet fox,' she says. 'They won't be tamed, but if they trust you, in time they may allow you to be a friend.'

The second reason is that they concentrate the major issues facing predators in Britain today. They have the audacity to stick their long, wet noses into our business, take what they want and then vanish. This ability to slip into our lives and thrive in the many environments we have created puts them in the thick of it and into direct conflict with us. There is not much about the human world that doesn't affect foxes. The huge processes that define modern Britain – intensive food production, urbanisation, spreading infrastructure, rewilding, nature conservation, field sports, even spiritual beliefs – all dictate the fox's place in the world and seal its fate.

We may love, hate, despise or revere foxes, but whatever image we lay on them and however we treat them, they are still here, spreading delight or fury in their wake.

In a shop recently I noticed an assistant had a running fox tattooed down her forearm. I asked her, why choose a fox? 'Because they are so adaptable and clever, they can do anything and I love that. I see them all the time here in Bristol, but I grew up with them in Wiltshire as well. I saw one the other day in the middle of Stonehenge. It's like they have always been here. I'd love one to be my Philip Pullman dæmon, but actually I don't think I am an all-rounder like a fox. If I'm honest, I'm probably more of a stoat. Still, I like to look at one every day, and it will be here [gently touching her arm] when I'm old.'

Foxes are the size of a medium dog and a flame-furred flash of brilliance with black on its feet and on the back of its upright ears. The tip of the long, thick tail is white. The pelt is so beautiful it was fashionable in the early twentieth century for women to wrap one around their neck, much as a fox curls up on cold nights. So attracted are we to the fine bushy tail we named them after it: the word 'fox' is derived from the ancient Indo-European word for tail – *puk*. A fox presents a flowing line from nose to tail, a sinewy form that slips around the country, from the mountains to the sea.

Exquisitely sharp senses allow them to hunt day or night. Ears, eyes, noses, whiskers, even an ability to 'see' the earth's magnetic field, means not much can escape their attention. Vertical pupils (like a cat's) make the most of low light, increasing their vision into the dark hours. A wet nose picks up drifting ephemeral scents. Long, deeply embedded hairs around the snout and feet detect the tiniest vibrations. Their funnel-shaped ears swivel independently and hone in on the slightest sound – a gnawing rodent, a rustle of grass, the tiny squeaking of chicks, even the movement of particles of soil. Professor David Macdonald, Director of the Wildlife Conservation Research Unit at the University of Oxford, found that (depending on the weather and time of year) a fox can get 60 per cent of its daily calories from earthworms alone, which means unearthing 120 from the soil, usually under the cover of night:

The fox walks very slowly with frequent pauses, often followed
by a change in direction. The animal's head is held in the
normal walking position (just above the horizontal line
extending along its back), and its ears are perked forward ...
Immediately prior to capture, the fox invariably moves its ears,
apparently locating the exact position of the worm. Sometimes
this takes several [seconds] and involves side to side
movements of the head. The fox then rapidly plunges its snout
into the grass and grasps the worm between its incisor teeth.[3]

Look into the sky on a clear, cloudless night and you may glimpse
a celestial fox trotting across the heavens carrying away a goose –
the constellation Vulpecula isn't easy to spot, and is as evanescent
as the earth-bound fox. The faint pin-pricks of white light in a vast
black sky are visible one second and gone the next. Perhaps from
its lofty position in the heavens Vulpecula sees the magnetic field
enveloping the earth below, a glowing and shimmering force-field
wrapped about us. Earthly foxes detect it as a diffuse ring using
receptors in the retina. It is used for 'mousing' – jumping into the
air with an arched back to land directly on top of prey that is
hidden under snow or vegetation.

The explanation is given on the website Wildlife Online:

Imagine wearing a miner's helmet (a hard hat with a torch
attached to the front); the torch points at an angle, illuminating
a spot on the ground two metres (6ft) in front of you.
Wherever you walk, that spot of light is always two metres
ahead of you. Now, imagine that you hear something moving
in the darkness and walk towards it until it's in the beam of
your torch – you now know that the object is two metres from
you and, if you're a fox and that object is a mouse, how far you

have to jump to catch it ... foxes do the same thing; they align
this ring up with where they hear the rustling coming from
(like a target bulls-eye) and then they know how far away
dinner is.[4]

All we may see is a fox peering at the ground, but its whole body
is caught up in the moment – hearing, smelling, feeling every sign,
honing in and focusing. So much happens to the fox when it hunts,
but we, from our lofty view six feet above the ground, know nothing of this world of hidden messages. 'There is always more to a
story than a body can see from the fence line', says Barbara
Kingsolver in her novel, *Prodigal Summer*.[5] Never was a truer word
spoken about fox-watching. What you see is most definitely not all
there is.

It is difficult to get an accurate estimate for the number of
foxes in the UK; figures range from 240,000 to 430,000 depending on how they are counted and the time of year. Numbers are
thought to have doubled between the 1970s and 1990s and there
has been a five-fold increase in the numbers of urban foxes to an
estimated 150,000. They now live in every UK city. Bournemouth
has the highest density with 23 foxes per square kilometre, but
they are more thinly spread further north. The southeast of
England, with its large areas of city and suburbs as well as extensive woodlands, heathlands and grasslands has more foxes than
the north and west with their harsher landscapes of moorland
and mountains.[6]

Some data suggest there was a dramatic decline in the rural fox
population of 40 per cent from the mid-nineties, but others believe
there has been little change for decades, an indication of just how
hard it is to get a handle on their numbers. Counting is made more
difficult by the sporadic outbreaks of sarcoptic mange, a potentially

lethal and distressing skin condition spread by mites. In Bristol, an outbreak of mange saw the fox population drop by 95 per cent between 1994 and 2004.[7] Numbers also wax and wane with the abundance of favoured prey such as rabbits and voles.

Tempting as it is to think there is a divide between city and rural foxes, they are often one and the same. City fox territories spill onto the green belt and beyond, and young foxes leaving their natal territory can travel long distances in search of a new home; 320 kilometres is the record so far for a juvenile fox tagged in Bournemouth. In 2017, research carried out by the Game and Wildlife Conservation Trust in the Upper Avon Valley close to Salisbury showed eighteen individual foxes using a one-kilometre-square area of grassland near the river Avon between March and June. Some of them were residents, but others were passing through, perhaps from Salisbury itself. But they don't all make it. Accustomed to city life and many friendly humans leaving out food, city-raised foxes can be naive. A nature reserve manager in Essex told me that foxes moving out of London are easy to shoot. 'They are totally unafraid of people and often walk right up to the marksman. Sometimes they come so close he has to shoo them further away to get a good shot.'

We are thought to have one of the densest populations of foxes in Europe,[8] with over 400,000 cubs born each year between February and March, but mortality is high. Both cubs and adults die through in-fighting, accidents and disease, and a handful through predation by eagles, but the majority of fatalities are at our hands. Around 100,000 are killed on the roads; 80,000 are shot each year by gamekeepers, farmers and on nature reserves, and a further 10,000 are estimated to be killed by pest controllers. There are a lot of foxes living and dying throughout Britain, but in roughly equal numbers, so the population remains stable.

The reason why Britain has so many foxes is not well under-stood, but there is some indication it is related to the two world wars. The changes that swept through both society and agriculture in the following decades were profound. The wars needed men on the battlefield, and rural life changed beyond recognition as farm workers and gamekeepers went to fight. The impact of their absence was summarised by the magazine *Shooting Times*:

> As gamekeepers, estate workers, male heirs and the general army of people who keep estates running were killed between 1914 and 1918, the British countryside, the landowning classes and shooting concerns were changed for ever.
>
> By 1911 there were more than twice as many keepers in rural districts as policemen (15,657 versus 7,041) and, as shooting thrived, so the numbers increased until World War I and then they plummeted, to decline to today's 6,000. This is not to suggest that during the war gamekeepers were disproportionately killed as compared with any other segment of society, but rather that their deaths uniquely affected many rural communities.[9]

The thinning out of young men was devastating for individual families and for society as a whole, but it also had the effect of removing pressure on the fox population. In addition, as a response to the near-starvation of Britain during the Second World War, farming went through a radical overhaul in a drive to increase food output. Those areas that were considered impoverished, such as heathland and low-nutrient wildflower meadows, were ploughed, drained, fertilised and reseeded with fast-growing grasses and crops. The use of pesticides and herbicides has increased more than tenfold since the 1950s. Large areas of woodland were felled, and

more than half of all hedges were torn out to expand field boundaries. Much of the uplands were blanketed with densely packed
cash crops of fast-growing Sitka spruce. Many small-scale farms
were subsumed into large, intensive agri-businesses and farm workers left the countryside for the cities. Urbanisation increased and
the human population of the UK began to rise.

In just a few decades, society was transformed. The changes saw
agricultural output triple, but it came at a heavy cost. Farmland
that fringed the cities was replaced by suburbia, motorways and
industry. The blossoming, buzzing, singing hedgerows and meadows of Britain's countryside went quiet as wildlife declined. Birds
such as turtle doves, skylarks, curlews, lapwings and nightingales
found their niches flattened, drained, mowed and stripped of food.
There are 40 million fewer breeding birds in Britain today than
there were in the 1960s;[10] there are half the number of hedgehogs,
and dramatic declines in water voles, adders, dormice and many
species of butterfly.[11] The once colour-rich tapestry of rural Britain
is now much coarser and plainer, lacking vibrancy and intricacy.
There have been winners too, of course. Adaptable, resourceful
foxes saw their population rise and rise as they took advantage of
new sources of food and shelter.

In urban areas people quickly got used to foxes, and many liked
the idea that something untameable was moving through the flow-
erbed and trotting over the lawn. Fox feeding and watching was a
safe way to touch the wild. A common misconception arose that
urban foxes rely on fox dinners and our food waste and that rural
animals eat wildlife, but this is too simplistic. Even in the middle
of towns and cities, foxes hunt birds, mammals, amphibians and
insects, despite the plethora of easy meals. Stephen Harris from
Bristol University showed that so much food was available in the
form of bird food, pet food and waste from bins or compost heaps,

that foxes could choose to survive without hunting at all, but they don't.[12] One study found that in each fox territory, nearly three times the amount of food required by a single animal was being put out every week. Yet still they obey their wild instinct to hunt.

But nature is not always an easy bedfellow. In 2010, two young babies asleep in an upstairs room were bitten by a fox that had crept into the house as their parents watched television. It is thought it had become so habituated that it had no fear of houses and people. The *Guardian* reported the bemusement of fox expert, John Bryant. 'I think it is a young fox cub. They are all teenagers, they don't know anything, they have no fear. They wander into houses, steal cat food and will even sleep on the sofa.'[13] It was a strange, rare incident as a fox would normally be curious but not vicious. There have been a handful of cases reported since then, and although it is distressing and alarming to experience, it remains uncommon. By way of contrast, nearly 7,000 people a year are treated in hospital in England alone for domestic dog bites and there have been over twenty fatal dog attacks in the UK over the last ten years.[14]

Out in the countryside, food is not put out deliberately, but there is plenty of it lying around. Studies in both Wales[15] and Scotland[16] in the 1970s showed that each square kilometre of sheep country yielded around 100 to 200 kilograms of carrion per year, enough to sustain large numbers of ravens, crows and buzzards, as well as foxes and badgers. These figures may well be lower today as there are fewer sheep overall, but carrion is undoubtedly still available. In addition, more human-provided calories come in the form of the tens of millions (one estimate is 50 million)[17] of game-birds, such as pheasant and partridge, which are bred and released each year in time for winter shoots. Only around a third of those birds are killed by shooting,[18] allowing the others to escape and settle in the countryside. Somewhat gawky and slow, birds like pheasants are often run over and they are easy to catch, and this extra flux of meat comes at a time when other food is becoming scarce. A paper published in January 2021 on the impact of pheasant and red-legged partridge release states:

> We estimate that around a quarter of British bird biomass annually is contributed by Common Pheasants and Red-legged Partridges, and that at their peak in August these two species represent about half of all wild bird biomass in Britain.[19]

It could be that gamebirds are a significant factor in maintaining high numbers of foxes in the UK, although research to prove a direct link is ongoing. High densities of foxes exist in countries with no gamebird shooting, so teasing apart cause and effect is not always as straightforward as it may seem.

We all fall into the trap of making easy assumptions, and the conspicuousness and sheer number of foxes makes them an easy target. An age-old and vexed question that has pitched farmers against conservationists for generations centres on just how much damage foxes do to livestock. Do they just eat the carrion from the sheep and lambs that have succumbed to the weather, starvation or disease, or do they actually predate livestock, in particular newborn lambs? The debate over scavenging or predation is raised time and again, and it applies to eagles as well as foxes (see Chapter 6). Conservationists insist few, if any, live lambs are killed, and if they are, they are weak, ill and destined to die anyway. Farmers strongly disagree.

Every year at lambing time, newspaper headlines tell the same story. 'Foxes Feast on New Born Lambs,'[20] 'Sheep farmer shoots dead 10 foxes after losing 33 lambs,'[21] 'Welsh farmer's anguish as fox kills one lamb a day for three weeks.'[22] The *Farmers Guardian* reported:

> In 2014, a survey of 650 Welsh farmers found 75 per cent had seen an increase in the number of lambs killed by foxes since foxhunting with hounds had been banned when the Hunting Act was introduced in 2004, while 95 per cent said they had lost money as a result of fox attacks.[23]

The peak lamb-predation period is the first two weeks after birth, and it is frustrating and distressing for farmers to discover that their lambs have been killed or injured. At 2019 prices, each lost lamb could cost the farmer anything between £40 to £140 for commercial lambs, depending on their condition, to a six-figure sum for high-quality, pedigree animals. Although there are many predators that attack lambs (dogs, badgers, larger birds of prey), if remains are found in the stomach of a fox, or a half-eaten carcass of a lamb is discovered in a field where foxes are known to operate, it is understandable that the spotlight shines on the fox as the killer.

Foxes certainly scavenge lambs that have died, but killing is not easy to prove. It is estimated by DEFRA (Department of the Environment, Food and Rural Affairs)[24] that across the UK, 15 per cent of lambs are lost at birth, or shortly after, due to starvation, hypothermia, disease, congenital defects or abortion, and that less than 1 per cent are lost to predation. Professor David Macdonald reports seeing foxes run past young lambs to chase rabbits and has often watched them travel through lambing fields with no obvious intention to take one. If they do kill a lamb, he says, it is more likely to be sickly, starving or abandoned, or have a mother that is inexperienced at protecting it. He agrees that foxes will readily eat the afterbirth and a lamb's faeces, which are rich in milky fats, but disagrees that direct predation is common. 'Considering the number of foxes in most areas, if most of them killed lambs habitually the losses would be astronomical. Since they are not, I presume that most foxes rarely or never kill a lamb.' No doubt there are some problem animals that have learned to take lambs, but Macdonald believes most are either too wary of defensive ewes or simply more interested in other prey. It would seem from the scientific evidence that fewer lambs are being predated by foxes than farmers believe is the case. In 2003, a study at the University of Bristol showed that reported losses of lambs (1 lamb killed per 1,250 ewes) was far lower than the perceived threat (1 lamb per 4 ewes).[25]

In personal communication with an upland sheep farmer, who asked to remain anonymous, I get the opposite viewpoint:

Most of the year no problem at all – they never take mature sheep or lambs over two weeks old, but most lambing times we get problems. I've heard all the claims that there is no scientific evidence of foxes taking live lambs but, frankly, that makes me laugh. I've seen foxes in broad daylight several times try to take lambs under an hour or two old and have probably lost fifty lambs in the last ten years to predation of this kind. Sometimes it may be a weak lamb, but all lambs are weak when born so this is a meaningless claim. They spend a lot of time taking the afterbirth in our lambing pastures – as do crows and buzzards.

It seems that over time, they learn they can snatch a lamb. The foxes I have seen are sneaky and circle the ewe just out of reach of her head and go round and round looking for an opening until she is confused, or a lamb is left isolated, then they grab it and run off. I have seen this happen two hundred metres away from where I stood – the fox was so desperate it ignored my shouting until I was quite close. They are brilliant and cunning predators, so why wouldn't they learn how to do this?

I hear people blaming poor shepherding, but it is a harsh criticism. Most are doing their best. There are few things more irritating and soul-destroying than producing lambs you were proud of, and relieved to have found healthy – and later finding them killed. You aren't getting much rest – you're tired – broke – and at your wits' end. But I can lose several lambs in a morning to other causes – so it is just one of a list of things we deal with.[26]

This farmer estimates it would cost £250,000 to build sheds large enough to house all his flock at lambing time, which are grazed extensively out of doors. Similarly, anti-predator techniques that are employed in the Mediterranean, such as using guard dogs and mixing fox-scaring llamas in with the sheep (foxes don't like llamas), is impractical across much of upland Britain. The solution is usually the gun.

We call a man with a rifle if we get a problem fox and he will kill it at night. This usually solves the problem – which makes me suspect that it is often a single animal and perhaps a vixen feeding cubs. Because farmers no longer trust environmentalists to listen to them or respect them for what they know, they simply sort their issues out at 2 a.m. with a rifle.[27]

One solution that is often suggested to avoid shooting foxes on UK sheep farms is to offer financial compensation for each lamb lost, but, as my sheep farming contact explained, that is missing the point.

I would stress that it isn't really a financial problem, it is an emotional one. When a lamb is taken, I don't think, 'Oh I just lost £45 and I'd be happier if it was insured with some clever compensation scheme.' In brutal truth I think, 'You sneaky, murderous bastard killing that lamb, you need a bullet.' It is like someone comes round your house and hits one of your children, you feel a rage. It isn't rational really.[28]

Adult foxes will always prefer to eat a rabbit or vole than most other things, and analysis of fox stomachs shows that rodents (rats, mice, voles and squirrels) and lagomorphs (rabbits and hares) normally account for around 50 per cent of their diet. But if these are in short supply, or if there are cubs to feed, foxes will take whatever is on offer. It stands to reason that concentrations of easy-to-catch meat, be that pheasants on a game estate or lambs in a field, will always be a magnet for predators – and conflict is inevitable.

Shooting foxes, however, also raises an ethical dilemma. If a lactating fox is killed, then her cubs are condemned to die by starvation. It is a point I put to Professor Ian Newton, who has written extensively on predation in both upland and lowland landscapes. 'While some broods of foxes may starve to death because of our control efforts, if the vixen lived, many broods of rabbits and other prey might starve as a result of what she kills. Starvation of young is an almost inevitable consequence of predation on any female bird or mammal species in the breeding season, by whatever predator.' It is a harsh reality of predation. The effects of the death of one individual ripple out beyond that one incident.

Foxes give birth in March when the breeding season is also beginning for ground-nesting birds, such as most ducks, gulls and terns, redshank, lapwing, snipe and curlew. Another flush of life appears in the fields, moors and meadows of the UK, and another source of tension arises. In the daytime the non-sitting bird can raise the alarm if a predator is detected. If there are a number of nesting birds in the same area, they may mob the intruder together and drive it away. At night, the advantage swings to the fox. Its night vision is excellent and it smells, feels and listens for clues as it quarters the landscape. A rustle of vegetation, the piping of chicks, scents from blood and fluids emanating from cracked eggshells as chicks hatch – there are many signs, and a fox is equipped to read them all.

The RSPB carries out fox control on some of its reserves to protect endangered birds, but will not allow a keeper to shoot a lactating fox. In reality, marksmen say, under many circumstances it is impossible to tell males from females, and non-breeding females from those that are lactating, especially at night or when the grass is long and the lower part of the body is largely hidden. It is a conundrum that makes the decision over what time of year to shoot more difficult. If foxes are not shot when they are most actively predating birds, then it raises questions about the efficacy of shooting them outside of their breeding season.

Fox predation of ground-nesting birds is natural and bird species can withstand losses if, overall, enough young are produced across a bird's lifetime to keep the population stable. Today, for some species, this is no longer the case. Curlew, lapwing and snipe, for example, need to produce just one chick every other year to maintain a stable population, but even these low rates are not being achieved. Predation is one factor, but nests are also destroyed by agricultural practices such as rolling and harrowing of fields in preparation for planting, trampling by stock and frequent cutting of grass for silage to feed cattle – up to four times a year from late April in some areas. No bird can nest and raise young in the few weeks between cuts. Add to these issues the disturbance from farm machinery, dog walking and leisure activities in the countryside and Britain is a landscape of killing fields. Reduced in number by so many pressures, it is then easy for foxes to finish off the few birds that remain.

Over the last few decades, numbers of many species of ground-nesting birds on farmland have plummeted. In a fragile and depleted area, foxes alone can cause a local extinction. In one study in Shropshire, out of thirty curlew nests monitored by nest cameras over two years (2015 and 2016), not one chick survived to fledging.[29] Two-thirds of the eggs were taken from the nest by foxes.[30]

Foxes are just one of a wide range of predators that will eat eggs, chicks and even adult birds. Others, such as badgers, mink, stoats, weasels, otters, hedgehogs, dogs, cats, brown rats, red kites, buzzards, goshawks, sparrowhawks, marsh harriers, grey herons, gulls and corvids, all take their toll. In 2018, the RSPB pulled together the findings from eighty-one peer-reviewed papers which looked at the effect of middle-sized predators on ninety bird species across the UK. The paper showed that predators such as foxes exist in high densities in the UK today compared to other European countries, but that their effects on their prey species is not uniform:

> Despite these high and increasing densities of predators, we found little evidence that predation limits populations of pigeons, woodpeckers and passerines, whereas evidence suggests that ground-nesting seabirds, waders and gamebirds can be limited by predation.[31]

The red fox was specifically highlighted in the report as 'numerically limiting' some ground-nesting birds such as lapwings and curlews.

In areas where ground predators like foxes are controlled by either lethal or non-lethal methods, nesting success rises. Ian Newton, in his book *Farming and Birds*,[32] gives an overview of the evidence and highlights one study where lapwing productivity more than tripled when an electric fence was installed. Studies in Germany[33] and Ireland[34] show curlew hatching success was increased by up to 80 per cent after the installation of a temporary electric fence. Taking predator pressure off these vulnerable birds does have a positive effect.

Many conservation organisations that own or manage land control a wide variety of predators to protect vulnerable species. Non-lethal methods include electric fencing, scaring devices, scent deterrents, sterilisation and providing alternative food sources, but as their deployment is not always possible or effective, lethal control may be the only workable option. Figures published by the RSPB for the period 1 September 2016 to 31 August 2017 show that 414 foxes were shot on their reserves to protect ground-nesting birds. In June 2018, Martin Harper, the Director for Conservation for the RSPB, wrote a blog about lethal predator-control when the latest figures were published:

Non-lethal methods, while always our preferred way of doing things, are not always practical. Lethal vertebrate control on RSPB reserves is only considered where the following four criteria are met:

- That the seriousness of the problem has been established;
- That non-lethal measures have been assessed and found not to be practicable;
- That killing is an effective way of addressing the problem;

- That killing will not have an adverse impact on the
  conservation status of the target or other non-target species.

If we can satisfy ourselves of all these things, then we can be
sure to make the right decision.[35]

For some people, shooting one animal to conserve another is always
unacceptable at any level and under any circumstances. Persuasive
arguments about preserving endangered wildlife by reducing the
number of predators that threaten them don't cut through.
Organisations such as Hunt Saboteurs and HIT (Hunt Investigation
Team) actively intervene to stop any control for any reason. In one
such encounter in 2018, a marksman shooting foxes for the RSPB
to protect a small population of curlews in the Peak District was
surrounded by the Sheffield Hunt Sabs, who then reported the
confrontation on Facebook:

A small team of locals took to the moors again last night to
prevent foxes being killed, as part of the RSPB's fox cull.

The 'predator control' programme, which began on five
RSPB sites across the UK last week, is billed as a way of
preventing curlew population decline. Evidence shows that
actually intensive farming is almost wholly responsible for
decreasing suitable curlew habitat. The RSPB themselves admit
'... drainage of farmland and improvement of grassland ...'
among other things, are responsible for curlew decline.
However, the RSPB still resort to the quick-fix, culling option,
which also offers employment for bloodsports enthusiasts.

A tragic spectacle, the shooter was caught on his home-
made, pickup-mounted, shooting rack ready for some fox
killing. After removing the towel cover from his rifle, he

decided the presence of three local people with bright torches meant he had better head home.[36]

Passion for a cause can, at times, cloud clear thinking, and result in confusion and mixed messaging. HIT concentrates on individual animals and is determined to stop harm to the foxes that the RSPB contract shooter was hired to remove. For HIT, the ends (conserving curlews) don't justify the means (shooting a fox), because each individual animal matters. The RSPB, however, are concentrating on preserving a species. They act on scientific evidence, which indicates that some predators may have to lose out for the greater good of maintaining biodiversity. The two groups are focusing on the same activity but not from the same stance. Animal welfare and conservation can often be at odds, and conflict arises when the two become embroiled. In addition, conflating the different worlds of blood sports (killing for entertainment) and wildlife management (killing for conservation) only serves to heighten emotions and makes rational debate more difficult. Balaclavas, flashing torches and threatening behaviour are intimidating for a legal contractor working alone at night, and this element of the RSPB conservation programme was stopped at this location.

Other wildlife organisations are not as up-front as the RSPB about their predator control operations, presumably because they fear losing members who object to discovering that killing some animals is part of their conservation strategy. It is understandable. The explanation for why control is done is difficult to present when emotions run high around particular animals – as in the case above. Building back biodiversity across Britain requires us to protect species many people don't know or particularly like, at the expense of some much-loved wildlife like foxes. It is complicated and time-consuming to present a coherent and reasoned thesis, and people may vote with their feet based on their feelings rather than logic, and some undoubtedly will resign their membership. But how many withdraw from an organisation is not known. Accepting there are extreme positions on both sides, it may be that the majority of people will understand that difficult management is necessary at times, and will become more supportive when the facts are laid bare. It can be argued that keeping quiet about the realities of managing mesopredators in Britain only makes it harder to do what science says is necessary. As society's involvement in recovering Britain's wildlife is becoming ever more important, bringing these issues out into the open can only be of benefit to conservation in the long term.

As an outsider to the day-to-day management for conservation, it seems that the present system of control across the varied landscapes of the UK is haphazard. It works efficiently in some places, but is certainly open to poor practice in others. Not everyone who shoots foxes is a good marksman, and not all predator control operators are scrupulous in the application of the law and ethics. If we are to control predators, then it must be done well, compassionately and ethically. As of 2021, post-Brexit environmental legislation is debating whether or not to include predator control in new environmental land management schemes (ELMS) in an attempt to revitalise the wildlife of Britain. Predation is not the only factor; widespread loss of good habitat is just as important in wildlife decline and the two cannot be separated. There is little point in restoring good breeding and feeding habitat for birds like curlew and lapwing if predator numbers are very high, nor will simply reducing predator numbers work if the habitat is too poor for the birds to survive. Both predator control and habitat restoration are therefore being considered in the way land will be managed in the future. The practical details on how this could be done are far from established. Significant issues arise from this move and are yet to be resolved. Ethically, it is vital that only trained operators should be allowed to shoot, but who pays for their training and deployment? Skilled predator control is expensive and may soak up much of the available budget, weakening support for other areas of management. What scale of predator control should be set across the country? What methods should we use? Should control be limited to low numbers and only in a restricted area, or more intensive and widespread across the country? Some people argue that a half-hearted approach to predator control is ineffective and and will only result in animals being killed for no reason. Who decides on these parameters? Is control a short-term solution while habitat is restored, or is it a long-term activity? Any control of native predators is controversial and will undoubtedly be the source of debate, if not hostility. It will also cause some to question this use of public money, especially if not everyone takes up the predator control option. There is little point in reducing predator numbers on one farm if the one next door does not. If it is to be done, then the scale and contiguity of control have to be considered carefully. All of these issues and more are being aired and solutions sought, but it is complex and difficult territory to negotiate.

The only long-term way to reduce the high numbers of predators in the UK is to remove what sustains them (namely easily available food and places to rear their young), and, in some places, to reintroduce the apex predators that once ate them (which is discussed in Chapter 8). This is neither a quick solution nor one that is universally accepted, so in the meantime we have to address what we can do now, with urgency. The inevitable result of the past few decades of agricultural subsidies, where farmers have been paid to remove wildlife and good habitat and to intensively grow crops and livestock, has resulted in uniformity and monoculture. If we are to tip the balance back towards a country rich in wildlife there needs to be a more varied and nuanced agricultural landscape that can provide for a wide array of wildlife species. Re-establishing a mix of vegetation, wet and dry ground, hedgerows, woodland areas and flower-rich, insect-rich meadows will support diversity, including foxes, but at a more balanced level. This is a fundamental change to the way we farm Britain, and it will take time and political will to implement. At present, until this process is underway, there seems to be no alternative but to combine short-term predator control with the introduction of long-term changes to our landscapes, with the ultimate goal of making predator control unnecessary. The involvement of the public is vital. No doubt there will be knock-on effects for food prices and the look of the British countryside, but unless we are all informed, we cannot make meaningful decisions.

This path towards the wildlife enrichment of Britain requires an open and honest conversation about the true nature of conservation. People have a right to know the facts and not simply be given a comforting, green-washed picture of a Britain that, in reality, does not exist.

The post-war years have created imbalances and stresses for wildlife at the ever-narrowing margins of the farming system. Tensions are rising as the extent of biodiversity loss in the UK and around the world gains greater attention. Conservation will need to be combined with steely conviction if certain endangered species are to be prevented from disappearing from British landscapes. At present, many of the debates and arguments generate more heat than light, but we have a moral duty to find a route through this quagmire of emotive discourse and work towards a system that is fair and just for all of life, not simply for our own species or those we favour on utilitarian or aesthetic grounds.

It is, of course, understandable to find shooting foxes unacceptable, but it is hard to imagine the same coordinated action being mobilised to protect the countless millions of rats and mice that are killed each year through poisoning and trapping, often to protect nesting birds. These highly intelligent and social mammals endure painful deaths from toxins that cause their internal organs to bleed. Rats and mice, though, don't have the same appeal as foxes, and few people are concerned for their welfare. They are viewed only as disease-carrying vermin, even though they are similar to foxes on many levels. Each are intelligent mammals that exhibit a wide array of complex social interactions, form social bonds and experience pain and pleasure, yet we treat them entirely differently. Very little about our attitude to wildlife is based on science and logic. We choose to protect some species over others based purely on our emotional reaction to them.

Mauritian conservationist Carl Jones, who has been responsible for bringing several endangered species back from the brink, muses on the hierarchy of animals we create, based on what we like or value. People are 'speciesist', he believes: 'I could shoot a rabbit and it wouldn't worry me too much. I'd find it difficult to shoot a deer and impossible to shoot a gorilla or an elephant.'[37] Carl Jones carried out widespread eradication programmes of invasive species that were destroying local wildlife and met opposition from animal-welfare activists who were opposed to his projects on the grounds that it's wrong to kill one species to save another. One such critic is Isobel Hutchinson, the director of Animal Aid, who is prepared for the consequences of valuing the individual lives of all wildlife equally no matter what the outcome: 'The species we prefer to succeed may not, but we should let that happen, rather than deciding to micromanage, control and inflict suffering on species we don't like.'[38]

In a conversation with David Macdonald, I asked if he, as a great admirer and promoter of foxes, would ever see a situation where shooting them is the only option to protect endangered species. 'I don't think you would find many people in this country who respect, idolise and who are as enchanted by foxes as much as me, but if there were a place where a species of bird is likely to blink out, I would probably kill some foxes – with a very heavy heart.'[39]

Whether or not to control foxes is a potent example in Britain of the collision of different world views; all of which came to a head with the passing of legislation to ban foxhunting in 2004.

> Fourteen couple screaming for blood, and every hound of
>   them knows
> This is his right from the ages – the heart-stirring 'Yonder
>   he goes!'
> Not for the lust of killing, not for the places of pride,
> Not for the hate of the hunted we English saddle and ride,
> But because in the gift of our fathers the blood in our
>   veins that flows
> Must answer for ever and ever the challenge of 'Yonder he
>   goes!'[40]

William Henry Ogilvie (1869–1963) celebrates the ancient 'gift of our fathers' in his rousing poem celebrating the tradition of hunting foxes with horses and hounds. Foxhunting was established as a sport in the sixteenth century. Not everyone found it glorious: Oscar Wilde memorably wrote of the English country gentleman galloping after a fox as 'the unspeakable in full pursuit of the uneatable'. Few wildlife controversies were as bitter and hard fought as the banning of foxhunting. It drew to the surface the complex mix of culture, tradition, community bonding and even royal favour that was woven through every level of society. Foxes were detected by their scent and chased down by packs of dogs and riders on horseback. The fox was either caught above ground and torn apart by dogs or, if it went underground, terriers were sent into the foxholes while 'terriermen' dug their quarry out from under the surface. The fox was then thrown to the dogs or shot. Foxhunting killed as many as 30,000 foxes annually, but in 2000 the Lord Burns Report[41] found it to be ineffective as a form of fox control. The argument that it was a traditional method for keeping fox numbers low was strained by some foxhunting groups raising foxes specially to boost numbers and, in the past, importing foxes from Europe just to feed the hunt.[42] Hunting with horses and hounds was banned in Scotland in 2002 and in England and Wales from February 2005, and attempts to overturn the ban have never gained widespread public acceptance. It is still legal, however, in Northern Ireland.

Rebecca Hosking, who grew up in a hunting family, described to me the violence not just of the hunt itself, but also the unregulated culture that existed in her particular hunting group. Foxes were used as a rite of passage for the young people into adult life – and, as a farmer's daughter, she had no choice but to participate:

I was bullied and intimidated by some of the younger male hunt followers. Two young terriermen in particular made my life a misery. Sidling up to my pony, they would graphically describe with glee how they tortured both foxes and badgers to death. To this day their sadistic tales bring tears to my eyes. I began to identify with the fox. I too wanted to escape these

plaguing monsters and flee, but back then in a close-knit
farming community I wasn't allowed to just quit.

Then came the kill. As a young rider you were expected to
witness a fox being killed, and for a long while I managed to
dodge this event. But eventually my luck ran out. The memory
that forever haunts me is how petrified that poor little vixen
was, how she screamed at her death. After she was killed, the
huntsman presented me with her tail, part of the tradition back
then, but I refused to take it and landed myself in yet more
trouble.

I was desperate to leave. So, on a hunt I purposely rode my
pony hard into a turn and flew off over her neck. I wanted to
hurt myself for this to cease. Luckily the worst I inflicted was a
bashed-up shoulder and a twisted knee. Yet none of the riders
around stopped to see if I, a girl of thirteen, could safely get
back in the saddle. I knew that would disgust the most ardent
in my family and get them to agree it wasn't safe for me to
hunt. I had found my escape.

Some twelve years later, I was told of an abandoned fox cub
that had been raised astonishingly by a local cat. The cat's
owner was at a loss as what to do with the fast-growing imp so
I offered to take the youngster on. I named her Red, and that
little vixen and I became inseparable. In her time with us she
managed to charm my whole family. Her influence alone
galvanised my father into banning the hunt from entering our
land again.

Red was never a pet, more I became her human. In the years
since, I've taken in other foundling fox cubs and raised them
on. I would say I've not so much rescued those foxes as they've
rescued me. They have populated my mind with gentle
memories. Now if I think of foxes I think of those wonderful

characters, my friends, and not so much of the childhood nightmares of hunting.[43]

Rebecca's experiences are hard to hear, and no doubt extreme, but they bring to the fore the feelings many have about foxhunting – namely that it is a cruel, unregulated activity for the entitled that has no place in modern Britain. Pro-foxhunting groups present a different picture. They insist that the majority of hunts were not sadistic and that hunting with hounds allowed the maintenance of precious habitats such as hedgerows and copses to support the foxes they like to hunt, which benefits other wildlife. Agreeing with Thomas Dale in *The Fox*, written in 1906, people who support foxhunting believe that 'natural history and sport are allies'. On the cultural side, they point to the community bonding provided by foxhunting, an important contribution to rural life at a time when making a living in the countryside faced great challenges. It provided employment for saddlers, feed suppliers and kennel and stable staff, as well as a focus for social activity for the followers and hunters themselves. It is a fact that not all hunts were run and attended by the upper classes. Some had working-class roots, such as the Banwen Miners Hunt, which targeted foxes that lived around the mining valleys and slag tips of South Wales. Foxhunting, say those who would like to see it return, was a valued part of British life that has been celebrated in song, art and poetry for generations; to lose it is to dismiss a countryside activity for all that has defined us for 400 years. Ahead of the vote on whether or not to ban foxhunting, over 400,000 people took to the streets to support it remaining.[44]

The pro and anti-hunt divisions remain deep and bitter. Differing visions are born out of mismatching expectations, ethics, priorities, knowledge, culture and how we view wildlife as part of society.

Whether or not we find it acceptable to hunt or shoot foxes is never simply a matter of scientific fact. Complexity has no single story, and which one we take to be our own individual truth will depend on who we are and to which communities we owe our allegiance.

A more radical solution to reducing fox numbers is increasingly heard as the calls to rewild Britain take hold of the popular imagination. The rewilding dream is to allow nature to restore the ancient relationships that have been severed over generations of the human-centred use of the land. It is suggested that if both lynx and wolves were reintroduced (both of which kill foxes), then fox numbers could be maintained at tolerable levels without the need for any further interventions on our part. For many it is a tantalising and exciting prospect, but for others it is a vision that instils fear and a dread of wildness spinning out of control. There is a wariness of bringing back animals that seem to belong to another era when there were far fewer people and much more wilderness. This tension will increase as the momentum behind rewilding grows, but whatever benefits rewilding with large carnivores could undoubtedly bring to degraded environments, reducing fox numbers isn't necessarily one of them.

One major problem with the reintroduction of large predators into places where they once lived is that their habitats may have been transformed beyond all recognition in their absence. This is especially true of landscapes that have since become dominated by people or agriculture. The Britain of bygone times, where the lynx and wolf still roamed free, has been transformed by urbanisation, farming and the removal of woodland. Wolves will actively avoid people, and lynx are notoriously secretive forest-dwellers (see more in Chapter 8), whereas foxes thrive in our presence. As the reintroductions of the larger predators will necessarily be in areas away from centres of human populations, they may have only a limited effect on fox numbers. Some European and American studies show that wolves actually benefit foxes as they leave carcasses to be scavenged, providing a good food source, especially in the winter months. So many foxes feast on this bounty that wolf researchers will often use fox tracks to guide them to kills. Wolves will certainly kill foxes if they can catch them, but as foxes quickly learn to avoid dangerous confrontations, they can often live parallel lives in the same area.

The lynx represents a bigger problem for the fox. Both adults and juveniles see foxes as competitors and will try to eliminate them from their territories by killing them, sometimes in large numbers, even though they rarely eat the fox carcass. One study in Sweden saw the fox population reduced by 10 per cent per year after lynx reintroduction. According to the authors, the results indicate that 'red fox populations can be significantly limited by allowing lynx populations to recover'.[45] Lynx, however, are restricted to woodland, are solitary and have large territories. It is estimated that Britain has enough habitat for a maximum of 250 lynx in the more remote areas of Scotland and northern England. Lynx reintroduction will, therefore, have little effect on most farmland and urban foxes, where most of the problems occur.

In other words, both the lynx and the wolf will only be able to do so much in the amenable, food-enriched landscapes of Britain. Foxes are too abundant to be controlled by the relatively low levels of predation by larger predators. This will be even more the case as the climate warms and more foxes survive the harsher months of the year, increasing numbers beyond anything large predators can cope with. In Sweden it is estimated that the lynx population will have to increase by 80 per cent over the next thirty years to

compensate for the climate-driven fox increase.[46] At present, therefore, we are the only species effectively controlling fox numbers.

*

I began this chapter on that cold, dark, January night, accompany-
ing a predator-control operator working in an area of rough grazing
and moorland where a vulnerable population of breeding waders
is being protected. By 11.00 p.m. the winter-frosted field was still
quiet. We had seen a badger trot along the river, and something
small and fast shoot across the open grass towards a hedge; perhaps
it was a stoat. The fox, though, was nowhere to be seen. We were
both chilled and tired. My companion jumped down from the van
onto the yard that now glistened with frost, saying 'I think we
should give up.' I took a last look at the heat signature of the
buzzard in the tree and took a deep breath of freezing air.
Somewhere out there was a fox, and tonight it had dodged a bullet.
The next morning, the camera trap showed that it came to the bait
at 5 a.m. We had been out-foxed by a survivor among a vast tribe
of survivors through the ages, and deep in my heart I breathed a
sigh of relief.

3

Ravens and Crows

'Three years ago, Bran got shot – it was pretty close for me as well. This lad came to do some shooting for a local farmer on the moor. He was very inexperienced. I was flying Bran as I usually do and he was coming back to my arm. As I was going through a gate in a hedge, I heard a loud bang and a rush of air past my face. Then Bran was on the ground in front of me on his back, twitching; I thought he was dead.

  'I couldn't understand what had happened for a second, but then saw this lad about twenty-five feet away, no more than that, carrying a shotgun. I was distraught and shouted, "You've just shot my raven!" He knew nothing about birds and said, "It's just a crow, I can shoot it if I want." Luckily, he was such a rubbish shot most of the pellets went between where Bran was coming down to my arm and my head, and that's what I felt whoosh past my face, the pellets. The shock, and the four pellets that got into him had knocked him down.

'I was panic-stricken, but I heard my wife Rose shouting, "He's not dead, Lloyd, he's not dead!" She was cradling him in her arms and he was looking around, dazed. We took him to the vet. He removed two pellets, but one was too deep in his pectoral muscle and the other was lodged in his neck by his vertebrae, so he left those. A few weeks later, the lad came over and apologised. I showed him the difference between ravens and crows. I've got an old crow called Zimba who is a lovely, friendly old thing. For the first time this lad saw crows and ravens as birds with character and personality, not just something to be shot. He said he understood why I was so angry; it must be like someone shooting one of his dogs. When he realised where I'd been standing, so close to where he had fired his gun, he was really frightened. He hasn't been back since.'

So much history, prejudice, ignorance, tenderness and affection are folded into the story of the near-fatal shooting of a tame raven named Bran. It was told to me when I visited his owners, Rose and Lloyd Buck, at their home on Tickenham Moor in North Somerset, in February 2020. Rose and Lloyd specialise in training birds for TV and film, and their dedication and their deep connection to Bran and their crow, Zimba, contrasts sharply with the aggressive disregard for corvid life that runs deep in some farming and shooting communities. A contempt as strong as this has ancient roots, a belief that any black bird is fair game and should be shot dead.

There are eight species of corvid in the UK – carrion crows, rooks, ravens, jackdaws, jays, magpies, choughs and hooded crows. Crows, rooks and ravens are the most commonly seen, all of which are black, except the hooded crow, which has some grey. Jackdaws are smaller and have a black head and grey plumage around the neck, while magpies are easily recognised, with their dapper black and white feathers and characteristic long tail. The chough has black plumage and a bright red curved beak and legs. The rarest of our native species, its range is confined to the cliffs of our western coastline. Hooded crows fill a similar niche to carrion crows and are mainly a lighter grey on their body, with black wings and heads. They are more common in North and West Scotland, Northern Ireland and on the Isle of Man.

The confusion is usually between the three black corvids; crows, rooks and ravens. The raven is by far the largest, weighing as much as 1.5 kilograms and with a wingspan of up to 1.3 metres. Ravens appear solid and composed as they soar or perch, and their call is a grating, 'raafen, raafen'. Their heavy bill and wedge-shaped tail make them easy to identify on the wing. Carrion crows and rooks are half the size and fly with rapid wingbeats rather than the gliding of ravens. They emit a higher-pitched 'caw, caw'. These black corvids are routinely clumped together as generic crows – as Bran's disturbing experience shows.

It is chilling to realise that not everyone wielding a gun knows what they are aiming at. The young man was no marksman, nor could he tell the difference between a raven and a crow, despite the fact that one is considerably larger than the other. Ravens are a protected species; it is illegal to kill them without a specific, strict licence. Crows can be legally controlled under what is termed a general licence, which has fewer restrictions, but the law still requires proof there is no alternative to lethal control after non-le-thal methods have been tried. This shooter's cavalier attitude to wildlife and the law could have destroyed in an instant what Lloyd, Rose and Bran have created over years, a touching relationship based on mutual trust. Bran has taken part in wildlife documentaries and is a trained, skilled performer, yet his life could have been ended by one ignorant and callous act.

Bran's brush with death is a distressing incident, but it is not a one-off. A decade ago, Lloyd and Rose's former raven, Loki, flew into a lambing field where carrion from perished lambs was strewn over the ground. It wasn't an area he would normally go to, but ravens have excellent eyesight and will investigate potential food. The farmer, assuming that the large, black, flesh-eating bird was implicated in the killing of his stock, walked up to the tame raven and shot him at point-blank range.

Running beneath all this killing of corvids is a deep dislike many have for creatures that combine intelligence and necrophagy (the eating of dead or decaying flesh). Fears as old as humanity itself surface, ancient associations we find hard to dismiss. Ravens eat carcasses and famously hung around gallows to feast on the executed. They also pecked the eyes out of the corpses on battle-fields, as they will out of any dead or defenceless animal. As if to underline this connection to darkness, they dress in funereal black and rasp a throaty rattle. In Swedish folklore, they are the ghosts of murdered people without Christian burials, and in German tales they are the souls of the damned. No surprise then, that an 'unkind-ness' is the collective noun for ravens.

Looking through my Twitter account recently, I came across a thread related to ravens. Someone had posted a picture of one and called it a 'horrible bird'. A whole string of replies came back, both for and against them. Some wanted ravens to be culled because they are 'too common' and predate songbirds or attack sheep; others praised them for their intelligence and asserted their right to exist as native birds that are recovering after generations of persecution. The wildlife photographer Peter Cairns added to the discussion: 'If we accept that nature is a wholeness woven from infinite complexity, we surely cannot pick and choose just the species we like, or profit from?' Someone else wondered if we were only supposed to like animals that don't eat other animals. The ancient love–hate relationship with ravens is nothing new.

Throughout time these avian black holes have absorbed our fear and disgust at the thought of dying and being eaten. They thrive on sorrow and we see them as the embodiment of bitter gall. In times of hopelessness and depression, a hunched dark bird, with fingered wings outstretched, shades our troubled souls from the light. Ravens and crows possess neither cuteness nor colourful beauty to make the idea of them more palatable; their charm has to be searched for. Fortunately, Lloyd and Rose Buck are part of a distinguished company of corvid-istas who do just that: Esther Woolfson's book *Corvus* is a touching account of sharing a home with different species of corvid. Bernd Heinrich explores their intelligence and their reputation as 'flying apes' in *Mind of the Raven*. John Marzluff's *In the Company of Crows and Ravens* examines the influence of corvids on human culture, and Joe Shute's *A Shadow Above* takes a personal look at the complexity of corvid–human relationships. These celebratory books challenge easy perceptions, and although I like to think of myself as someone who values all wildlife, I still found myself marvelling with fresh eyes when I met Bran in the flesh.

On a February afternoon, I joined Lloyd on Tickenham Moor to take Bran for his daily flight. Once out of his cage he took to the air with powerful beats and sailed above us as we waded down the submerged path from the aviaries to the open fields. When I say path, after weeks of unprecedented rain, pond would be more accurate. Water lapped the base of tree trunks and drowned the wintry grey and yellow grasses along the verge; at times it slopped over the top of my wellies. Many of the surrounding fields held standing water, a reminder of the true nature of this landscape. Before widescale drainage, medieval West Country folk would have rowed through a watery world, drifting between the small islands that rose out of the tidal floods. Miniature citadels, complete with compact villages, towers and churches, dotted the patchwork of wetlands that stretched from the Severn Estuary to Dorset. They would have appeared and disappeared with the mist, becoming natural gathering places for mystical lore – enchanters casting spells and Arthurian knights brandishing their swords above the waves. I allowed myself to indulge in just a little of this over-romanticised magic on that wintry day; after all, the village of Glastonbury, the centre for all things New Age, was only a few miles away as the crow flies.

John Steinbeck fell under the spell of the floodplains of Somerset. In a letter to his agent in 1959, he wrote, 'I wish you could feel this place, just let it seep into you … It isn't really country. It's the most inhabited place you ever felt.' And there was Bran, named after a mythic Celtic king, flying over it. Today, drained, canalised and cultivated, the low-lying plain that stretched before us is a combination of SSSI (Site of Special Scientific Interest) and grazing land, framed by ridges of woodland and the M5.

Bran soared above, allowing the winter breeze to carry him over a land he knows intimately. He recognises and situates every feature and is aware of every change. Even the movement of a piece of machinery from one part of a farm to another is enough to make him wary. His world is one of order and certainty, a mosaic of the known, because only then can he detect potential threats. At times he flew so far away, he appeared as just a dot in the distance, but the slightest movement of Lloyd's arm, to take a piece of chicken out of a pouch strapped to his belt, caused Bran to wheel round and glide back. This raven is all-seeing and ever-present; constantly monitoring, observing, calculating. Totally bonded to Lloyd, he checks on him as he would a mate. Lloyd loves Bran, Bran loves Lloyd. Like old mates they chatter gently to each other, Bran hopping deftly from Lloyd's arm to shoulder and back in an intimate display of trust. But, if Lloyd had not completely closed the pouch where he kept the pieces of chicken, even by a centimetre, within seconds Bran would have dived down, opened it and had his head thrust inside.

Communication between Lloyd and Bran is as physical as it is oral. In her book, *Corvus*,[1] Esther Woolfson describes how she experienced a similar connection to a rook that shared her house, how they knew each other's intentions and moods by a turn of the head or an attitude in a walk. She describes the movement of corvids as possessing 'a sharp, tenebrous grace'. On that damp, February day, the air was filled with raven-presence, a searing, intense curiosity.

When Bran was a mere pinprick over distant woodland, Lloyd fished a small stone out of his pocket and threw it on the ground, where it was quickly lost among the mass of other small rocks and pebbles on the track. We were partly hidden by a high hedge so it would have been impossible for Bran to see the detail of what we were doing. There was nothing to distinguish this stone, not its colour or shape, and Lloyd even kicked some debris to partially cover it. After walking on a little way, a piece of chicken drew Bran back to us. 'Where's your stone, Bran?' Immediately he was alert and hopping in circles on Lloyd's shoulder, head cocked, eyes like lasers. Seconds later he retrieved it, tossing other stones aside. 'That's one of the things about ravens, that people don't realise,' says Lloyd, 'just how good their eyesight is. I think it's better than a raptor's. When we were filming once in the centre of London, I was standing with about five hundred people in Trafalgar Square and Rose flew Bran from the top of Trafalgar House. I wasn't behaving like I normally do, not holding my arm out, but he picked me out immediately and flew straight to me.' The stone trick was an astonishing display of accuracy and I marvelled at how much more information Bran's high-functioning brain could gather compared to what we collate with our constrained, earth-bound senses.

In the Viking age, the seafaring Norse explorers are said to have used the far-sightedness of ravens to direct them to land. The saga of Floki tells of three ravens that were taken on a boat to search for what we now call Iceland. It is an epic tale that highlights the different personalities of ravens as well as their good eyesight. When released in the middle of the ocean, the first raven turned south and flew straight home, the second circled the boat and then landed back on deck, but the third raven was more intrepid and headed north. Following it, Floki arrived at the bay where Reykjavik now sits. This story of bird leading man to safety, or indeed into a new future, has echoes of a more ancient, darker tale. The book of Genesis, perhaps written as early as 1000 BCE, relates the story of Noah who was directed by God to build a large boat, or ark, to survive the floods that were soon to arrive as a punishment for people's sins. Noah and his family took a male and a female of each kind of creature into the ark as the rains began to fall. For 150 days they floated on rising waters while all around life perished. When eventually the rain stopped and the water level began to drop, we are told that the first bird Noah released to find land was a raven, followed by a dove. The dove, unable to find hard ground, returned to the ark, but the raven never came back. Some interpretations of this are macabre. Perhaps, it is suggested, the raven survived by feeding on the floating carcasses of those who had drowned, a gruesome image that further cements the association that runs deep through many different cultures between ravens and death. Ravens are otherworldly messengers that move freely between creation and destruction.

After a while Bran leaned forward on Lloyd's arm, his gaze fixed on me. I was suddenly aware of a tangy, musky odour, an eau-de-raven, which was both alluring but with an acrid edge. He then, astonishingly, began to whisper in a hoarse, eerie tone. Ravens are superb mimics of the human voice. Rose says that when Lloyd is away from home, Bran sounds so much like him, complete with London accent, that she thinks he has come back and is in the garden. That afternoon, though, the sound he made was ghostly. His 'eyebrows' were erect, parallel ridges of feathers running front to back over the top of his head that made him look a little like Batman. It was a sign he was agitated. At the end of each breathy word he snapped his thick-set beak. 'Hello', snap. 'Hello', snap. 'He's being dominant over you,' said Lloyd, 'He's testing you. He's not met you before so he's trying to work you out, to see how you react to him; ravens do that. They're different from other corvids – they are more knowing. Ravens don't look at you, they study you.' It certainly felt like my inner self was being examined by an intense and intelligent creature, and that voice was unearthly. Bran then flew from Lloyd's arm onto the ground and started to walk right in front of my feet, almost on top of my boots, causing me to stop and change direction with every step. He was telling me he was in charge and that Lloyd was his. Never before had I felt controlled by a bird that was channelling a spectre.

Perhaps Edgar Allan Poe had heard that eerie raven-voice, and it stirred his dark, creative forces to coalesce into his most famous poem of desolation – 'The Raven'. A bird flies into the author's room in the dead of night and will not leave; it taunts him with just one repeated word: 'Nevermore'. Poe cannot rid his life of this dark pyschopomp, which he describes as a 'grim, ungainly, ghastly, gaunt, and ominous bird of yore'. No matter how desperate his pleading, it only replies, 'Nevermore.' At the end of the poem, in desperation he cries:

> Take thy beak from out my heart, and take thy form from
>   off my door!'
> Quoth the Raven 'Nevermore.'

In my home town of Stoke-on-Trent, we have our own seventeenth-century tale of black-bird black magic. Molly Leigh lived alone with her raven (or was it a crow or rook?) in woodland outside what is now the town of Burslem. Her raven was believed to be the outward manifestation of her inward witchiness. Molly suffered the same superstitions that were applied to many old, single women, and she and her bird were accused of being responsible for all kinds of unnatural happenings. The hawthorn bush by Molly's house, on which the bird often perched, was said to have never produced flowers. When the raven appeared at the local pub window, people swore blind that all the beer went sour and the drinkers developed rheumatism. Some said that Molly and the raven put a curse on the local pastor, which made him appear drunk for three weeks. In the end, when poor, maligned Molly died (of natural causes), the pastor buried her facing north–south, not east–west, as is the norm for a Christian burial, and her hapless raven was buried alive with her.

On the other hand, it isn't all death and dread; ravens possess desirable attributes that we can only admire. Even though their brains weigh a mere 15 grams (a chimp's is over 400 grams), the density of the forebrain neurones, the area that controls spatial awareness, language, thinking and memory, exceeds that of most primates and they are comparable to great apes in intelligence tests.[2] They can quickly solve problems, use tools, have canny bartering skills,[3] can plan activities[4] and play games. Like children, they are sensitive to unfairness and refuse to deal with experimenters who promise them a treat but then withhold it.[5] They will also punish cheats, as Rose and Lloyd Buck found out.

Ravens, like other corvids, are politicians. They study their extended social group to understand character and motivation; it is essential for survival. As anyone who has shared a communal kitchen will know, stealing food can cause social breakdowns. Ravens are no different. If a new raven appears on the scene, it pays to find out if it is trustworthy. The character of a new bird is tested by burying a morsel of food in plain sight. If that bird then steals the cache, they will never be trusted again and caching will always be done in secret. Conversely, if the food is left alone, a pact of honour is sealed and trust is established. Loki never again trusted humans with his treasures after an incident with Lloyd and Rose when they were working on a film set. Rose was asked to repeatedly unearth Loki's cached food to reset the scene for the cameraman. In Loki's eyes, this was high treason. To exact revenge, Loki would steal bunches of car keys or earrings, things he knew were precious to Lloyd and Rose, and hide them. Every so often he would appear, dangling the object in his bill, flying around and over them, showing he had what they wanted. He would never allow them to take them back and they would be returned to the secret place, which Lloyd and Rose to this day have never found. Although Loki, Lloyd and Rose continued to work closely together for many years, that aspect of their relationship had been broken.

The faithful bond that Lloyd and Rose developed with their ravens is also found in the extended social groups of wild birds. Although a pair will mate for life, they form part of a wider, complex social structure whose hierarchy shifts over time. Politically astute, ravens intervene in relationships if they want to disrupt alliances and ingratiate themselves with higher-status birds.[6] Recent discoveries show that ravens can express empathy and console a member of their group who has been attacked.[7] They possess phenomenal memories, and, along with crows, remember who is their friend or foe, even after many years have passed.[8] Creating bonds as strong as those between humans and domestic dogs, ravens form unique relationships with different people. Recognising these traits, and admiring their confident demeanour, we have placed them on heraldic coats of arms to indicate acumen and fidelity. In what seems a provocative tempting of fate, according to Victorian folklore, if the ravens ever fly away from the Tower of London, the United Kingdom will fall apart. Just to tip the balance in favour of stability, the Ravenmaster clips their wings, making flying any distance very difficult. Even today, six pinioned ravens perch around the battlements of the Tower of London.

We have also been inspired by their wild, free selves and envied their soaring on mountain winds, swooping in abandon. In bright mountains, their croaking call is not sinister, it is a shout of joy. And yet, on those same hillsides, they peck the eyes out of the defenceless and tear flesh from the cadavers of sheep. Joy and pain, life and death, loyalty and ruthlessness – we bind ourselves to the raven in an intertwining of bittersweet complexity. David Gray, in his ballad of grief and love, 'The Other Side', picks up these dualities and spurns the common image of love as cooing doves. Instead, he chooses a black bird that is at once light and airborne yet still infused with pain, 'Love is a raven when it flies.'

In truth we don't know what to make of ravens, we cannot pigeonhole them. In Lewis Carroll's *Alice in Wonderland*, the Mad Hatter famously poses the riddle, 'Why is a raven like a writing desk?' No answer is forthcoming, but maybe it is because anything we wish can, and has, been written onto the raven.

Edgar Allan Poe wrote 'The Raven' in 1845, the middle of a century of intense persecution for ravens on both sides of the Atlantic. The industrialisation of the western world saw ancient relationships replaced with a more utilitarian approach to nature. If wildlife hindered the serious business of producing food and game, it was removed. Ravens, like crows, are omnivorous and in addition to carrion, they will eat the eggs and chicks of wild birds, gamebirds and domestic fowl, mammals, small birds, reptiles, insects or anything they can find – including grain. They will peck the eyes, anus and tongue of any incapacitated animal, old or young. Ravens are the farmer's pest, the shepherd's curse and the gamekeeper's nemesis.

The nineteenth century saw widespread shooting, poisoning and trapping of ravens (and many other species considered 'vermin') and their numbers plummeted. By the turn of the century in Britain, they were reduced to nesting on rocky outcrops in the far west.[9] Numbers recovered during the twentieth century as game-keepers left to fight in two world wars, and the introduction of the Wildlife and Countryside Act of 1981 added a further boost to their return. Since the 1990s they have increased rapidly and are expanding east once more. There are now over 10,000 breeding pairs in the UK. In Scotland, where most of the increase has occurred, the population of ravens has increased by 50 per cent over the last twenty years. There are ups and downs associated with these figures, especially in areas of afforestation, where plantations provide some nesting areas, but they also take away feeding grounds. Sustained population declines have been recorded with the establishment of softwood plantations, and this is likely to become a significant problem in the future as more forestry is planned.[10]

Taken as a whole, ravens are recovering, with signs that the size of the population is beginning to level off. I often see them in the middle of Bristol where they nest in a large Scots pine in a city-centre park, and surprise me on my dog walk with their mountain cries. They also enjoy a more widespread affection and appreciation than in the past. In 2018, when the Scottish statutory environmental protection body, Scottish Natural Heritage (shortened to SNH, now NatureScot), issued a licence to kill over sixty ravens each year for five years to protect ground-nesting waders in Strathbraan in Perthshire, there was an outcry from both sides of the border. Gamekeepers and farmers in the area had reported an increase in the number of ravens and a decrease in nesting wading birds, like lapwing, curlew and redshank. The plan to cull ravens was devised to test if the correlation was valid, and to see if wader breeding success increased with a reduction in raven numbers in the valley. Many people condemned this approach as unscientific, accusing NatureScot of listening to hearsay rather than acting on scientifically gathered data, and arguing that the cull was therefore unjustifiable. A government petition to stop the shooting quickly reached over 100,000 signatures. By August, after thirty-nine ravens had been shot, the cull was suspended. The power of social media and the involvement of celebrities like TV naturalist Chris Packham helped raise awareness of an issue which would previously have been left to licensing officials and land managers.

Licences to control ravens legally continue to be issued throughout the UK, mainly to protect sheep and gamebirds. Applicants have to show that the birds are seriously impacting their business or conservation efforts, and that non-lethal deterrents have been tried. Between 2015 and 2018, around 3,000 ravens were killed under licence in Scotland, although the figure applied for was 4,000, perhaps showing an over-estimation of the problem. In England the figure is far lower, with fewer than a hundred birds killed in the same time frame. In Wales it is around fifty birds.

However, persecution continues in pockets across the country-side. In a throwback to the bad old days, in April 2018, ten ravens, a crow and a dead lamb were discovered on a farm on the Wales–Shropshire border. The lamb carcass had been laced with Diazinon, a powerful insecticide that farmers formerly used in sheep dip, and lethal to a range of wildlife. Baiting to attract carrion eaters like ravens, crows, red kites, eagles and buzzards was once common practice and was indiscriminate in its victims. On 6 May 2019, two ravens were shot in Staffordshire, and as the story of Loki and Bran shows, there are potentially many more victims that are never reported. The National Wildlife Crime Unit also identifies ravens as being particularly vulnerable to egg collectors: 'This may be because it is one of the earliest nesters or because the nests are a challenge to climb up to (or abseil down to). Ravens nesting in coastal areas of north Wales are often the population that suffers most from this strange breed of criminal.'[11] Another draw could be the allure of a rare colouring on some clutches of eggs. Ravens' eggs are normally blue or green with dark markings, but some lay highly prized and valuable red-coloured (erythristic) eggs with pink back-grounds and dark-red streaks or blotches.

Despite sporadic persecution, the raven is returning to once again infuse our skies with meaning and majesty. Nature can recover, even after centuries of persecution. The world they are recolonising, however, is not the same as the one from which they were removed. Over the intervening centuries, farming practices, industrialisation, human population growth, climate change and global trade have transformed how we use landscapes; and alongside, we have changed too. Plantations, monocultures, high numbers of livestock, drained and tamed lands now present a different vista and an altered platter of food for wildlife. Our relationship with the land is fundamentally different in this age of mass production. The abundance and resilience of many species has shifted in response, with fewer specialists and more generalists than there have ever been in human history. The raven occupies this space, an exultant survivor and exploiter of change. The 23 million sheep, for example, that graze both the uplands and lowlands of the UK provide carrion in abundance, especially over the lean winter months, as do the millions of gamebirds that escape the gun and naturalise. Plentiful food also comes from cereal fields, rubbish tips and overflowing bins, with their attendant tribes of rats and mice. The raven has made the most of these opportunities and thrived.

Standing in a courtyard with two dead sheep at his feet, casualties of a hard winter, farmer and author James Rebanks describes a raven peering down at him from a barn. Minutes earlier it had been feasting on his prized possessions.

Coal black. Scared of nothing and with a bellyful of the dead. Ravens live on our failures. Brutal. Arrogant. Cruel. And sometimes stunningly beautiful … His thick, black, hoary neck ruffles as the wind catches his feathers. Greedy. Delirious. He rises like he has a stone in his belly, punch-drunk on carrion.[12]

Those creatures that cannot eat a range of food, as corvids can, have gone into decline. Specialists are fading from the land, and with them a nuanced, varied palette of habitats. It is the way of things in Britain today, in the world today. The scales are shifting in favour of the creatures that can live off our way of life. It is up to us to decide whether to help redress the imbalance, or let things take their course.

As I journeyed around the UK, researching for this book, I talked to people from very different walks of life. I may have only travelled from the city to the nearest farm, yet I crossed invisible attitudinal boundaries as impenetrable as concrete. Like the crew of the *Starship Enterprise*, I materialised on different planets that were a universe apart, and each held its own opinions, priorities, traditional values and mores. My empathies swayed with each conversation, and my mind swirled with alternative visions of the world. I felt tossed around on an ocean of opinion. At the end of the day, head in hands, I didn't know what to think or who could compassionately lay out a way forward that embraces both the needs of people and of wildlife, because we all matter. I wondered if such a pact were even possible.

Meeting Bran, that highly intelligent, communicative, extraordinary, ordinary bird, I was forced to confront hard questions. Should ravens be killed to protect rare, ground-nesting birds, a group that are particularly vulnerable to predation by ravens? A pair of ravens can do serious harm to a few isolated wader nests. If, as in the past, there are lots of alarmed parents to see off the danger, and if the habitat is varied enough to provide hiding places for the nest and chicks, then the damage is limited. Ravens can be put off by screaming, angry adults with long, sharp beaks, and the chicks can dive for cover; but in many areas this is simply no longer the case. Reduced to a thin scattering of tasty morsels in over-grazed landscapes, wader nests stand little chance. Corvids are just one of their problems, but a serious one. The problems are the same for terns, ducks, gulls, larks and many other ground-nesting species. This is a situation we have created. It is incumbent on us to make amends if we want to retain some of these vulnerable birds for the future, while we make every attempt to restore degraded habitats. It is a choice we must make. That may well mean taking out a limited number of predators for a limited amount of time in the most affected areas while the habitat is restored and the numbers of endangered birds recover; a temporary measure. Try as I might, I can't see an alternative.

Ravens and crows are now attaining greater numbers on human-generated food than they ever achieve in more natural settings. We cannot roof and fence in whole ecosystems. Does that mean a raven's life is worth less than a wader's? No. But the balance is tipped against many species of wader surviving into the future if we don't do something to help them produce eggs and chicks that survive to fledging. I find myself constantly returning to the conversation I had with Professor David Macdonald, first mentioned in the Introduction: 'I think people find themselves having to acknowledge that different views of the landscape lead people to have different conclusions. Accepting that is the case, then we have to take a philosophical position on what is the right thing to do – what should we do.'

Knowing this reality, would I pull a trigger on a raven? No, I simply could not. I know that makes me weak, with no stomach for the real world. I know I am unable to put aside my feelings and face, head-on, the ruthless world of conservation in the raw. I am happy to let others do the dirty work and then glow with joy as a curlew bubbles and soars overhead or a redshank erupts from a pool and twists into the mist. I know I belong to a vast throng of 'nature lovers' who desperately want wildness to be left to be wild, unencumbered by our meddling. The evidence on the ground, though, shows that given the present state of the UK, that doesn't favour the few. When the last wader nest has been emptied, the adaptable, omnivorous predators simply move on to another source of food. The end result is no waders to keep the population viable into the future; and what a desolate future that would be. I despair at being faced with this awful reality; an unbalanced world turning its face against the long-legged, light-touch birds of liminal places.

The next question is, if we accept that some predator control must happen to protect the most precarious populations, who does it? Leaving it to unskilled people, like the young man who thought Bran was a crow, is clearly not acceptable. Knowledgeable, skilled marksmen, however, are expensive, and it is not clear who would pay for their training and services. In the long term, putting back the habitat that allows specialist creatures to protect themselves is the key, but that takes time; time many don't have. In the short term, is there an alternative to some predator control? It seems not. I wish it was different.

*

I am walking through moorland in spring as skylarks sing overhead, their notes dancing on the breeze. The warm heather and grass emit the beautiful scent of growing life, pushing fragrant air skywards. I am with a land manager who is using two methods to control crows to protect waders. This afternoon we will be checking his Larson traps – a cage in which a 'call-bird' is kept to entice inquisitive crows to investigate and find their way in through a trap door. As they are intelligent, self-aware and sociable birds, it usually works well. Then, tomorrow morning, the land manager will employ the second method of control. At dawn, we will shoot crows drawn to a decoy placed on a wall in the middle of fields. These two tried and trusted ways of reducing crow numbers are widely used.

As we make our way along a well-worn footpath, two walkers come past and we exchange cheery hellos. They are wearing

shorts, have rucksacks and carry a map; happy to be out of winter
and out of doors. I'm glad they don't realise that near the stile
they have just climbed over is a caged crow. My companion waits
until they have gone, then jumps over the wall and pulls out the
Larson trap that is tucked out of view. The call-bird hops from
perch to the floor and back again in obvious agitation. It is anxious
but defiant, and it is alone; no other bird has entered the cage. I
am relieved that I won't have to see a newcomer dispatched by
having its head hit against a wall. I crouch down to get a better
look at the call-bird and feel I am staring at an imprisoned piece
of the sky. Its eyes are bright but wary as it looks straight back at
me. After filling the trapped crow's water bowl and replenishing
the food, the cage is replaced, making sure part of it has some
shelter and shade from the branches of the hawthorn. The keeper
will return tomorrow.

Larsen traps, and the larger ladder traps, which can hold more
birds, have been in use since the 1950s as cheap and efficient
methods for catching corvids. They are most useful when placed in
a breeding territory to catch the resident birds, who do the most
damage to ground-nesting birds when feeding their own young.[13]
Rules abound about their proper and ethical use, but the bald fact
is that the call-birds remain in an avian prison from which there is
no escape. There are laws around their correct use to reduce as
much as possible the distress to the call-bird, but the extent to
which these traps are operated humanely relies entirely on the
operator. Undoubtly there are less than scrupulous ones, and
policing their use is nigh impossible in remote areas. As we walk
away, my companion tells me that he kills any trapped crows away
from the call-bird to avoid distressing it and he avoids eye contact
with the crow; it makes his job easier. 'They look at you straight
and there is a connection.' Nothing about this method is

comfortable, and it is understandable that Larsen traps are frequently vandalised by passers-by and animal-rights activists, but the alternative – shooting – is much more difficult, expensive and far less efficient.

By daybreak the next morning, we are already sipping coffee in a truck parked in a track with a fine view across the best that upland farmland has to offer. An absurd plastic crow has been attached to a drystone wall in the distance. The valley is beyond lovely in this morning hour. The rising sun is a red ball of fire, throwing pink rays onto a gentle landscape of rough fields and isolated trees. The bubbling and trembling calls of curlews lie soft on the breeze, occasionally punctuated by the sounds of cuckoo and grasshopper warbler. In contrast, the keeper's rifle resting on the open car window looks like an affront to nature. He is poised and ready to fire. I am trapped between pragmatism and distress. Soon the corvid rush-hour will begin and commuter crows will fly back and forth across the valley in search of food. As with ravens, their eyesight is superb and a strange, lone crow is worth investigating. It doesn't take long before one swoops down and flaps onto the wall next to the dummy. The bullet is a violent assault on the tranquillity and shatters any attempt I make at professionalism, but there is no alternative but to lean into the discomfort and move with the day. It is why I am here, to experience the hard, bitter taste of crow control for conservation. The valley is no longer quiet; it is silent.

So, this is how it is done by professionals, calm, clean (one hopes) and practical, and it is infinitely preferable to an alternative method of corvid control described so well by James Rebanks in *The Shepherd's Life*. He recalls a springtime ritual in the Cumbrian valleys where marauding groups of men blasted away at anything black and airborne; venting spleen for the damage they believed

these birds had inflicted on the lambs they worked so hard all year
to produce.

> The whole valley echoed with cawing and the thuds of
> cartridges. Twelve bore retribution for one-eyed lambs and
> maimed corpses. Shattered twigs blown skywards as nest floors
> crackled back down through the branches. Ravens, rooks, dopes
> (carrion crows), magpies and jackdaws, all wanted for murder
> or GBH. Anything with black feathers was a 'dope', a robber, a
> killer and a cheat. In a valley where men lived for their sheep
> these shadows of the lambing field were guilty. The morning
> after they were black specks in the rushes by the wood's edge.
> Crumpled wings, perforated flight feathers, specks of blood,
> porcelain legs twisted and broken like cocktail sticks. The angry
> caws of the survivors reprimanded the valley and its shepherds.
> A dope rose and twisted like a broken kite before crumpling to
> earth like a bi-plane with torn canvas wings.[14]

One farmer said to me in the Peak District recently, pointing to
some trees with a flock of rooks (which eat mainly grubs in the
soil), 'Them black birds, they want dealin' with.' We find dark,
meat-eating birds hard to like. We perceive a black stew of ill-intent
simmering in their brains.

> Black was the without eye
> Black the within tongue
> Black was the heart
> Black the liver, black the lungs[15]

Ted Hughes' intense collection of poems, *Crow*, is pure darkness, a poetic representation of scratching fingernails on a blackboard, a cry of utter despair, where some of the bleakest images ever written are given form. In a 2014 survey of 1,200 people, quoted in the *Daily Mail*, crows, ravens and rooks are high on the list of the most disliked birds in Britain, reminding people of horror films (though gulls, for different reasons, are the most detested).[16]

Today, crows are common in towns and cities as well as the wider countryside. According to the British Trust for Ornithology, there has been 'an ongoing, steep increase in England offset by stability or minor decrease in Scotland, with a fluctuating trend in Wales'.[17] There are over a million breeding pairs in the UK, and the population growth now seems to be flattening.

With so many crows, and so many farmers and landowners concerned by their presence, for many years their fate has been decided by the general licences, mentioned earlier. These allow for the control of a range of birds that are considered a threat to farm animals, crops, gamebirds and endangered species. The general licence covers most corvids – crows, jackdaws, jays, magpies and rooks – but not ravens or choughs, which are given more stringent protection. Although not designed to be such, the general licence was often taken as permission to kill more indiscriminately, without having to produce evidence of the supposed damage done by the victims.

In February 2019, environmentalists Chris Packham, Mark Avery and Ruth Tingay set up Wild Justice, an organisation that fights legal battles to protect wildlife. It immediately launched a challenge to Natural England to end the general licence in its present form, which they saw as enabling the unjustified, casual killing of wild birds. They argued that applicants were not required to prove they had tried other methods of control before issuing a licence, which allowed for widespread persecution. The challenge succeeded. In April 2019, all shooting of crows and other 'pest' species was suddenly, and without warning, stopped until the regulations were tightened; a process which is still ongoing. It was a rapid and astonishing victory. Wild Justice was taken by surprise at the speed of the response from Natural England, which they expected to take months, not a handful of weeks. The suspension produced a wave of outrage among land managers, farmers and gamekeepers, and disconcerted some conservationists, worried at the withdrawal of a conservation tool at a crucial time of year. Battle lines were immediately drawn and the rapid fire of angry insults began. I went to find out for myself what effect the suspension of the general licence was having on the ground, in particular for nesting lapwings and curlews in Yorkshire.

'Normally, we'd have 70 per cent fewer crows at this time of year,' said Craig Ralston, senior reserve manager at a National Nature Reserve (NNR) on the Lower Derwent Valley near York. It was May 2019, and we drove around the fields watching lapwings wheel like mini kites, filling the warm air with their otherworldly, space-invader calls. Occasionally one scuttled past the verge, hurried and important-looking. Crows sat in the bushes and cawed before rising on their fingered wings.

This floodplain is wader heaven. The wet grassland bordering the River Derwent is a jewel of protection in an area surrounded by housing, industry, dog walkers, smart villages and farming. The birds are hemmed in by humanity, but just here, the 'Ings', as they are called, provide wide-open fields bordered by high hedges, which literally sing and tremble with birdsong. It was a heavy-sky day, warm and grey, which fitted the mood. 'We have found twenty-five lapwing nests this year; half have already been predated, most probably by crows. We have done less monitoring because the crows watch to see when you find the nests, so it's best to stay away. It's unfortunate timing, the general licence withdrawal, but hopefully it will be better next year.'

The breeding season of 2020 wasn't better, though. In fact, it was worse. Despite applying early, the general licence failed to come through (many land managers had the same problem) and the country was shut down by the COVID-19 pandemic. Craig and his colleagues could not get out on site, and neither could they manage the public. He wrote to me at the end of July 2020:

The year started out looking good with good numbers of breeding adults returning and an estimated 70 pairs of curlew again before lockdown and average numbers of lapwing. NNR staff worked from home during the lockdown with a gradual return to work thereafter. However, what we saw on those visits, and from reports from local birders doing their daily permitted exercise, was that lockdown caused the whole place to go 'wild'. With the valley being bordered by several local villages it seems that the majority of the local community chose the 'Ings' as the first available green space to do their exercise – some taking that literally with people walking or dog walking all over it, cycling, exercising, picnics, horse riding, 4x4 off-roading – we had it all reported. I was at home getting several reports every day from all around the site – with signs being pulled down, chains and padlocks being cut – very strange as we don't usually suffer any problems. Since the easing of lockdown that pressure has eased but our visitor numbers are still well up (200–300 per cent) having been 'found' by the local communities. And although behaviour is better now we are finally back to warden the site, it's taking a while to turn this behaviour around.

   That disturbance, along with predation (we didn't get our
general licence for the second year), has had a significant
impact – and it was clear on my return to the valley in early
May that large numbers of curlew pairs, and most lapwing
pairs, had deserted. This may have been further impacted by
the very dry drought-like conditions that produced very little
growth and cover in the meadows at this time. Those pairs that
remained appeared to do well, especially later in the season
when we got some grass growth as cover and carrion crow
predation reduces.[18]

The transition to the new, more focused general licence has been
difficult in many areas, with ground-nesting birds suffering particularly badly. But whatever the disruption now, the long-term
outcome could be beneficial and mark a new era of respect for
native birds. Corvids can cause problems, but if they must pay the
price for their success in our human-made landscapes, at the very
least their control must be done with good reason, efficiency and
humanity.

*

I wish I could climb up to a crow's nest and have a raven's-eye
view of the future, to see how ravens and crows will fare over the
rest of the twenty-first century. Will we still be telling the old, dark
tales of witchery and bad omens? After all, our understanding of
wildlife is shaped by the stories we superimpose on it. But what
will we choose to write next and what will be the outcome? I
believe that if we could see like birds, if scientists could develop
the technology to allow us to detect the array of colours birds can
see – into the far ranges of ultra-violet light – then we would create
tales of wonder and magic. Seen with birds' eyes, ravens and crows

would shimmer and glint with a fantastic display of bright colours. Far from being monochrome, a crow cawing atop a tree would be a glitterball that flashes with every turn of its body, firing out colours that would dazzle and amaze us. We would no longer call them omens of death, but emitters of light.

If we fail to halt the decline of nature and we find ourselves alone in a threadbare world, the superbly adaptable crow may well be one of our few constant companions. They will be one of only a few wild creatures to connect us to wonder. Two hundred years ago, the peasant poet John Clare loved them. For Clare, a crow was home for his weary soul. Its evening flight drew to the surface a deep joy at the end of a hard day:

> How peaceable it seems for lonely men
> To see a crow fly in the thin blue sky
> Over the woods and fealds, o'er level fen
> It speaks of villages, or cottage nigh.[19]

A jet-black bird sailing across a blood-red sky was his spirit heading to a place of blessed rest. There was no anxiousness, no resentment towards this bird of the woods, just the recognition that in our man-made world, the crow keeps step with us. They always have.

4

Badgers

I was a little disconcerted when a man who had spent six weeks living as a badger invited me for lunch. What would be on the menu – a plate of worms? After all, worms can make up 85 per cent of a badger's diet. I was intrigued, though. Charles Foster's book, *Being a Beast*,[1] which recounts his experiences of living like animals, revealed that a worm is not just a worm to those with a discerning palate. I had imagined that eating a plate of *Lumbricus terrestris* would be like tucking in to thick, bitter, well-oiled spaghetti, but according to Charles, the worm-eating experience is in two parts: the outer body slime and the soft innards.

Apparently, the taste of the external slime is unrelated to that of the entrails, and can be savoured on its own by sucking it off the body before chowing down on the body sac. Advice from Charles is to avoid worms from the Kent Weald as their slime has overtones of 'burning flex and halitosis'. Far better to revel in those matured in the soils of wine-growing regions, where in the spring you'll find hints of 'lemongrass and pig shit'.

Worm innards are just as varied and display distinct terroirs that reflect the high notes and low notes of the earth where they are found. If Wealden slime is distinctly foul, the soft insides are fresh and uncomplicated: 'They'd appear on a list recommended with grilled sole.' If you prefer a more pub-grub approach to food, the innards of worms from the Somerset Levels have 'a stolid, unfashionable taste of leather and stout'. Who knew? Badgers, I assume, and now Charles Foster.

We did meet for lunch (delicious pasta and salad) in his delightful family home in Oxford, and I was keen to find out what he had discovered was the essential difference between being an Oxford don and a badger. The trick to turning into a nocturnal predator, it seems, involves swapping the dominance of eyesight for a near total reliance on two other senses: smell and hearing. Badgers are, in effect, dark-adapted noses with ears, with an inordinate fondness for worms.

Nocturnal wildlife lives to the rhythm of the revolving night sky and its soft pin-pricks of light. Badgers occupy the mouldy ground floor; a dense, tangled, wriggling, scuttling, creeping, odorous, vibration-filled world of underground burrow and the decaying detritus of woodland and grassland. Badgers do not experience wide horizons; their universe is tight-knit and close by. They have exchanged the world of sunlight for a low-level life.

As badgers go forth into the night and criss-cross the moonlit fields and glades of Britain, they can eat 200 worms apiece. Worms really are important to them. Badgers that were monitored in six areas in Scotland in 1981,[2] for example, showed that earthworms were their staple food in every location, and a similar study in southwest England found that 75 per cent of the badgers had worms in their stomach, with over half having worms alone. Every badger would agree with the eighteenth-century naturalist, Gilbert White, that 'Earthworms, though in appearance a small and despicable link in the chain of nature, yet, if lost, would make a lamentable chasm.' But if worms are in short supply, badgers are adaptable enough to switch to a smorgasbord of seasonal fresh food in the form of birds' eggs, chicks, hedgehogs, small rabbits, insects, carrion, fruit, tubers and crops. This platter of delights is usually sought out alone, as Kenneth Grahame reflected in *The Wind in the Willows*: 'Badger hates Society, and invitations, and dinner, and all that sort of thing,' says Rat to Mole. Despite often living in a group or clan, badgers tend to be solitary foragers once they leave the area around their underground home of tunnels and chambers, called a sett.

European badgers *Meles meles* are related to weasels, stoats, polecats, pine martens and otters and are Britain's largest land predators. They are common right across Europe, from Ireland to the Volga River and down to the Mediterranean, and occupy a range of habitats – lowland farmland, forests and grassland, moors and rough pasture. As long as they can dig a sett and find food, they will move in. The average group size varies depending on the amount of food available, with only one or two per sett in poor terrain, but over twenty have been recorded in rich grasslands. The average is around six badgers per sett. They prefer to dig their homes in the tangled understorey of hedgerows and woodlands, particularly on well-drained sloping ground, where the roots and branches shelter the entrance and minimise the risk of flooding.

Badgers are both endearing and impressive. Adult males can weigh thirteen kilograms, most of which is their hairy, grey and white, rotund torso, supported on short legs. They carry their stumpy solidity with an easy grace and can sprint at twenty miles per hour for short distances. Their most distinctive and defining feature is their humbug head. Broad, black and white, zebra-crossing stripes run lengthways from the snout through small, oval eyes and compact round ears (trimmed white at the top) before fading into the grey pelt. A badger's face is a graphic designer's dream and is used as the symbol for the Wildlife Trusts, as a logo for craft beers, as the emblem of sports teams and as a symbol of tenacious fortitude on heraldic shields. There are three badgers on the Tesco supermarket coat of arms, supposedly chosen because badgers are good housekeepers and will drag soiled bedding out of their sett and replace it. Badgers are widely recognised, and their roly-poly form is an endearing and cheerful reminder of the secretive wonders of the wildwood. Badgers tug at the heartstrings of our vestigial connection to nature.

For a creature of the night their eyes are surprisingly lacking in vigour; small and dull-looking, they give the impression they are short of sleep or in need of spectacles. A badger's eyes look like an afterthought, as though taken from an old teddy bear and added at the last minute. Nocturnal animals usually have outsized eyes to gather as much light as possible, but vision has limited use in underground tunnels, and large eyes are a liability when digging and snuffling through grit and dust and among a tangled, thorny undergrowth. They are thought to be colour-blind as well as light-sensitive, and in bright light badgers will cover their eyes with their paws and retreat to dark corners. In low light their vision is good enough to pick out individuals in their clan by their unique patterning of black and white stripes, and to detect shifting shapes in the gathering gloom, which their other senses then form into a clearer picture of friend, foe or food.

Sharp teeth set within powerful and non-dislocatable jaws make them fierce fighters. Once locked onto flesh they won't let go. Their front claws are two and a half centimetres of dagger-sharp weaponry, used for digging earth and dismembering prey (the back claws are just half as long). Wildlife cameraman and presenter Simon King recounts in his *Wildguide* watching a badger eating a petrified, screaming hedgehog, and his description is not for the faint-hearted:

Of all the predators in Britain, badgers seem best equipped to deal with hedgehogs as a meal, digging a shallow pit next to the curled pin-cushion, rolling it in with muzzle or forefeet, and then using enormous power and long front claws to prise open the packed lunch. This whole procedure is usually punctuated by very loud and pitiful screams and grunts coming from the terrified hedgehog.[3]

Their predators' teeth and claws are also used to neatly skin young rabbits, to crunch up nestlings and eggs and to tear the flesh off dying or dead livestock. Back in 1958, *The Countryman* published a letter from an Oxfordshire farmer describing what seems to be highly unusual behaviour. It recounts how two badgers dragged a newborn calf across fields and into their sett, leaving only the hooves poking out of the entrance. The calf in this instance was successfully rescued.

Despite hearing being very important to badgers, their ears are small and round – another adaptation to an earthy life. They work well, though, as well as a fox's, because even the faintest rubbing of soil particles made by a worm surfacing at night is enough to seal its fate. Trail camera footage shows a badger sniffing along a track but suddenly stopping, ears twitching. It then turns around and traces back to the moving earth behind it and gently extracts between its teeth the long body of a worm.[4] In contrast to the smallness of the ears, a badger's nose is large, black and oval, an indication of just how important a sense of smell is to every aspect of their lives. Scent marking is used to trace out the boundaries of territories, to mark objects and to identify other individuals, as well as to detect food. Block up a badger's nostrils and you have condemned it to confusion, disorientation and starvation, even if it is surrounded by food. The oft-heard sneezes and snorts are essential maintenance for that all-important snout.

From our lofty two-legged position, with our noses in the air, we are mostly oblivious to the variety of life at our feet, each one of which has its own scent signature. Discerning and choosing prey is an all-consuming activity, which Charles Foster discovered when he channelled a badger and got down and dirty in a Welsh woodland. An array of swirling smells greeted him on his nocturnal fossicking – a complex world of scents and mucousy odours that changed in intensity and character with the time of night, humidity and the weather. He would emerge from spending the day sleeping in a tunnel, crawl out on all fours and push through the undergrowth, nose down. 'I'd dropped six feet and several million years into the badger's world.' His face was brushed by wet grass and scratched by woody stems. Backache and sore knees were part of the deal, but for Charles it was a nose-opening experience.

'I was aware of how much more alive I could be as a human by being aware of all those scent particles streaming into my nose. I was awakened to the charisma and the colour and the variety of an olfactory landscape, to how fantastic the material world is, and how relatively impoverished my abstracted world is. We constantly interpret the world through giving things names which have layers of meanings and ideas attached to them, but when we let go of all that, or try to, the world is real and the present more immanent. We are so much more alive when we are predators, we are sensorially half-cocked in our civilised lives.'

Experiencing the world as a badger is not possible in any quantifiable way, but that was not the intention. We can no more be a badger than a badger can be a stockbroker; but we may glean an inkling of what the nineteenth-century eco-philosopher and writer Ralph Waldo Emerson described as 'being moved by strange sympathies', an ancient connection to our shared ancestry that lies deep within. For Emerson, this connection drove his life's work: 'I feel the centipede in me – cayman, carp, eagle and fox.'[5] There is still enough of a badger within us to attract our attention and enough difference to intrigue us.

Humans evolved to navigate a bright planet from about 1.5 metres above the ground, and we largely rely on the patterns of bouncing and refracting light and sound waves to make sense of our surroundings. Like badgers we sniff the air, and each other, to gain all kinds of information. Our noses are extremely good at detecting wholesome food, and they also extract subconscious data such as another person's emotional state, health and mating potential; but mostly the information is not hard-edged. Various smells drift through our day as a diffuse collage of odours that merge and disperse through the air. Modern life confuses the picture even more with our range of synthetic scents and pollution. Not so out in the woods. When a badger makes its way down its foraging tracks and sniffs the soil and the cool air, the darkness reveals to it a well-stocked supermarket. And when the night's foraging is done, the sensory experience continues, as Charles Foster found when he retreated underground as the sun rose higher in the sky. In the comfort of his home, he told me:

'This kitchen we're in now is a really boring, static place; the walls of a badger's sett change all the time. The whole wall writhes. Worms and larvae and beetles come out of the sides and ceiling and drop on you; it is a changing kaleidoscope of sensation. Lots of those things are food, so you're constantly sniffing and snapping at your walls. It's a bit like sitting here and a shepherd's pie oozes out of the wall next to you.'

My own encounters with Brock have not been so adventurous. For much of my life they were rare in the wild and I only met them remotely in children's books as independent and strong characters, sometimes grumpy but always magical – the keepers of country-side lore. At times they were portrayed as kindly and wise, mentors to the flightier characters in stories. At others, as viewed by the rabbits in *Watership Down*,[6] a badger was a shocking and terrifying animal whose eyes were 'full of savage cunning' and who grinned with menace while blood dripped from its lips. Badgers defy easy characterisation, but they are never presented as weak or stupid and they are always knowing.

Humanity is prone to believe that our fate is guided by forces unseen and unbidden. In the days before scientific weather-forecasting, when we depended on a fickle planet for survival, it was important to gain intel. What dictated the warmth of the breeze or the wetness of clouds? When would storms batter the crops and ice freeze tender shoots? A badger seemed to know, but we did not, and so we looked to them for guidance. The ancient pagan feast of Imbolc (later adopted by Christianity as Candlemas) is celebrated in early February and signals a turning of winter and the strengthening of light. It was believed that if a badger emerged from its burrow at Imbolc and could see its own shadow, it would return underground for another six weeks as cold weather would continue. It inherently knew what we yearned to learn, and we watched them carefully. Enduring celebrations to mark the coming of sunlight to warm the earth, the purification of the soul and the promise of new life and nourishment found a meaning and a holding in the daily activities of a badger.

But, as with the black and white of a badger's face, the hopefulness of Imbolc had a counterpoint, as an old superstition warns us:

> Should one hear a badger call,
> And then an ullot [owl] cry,
> Make thy peace with God, good soul,
> For thou shall shortly die.[7]

Our lives could turn on portentous serendipity, merely by how our paths crossed. Another saying tells that if a badger crosses behind you, you will be lucky, but if it is ahead of you, death is imminent. Our self-appointed place at the centre of the natural world assumed that badgers (and other creatures) were concerned with our fate. They could bring good fortune or bad luck, and we had no way of influencing which it would be. A beetling, worm-grubbing, humbug-head was endowed with the power to change our world in an instant. Suspicion and fear swirled around the old brock of the woods. As we battled with feelings of powerlessness in the face of this all-knowing natural world, we tried to take control by appropriating their bodies. Badger heads adorned Scottish sporrans, severed paws were used as amulets and their penis bones were a revered token of fertility.

Widespread belief in the wiles of wildlife has largely drifted into the mists of the pre-industrial age. As cities expanded and agriculture itself has become more industrial, our concerns and affiliations have shifted in response. A more utilitarian approach to nature now dominates. Few people today look to a badger as a weather forecaster or dealer of fate, but they may do so for a good shave, as badger hairs form the expensive bristles for high-end shaving brushes. So intertwined is the act of shaving with a badger's coat that the French word for both a shaving brush and a badger is the same: *blaireau*. Today, these badger hairs are taken from animals removed from the wild, caged and killed in China, an industry that has been highlighted for its cruelty.[8] But the moral ground is not so high – we should all hang our heads in collective shame. A closer look at a more hidden side of British society reveals a persistent, age-old savagery towards badgers.

For generations the deep-seated fear of creatures of the night drew to the surface the poison that is the uniquely human aptitude for barbarity. Few animals have suffered at our hands as much as badgers. Pitched against packs of dogs, beaten to death or hung from trees and tortured – the list of abominations is as long as it is gruesome. As they are so physically tough the contests were often prolonged and bloodied, with the supposed intention of making the spectacle more satisfying. In 'The Combe', by Edward Thomas, a pall of evil hangs in the air where a badger was tortured and killed.

> But far more ancient and dark
> The Combe looks since they killed the badger there,
> Dug him out and gave him to the hounds,
> That most ancient Briton of English beasts.[9]

Thomas spares us the details, but the early nineteenth-century poet, John Clare, describes a badger battling to the end, attacked by both a pack of dogs and a braying crowd of men.

He drives away and beats them everyone,
And then they loose them all and set them on.
He falls as dead and kicked by boys and men,
He starts and grins and drives the crowd again;
Till kicked and torn and beaten out he lies
And leaves his hold and crackles, groans and dies.[10]

This form of sadistic entertainment is ongoing. Today badger-baiting is streamed around the world, increasing the money to be made by gambling on the outcome. Legislation has helped curb the more obvious physical gatherings – a £5,000 fine and up to six months in jail is a deterrent for some – but the persecution continues in out-of-the-way fields and barns.

Why badgers should incite such ferocity in today's supposedly superstition-free world is a question I posed to Charles Foster: 'That's more of a theological issue than a wildlife one. It is to do with the existence of evil and an unfocused, de-humanised brutality. If it wasn't the badger it would be something else.' Dominic Dyer, former CEO of the Badger Trust, is less philosophical and more prosaic. 'Badgers are large, particularly big males, and they are ferocious if provoked. So, for some people they play to our innate fears. They are extraordinary creatures that both inspire us and incite us to violence. In the absence of wolves and bears, they are the only large [predatory] mammal we have left. Maybe being nocturnal is a factor too.' Like a Venn diagram where many circles intersect, badgers occupy that space where negative factors merge, and it is a deadly one to occupy.

Some of the killing of badgers by landowners, gamekeepers and farmers is out of frustration at the damage they can cause. Badgers on a mission are like bulldozers without a brake and they can barge through fencing to make short work of the eggs and chicks of gamebirds or poultry. Some believe they will kill lambs, although it is more likely they scavenge carcasses. They can also shovel huge amounts of earth. A study of one particular underground sett estimates that 25 tonnes of soil were moved to create a network with twelve entrances and tunnels measuring 325 metres.[11] Over time, weather and erosion may cause a labyrinth to collapse, which creates danger for livestock and machinery. Badgers also dig up crops as they search for invertebrates, and they tunnel under, or barge through, fence lines which cross their foraging routes. One landowner expressed his frustration to me in an email: 'Like many others, we have no hedgehogs, I have not seen one this year and we used to have loads. My tractor is always in danger of being driven by inattentive me into craters, dug by badgers when they destroy and kill our bumble bee nests. Will anything ever change to alter the balance?' All in all, a large mammal capable of eating livestock and damaging property was never going to be a welcome presence in rural Britain, and the measures taken to reduce their numbers were often cruel and efficient.

Because of persecution, badgers were relatively rare throughout lowland farmland until the latter part of the twentieth century. As late as the 1970s and 1980s it is estimated that up to 10,000 badgers were killed every year.[12] Their situation eased from 1973 onwards when a series of legal protections was enacted, culminating in the Protection of Badgers Act, 1992. Numbers are now increasing dramatically, by 88 per cent since the 1980s, and a national survey published in 2017 showed a doubling of setts since the 1990s, although the actual density of animals occupying each sett varies depending on the habitat.[13] One study in Wytham Wood in Oxfordshire saw the population treble from 60 to 228 in the last two decades of the twentieth century.[14] Today there are around half a million badgers in the UK, but the official figure fluctuates.

Hot, dry weather can make the ground too hard for foraging, which impacts the survival of cubs which are born between January and March. Weeks of rain can cause extensive flooding, which both reduces feeding areas and can drown cubs that are too young to leave their chambers. Both of these weather extremes are more common as climate change takes hold and adds extra pressure to cub and juvenile survival, which is only one in three under normal conditions. The illegal killing of badgers on farms and game estates still takes place, but obviously numbers are difficult to obtain. Our restless and relentless world-on-the-move lifestyle also brings its own issues. Millions of tonnes of fast-moving rubber and metal hurtle along UK roads day and night, resulting in 50,000 badger deaths each year.[15] Nevertheless, it appears Britain today has more badgers than foxes.

The world which this expanding population inhabits is not the same as the one its ancestors knew. Hedgerows have been ripped out, copses replaced by fields, and wildflower-rich meadows reseeded by monocultures and plantations. There is more livestock and human rubbish than ever before, and villages, towns and cities have spread outwards. In many ways, as with the fox, some of this change suits the omnivorous, resilient badger and it has adapted and thrived.

Conversely, its sometime prey and cohabitor of hedgerows, the hedgehog, has declined rapidly over the same timeframe. Estimated to number many millions in the 1950s, there are now thought to be fewer than a million left. Between 2000 and 2015, hedgehogs decreased by half in rural areas and by a third in more urban habitats.[16] The decline of the hedgehog is a tragic casualty of modern life. There are many reasons for this disappearance; the loss of hedgerows where they can hide and forage, the lack of rough, invertebrate-rich margins around fields and the widespread use of pesticides and molluscicides, which they ingest through their food. They also succumb to rodenticide put out for rat control, are killed on the roads, mown over by agricultural or garden machinery or drown in steep-sided ponds. Some are burned as they hibernate under bonfire piles. In towns and villages, where the decline is less severe, they are harassed by dogs, cats and foxes and have their foraging routes blocked by impenetrable fences. There is no mystery surrounding the decline of the hedgehog – their food source and habitat have been changed – but there is also the added pressure of an increasing number of predators, including the badger.

Many people equate badger success with hedgehog demise, as with the landowner quoted above. It is an increasing focus for human–wildlife conflict in modern Britain. There is no denying the fact that badgers do eat hedgehogs. From a number of studies, it is clear that hedgehogs are more secretive and spend less time foraging in areas with high badger numbers. If they can, they move away and prefer to settle where badgers are less common, such as near buildings and people, which may help explain the slower decline in hedgehog numbers in villages compared to farmland. As a rule of thumb, if there are lots of badgers there are fewer hedgehogs, but the relationship is nuanced.

Both badgers and hedgehogs are consummate worm-eaters. If there are lots of worms and other foods to share, badgers and hedgehogs will peacefully coexist. A wealth of trail-camera footage from gardens placed next to feeding stations shows them eating side by side, with no aggression or fear. The converse is true in a food-stressed landscape, where big badgers can intimidate little hedgehogs and make foraging for food a dangerous activity. In addition, badgers are large predators and can readily turn to hedgehogs to supplement their diet. This is particularly true if the landscape is uniform and lacks good places like hedgerows and undergrowth where the hedgehogs can hide. In these areas, badgers may well drive numbers down to unsustainable levels. Therefore, if there is enough food and plenty of hiding places, badger predation is not a major factor for the hedgehog. This situation is yet another example of the running theme throughout this book, namely the problems posed by modern, uniform landscapes, both in agricultural and urban areas. They favour the adaptable generalist and seal the fate of those creatures that require nuance and variety. Too often though, we remove ourselves from the problem and draw easy conclusions. Simply equating recovering badger numbers with the decline of the hedgehog leaves out the crucial role we play in creating an unbalanced world.

Badger predation of hedgehogs is not the only source of cognitive dissonance for wildlife lovers. Badgers will also readily eat the eggs and chicks of rapidly declining ground-nesting birds like lapwings, terns, curlews and skylarks. There is no national study to quantify the extent of the problem, but there is plenty of anecdotal and circumstantial evidence. In 2014, the BBC wildlife programme, *Springwatch*, recorded a badger swimming to an island in Suffolk and predating the eggs and chicks of an avocet colony. In 2015 and 2016, the Shropshire-based curlew conservation group, Curlew Country, placed nest cameras on a total of thirty curlew nests and in each of those years only three nests hatched chicks.[17] From the camera footage it was concluded that a quarter of the nests were lost to badgers, with the other failures associated with foxes and crows. It is thought that badgers predate nests opportunistically rather than hunt them out, and they are less successful in finding them if the habitat is good and nests are hidden in varied sward and tangled vegetation. Nevertheless, badgers are caught in the midst of the conservation angst around protection for declining species that are struggling to survive in the modern world.

Calls to reduce the numbers of badgers are increasing in intensity. Some sectors see their high population numbers as a black and white issue that has to be resolved quickly. They see a simple and intuitive equation. Lots of badgers equate to the loss of struggling species; fewer badgers will aid these species' recovery. Or maybe not. The complexities of ecosystems can mean that if badgers are removed, a whole host of other predators may step into their empty paw prints. In the Wildlife Online blog, Marc Baldwin lists the other predators which will readily take hedgehogs (and eggs and chicks).

> Other species known to opportunistically take various life-stages of hedgehogs include brown rats (*Rattus norvegicus*), wild boar (*Sus scrofa*), otters (*Lutra lutra*) and various species of small mustelid, including pine martens (*Martes martes*), weasels (*M. nivalis*), mink (*M. vison*), stoats (*M. erminea*) and polecats (*Mustela putorius*). Indeed, in his book *The Hedgehog*, Maurice Burton described the polecat as the hedgehog's '*most deadly enemy, by common consent*'; apparently, they leave nothing, eating flesh, bones, bristles and spines.[18]

Simply removing one predator may well just give another the opportunity to thrive. If badgers are removed, then foxes and stoats may increase, for example, and the hedgehog still loses out. A paper produced in 2008[19] looked at the response of fox populations to badger culling and found that 'Following the initiation of badger culling, mean fox density increased by 57% in culled areas within 24 months … Given the importance of the fox as a predator in the areas likely to be subject to badger culling, any such population response could have significant knock-on consequences.'

On the other hand, and there is often another way to look at a situation, a study in 2014[20] found that in areas particularly favoured by hedgehogs, such as amenity grassland (parks, sports fields, village greens and grassy areas around buildings) their numbers more than doubled after the removal of badgers by culling, indicating that in some places badgers may well be suppressing hedgehog numbers, as discussed above.

Trying to pick apart the intricacies of the relationships between predators and prey across the UK is hugely challenging. Every situation has to be assessed on its own merits and it is not possible to make universal and sweeping statements about the connection between badger numbers and hedgehogs, tempting as it is to want to find easy answers.

The world we have created to provide for our growing population, with its focus on food production, compartmentalised landscapes, housing and industry, has placed stresses and strains between wild creatures as they adapt, or not, to their rapidly changing surroundings. Some species sink, some swim, others just about manage to keep their heads above the rising tide. Depending on where our own allegiances lie, we are often quick to assign blame and identify a culprit. Badgers are large, obvious and increasingly widespread, but hedgehogs and ground-nesting birds are more difficult to find and their populations are fragile and declining. It is easy to jump to conclusions and make rash decisions, and all too often we remove ourselves from the blame game. And nowhere is this more obvious than with the highly contentious issue of badgers and the spread of disease in cattle.

The southwest of England has the highest concentrations of badgers of anywhere in the UK and it also has a lot of cows. The mild, wet climate, extensive grassland and farmland suits both cattle and badgers well, and the increasingly abundant *Meles meles* in these rolling pastoral counties has caused a souring of relationships with badgers over recent years. In 1900 there were around 7 million cows in the UK, mainly in small, mixed farms spread throughout the country. Today there are 9.6 million cattle, usually kept in large herds in specialised farms, and many of those are concentrated in the southwest. Maps showing the population densities of both cattle and badgers almost exactly coincide. This would not be a problem were it not for the fact they share one particularly problematic disease.

Bovine Tuberculosis (bTB) is an infectious bacterial disease in cattle which, as in human TB, primarily affects the lungs. It is also a 'zoonotic disease', which means it can be transferred from animals to humans, which makes it of particular concern. People can become infected with bTB through ingesting unpasteurised milk and cheese, through contact with blood during the slaughter process or from inhaling the bacteria-infected aerosol droplets in air.

Bovine Tuberculosis is most commonly transmitted from cow to cow through inhalation, where one animal coughs and infects cows near to them. If cattle are kept in large herds, the cross-infection rate can be very high. If bTB is detected (and tests are not reliable, and can miss 1 in 5 cattle tested[21]), the whole herd has to be slaughtered. In the 1980s up to 700 cattle per year were slaughtered in the UK because of bTB. In the twelve months to June 2020, the figure had risen to a staggering 39,000.[22] Tracking the disease, culling cattle and compensating farmers is expensive and is estimated to cost the UK £100 million per year. Over the last decade the UK taxpayer has paid out more than £500 million, and it is predicted a further £1 billion will be needed over the next ten years.[23] Bovine TB has spread rapidly through the country as cows are moved around. In 2018, nearly 5,000 new herd incidents (herds that were clean but have become infected) were recorded, most of them in the southwest. There is no doubt that it is a serious problem.

If this was just about cows, it would be more straightforward to solve, but bovine TB can be passed from cattle to a range of wild mammals, including badgers. The first bTB-infected badger was discovered in 1971 in Gloucestershire, and today badgers are thought to be the most significant wild reservoir of the disease, especially where their populations are high – in the midlands and the southwest. As badgers snort and snuffle through the same fields as cows, it is possible they pick up the infection through physical contact with infected cattle and from their urine and faeces in the grass. These bTB badgers may then carry the disease to uninfected cattle as well as to other badgers as they trundle around the countryside. This is a highly complex, vicious circle of disease from cattle to wildlife back to cattle, and its effects ripple outwards, bringing distress and division to rural Britain.

The culling of badgers to reduce the transmission of the disease began in 1975 and was concentrated in bTB hotspots. The practice has grown in scale and controversy ever since. Poisoning by pumping hydrogen cyanide gas into their setts was the first method used to kill them. In 1982, this was replaced by trapping and shooting, the method still in use today. Badger culling in England is now carried out in over forty areas, with over half of the killing zones in the southwest. Up to 40,000 badgers per year are shot, with the total figure estimated to be more than 100,000 animals since 2013.

Much ink continues to be spilled on the pros and cons of the efficacy of badger culling. There is evidence from what was called the Randomised Badger Culling Trial, carried out between 1988 and 2004, that culling reduces the level of TB in cattle by 12 to 16 per cent. However, opponents say that the badgers that escape the bullet merely spread the disease further afield. Furthermore, they maintain that the cows themselves are by far the most potent vectors of transmission, made worse by their being kept in large herds and transported long distances. They say that killing a native, protected species that is recovering from centuries of persecution is an unacceptable price to pay, and that it is farming and animal husbandry that should change and shoulder the cost, not the badger.

Some passionate animal welfare advocates don balaclavas and try to disrupt the shooting by intimidation. There are arrests, fights and bitterness in the quiet country lanes of Britain. It is unedifying and upsetting. Patrick Barkham, in his book, *Badgerlands*, describes a night spent with cull saboteurs seeking to disrupt government marksmen. They meet in a country lane as night falls, and somewhere out in the darkness, guns were pointing at the entrances to badger setts. As the sabs made their plans, Patrick's flashlight lit up the gentle countryside of Somerset:

'Remoter than most classically beautiful pieces of rolling English landscape, it was still proper working territory, not buffed and gentrified into a film set. During the cull, however, its atmosphere of suspicion, paranoia and division was almost heartbreaking.'[24]

Shooting badgers is far from easy or a straightforward solution. It is virtually impossible to kill every badger in an area, and those that remain will range more widely, taking the disease with them to possibly infect clean herds as well as other badger clans. Nevertheless, even though the efficacy of the cull is still fiercely debated, many farmers believe it is having a positive effect, stressing that if they are to meet the increasing consumer demand for meat and dairy then culling should be available as one of the tools to help them counteract the rising levels of infections and to protect their livestock. The badger culls continue.

Apart from the expense to the taxpayer there are multiple hidden costs to the badger cull in the form of policing, political division and the emotional and psychological problems for both farmers and opponents. It is hard to think of any other species that has been the focus of so much attention, money and passion.

As an alternative to shooting, vaccinating badgers against TB has been proposed, but that too is highly controversial. It is a herculean task to vaccinate all badgers in an infected area, and to keep doing so. Vaccinating cattle is also an option, but as yet there is no reliable method of distinguishing between a cow that has the disease and one that has been vaccinated. To further complicate the picture, the vaccine itself is not 100 per cent efficient and there is a reluctance to implement a large-scale programme until it is improved. Vaccination programmes are very expensive and there is the thorny issue of who will pay. At present, the dairy industry produces 15 billion litres of cheap milk per year; any extra costs imposed by vaccination programmes will inevitably result in higher prices in the shops.

All this is taxing some of the finest scientific minds in Britain. Successive government ministers have attempted to balance the different agendas – but there is still no accepted solution. Angela

Cassidy of the Centre for Rural Policy Research (CRPR) at Exeter University sums up the situation succinctly in her book *Vermin, Victims and Disease: British Debates over Bovine Tuberculosis and Badgers*.

> Over the near half-century that badgers and bovine TB (badger/bTB) have been debated in Britain, the issue has passed across several generations of scientists, veterinarians, farmers, policymakers and politicians. So far, it has been the responsibility of nine prime ministers, fifteen government administrations and twenty-one Cabinet Ministers. As of 2018, there will have been nine expert led reviews of the situation.[25]

The people-shy badger finds itself in an uncomfortably hot spotlight and is, yet again, a figure of division and controversy. It has become a symbol of the divide between farmers and conservationists, rural dwellers and urbanites, idealists and pragmatists. The badgers' road to recovery from cruelty and persecution has not been an easy ascent to sunlit uplands, but is fraught with protests and the threat of the marksman's bullet. There seems no end to their tribulations.

The river of fate, however, makes sweeping twists and turns, and two momentous challenges are altering the direction of travel for the world's nations. Climate change and the COVID-19 pandemic are both terrifying in their potential to destroy and are both forcing fundamental change upon the planet. Among all the chaos, the humble badger may be one of the beneficiaries.

The earth's climate is warming due to the relentless build-up of carbon dioxide and other gases emitted by our various carbon-reliant industries. The agricultural industry contributes around one fifth of all global greenhouse gases,[26] 80 per cent of which is linked

to livestock production.[27] Faced with the enormity of the consequences of climate change, many people are switching to a more
plant-based diet and reducing or eliminating their consumption of
dairy and meat. One survey suggests one in eight Britons are either
vegetarian or vegan, and a further 21 per cent have cut down their
consumption of animal products.[28] This is a trend which the former
CEO of the Badger Trust, Dominic Dyer, sees as a glimmer of
hope:

> The next decade will be crucial. The next 10 years will decide
> if badgers become locally extinct in some areas of England or if
> we come to terms with the idea that the livestock industry has
> to change. With more people moving to plant-based diets, it
> may not be viable in its current form in the long term
> anyway.[29]

If dairy and meat consumption decline then it follows that the
intensity of production will also fall. Cows will be less crowded
together, stocking densities in the fields could be reduced, and
badgers may well be able to breathe more easily in a less livestock-
intensive countryside. The same consequence could arise through
the rapid spread of COVID-19 early in 2020.

Thought to have originated in the so-called wet-markets in
China, where wild animals are slaughtered and sold in close proximity to people, the virus was transferred from animal to human
and rapidly spread around the world. The effect was unprecedented. By February 2022, 381 million people were thought to
have contracted COVID-19 and 5.7 million people had
died. Whole countries went into lockdown as governments
fought to halt the infection rate. One of the many debates the
virus has prompted is the way humanity interacts with nature. A

reassessment is underway of how we encroach on wilderness and disrupt natural ecosystems, releasing potentially deadly viruses into the human sphere. We are being forced to look afresh at the way we intensively farm animals, trade animal products and exchange wild habitats for farmland. Four years before the pandemic, the United Nations Environment Programme warned of the consequences of ignoring zoonotic diseases:

> The 20th century was a period of unprecedented ecological change, with dramatic reductions in natural ecosystems and biodiversity and equally dramatic increases in people and domestic animals. Never before have so many animals been kept by so many people – and never before have so many opportunities existed for pathogens to pass from wild and domestic animals through the biophysical environment to affect people causing zoonotic diseases or zoonoses …
>
> Around 60 per cent of all infectious diseases in humans are zoonotic as are 75 per cent of all emerging infectious diseases. On average, one new infectious disease emerges in humans every four months. While many originate in wildlife, livestock often serve as an epidemiological bridge between wildlife and human infections. This is especially the case for intensively reared livestock which are often genetically similar within a herd or flock and therefore lack the genetic diversity that provides resilience: the result of being bred for production characteristics rather than disease resistance. An example of livestock acting as a 'disease bridge' is the case of bird flu or avian influenza pathogens, which first circulated in wild birds, then infected domestic poultry and from them passed to humans.[30]

Ebola, SARS, bird flu, TB, salmonella ... the list of animal-to-human diseases, some using domestic animals as bridging species, is an increasing threat to global health and economic security. COVID-19 may come to be seen as the hidden danger unleashed on the world by our disregard for the integrity of wild systems and may force a dialling down of intensive animal farming. Both climate change and COVID-19 may help us realign our food production to systems that are less intensive and more sustainable, with knock-on effects for a whole range of wildlife, the badger included.

With such wide-ranging global and local issues at play, what is the outlook for badgers in Britain today? Of all the predators in this book, badgers present the most complex picture. They are undoubtedly much loved. Their shape, colour, endearing gait and snuffly demeanour, combined with their associations with ancient woodland, give them the prefect characteristics for children's stories and for winning adult affections. And yet, they can predate endangered birds and hedgehogs, transmit disease to cattle and can damage farmland. Increasingly, landowners want the power to control them. Many say that badgers are a 'new' phenomenon on their land and they cannot see why, as numbers are increasing, they are afforded special protection. On the other hand, after genera-tions of terrible persecution, badgers are at last regaining a foot-hold in their ancestral homes. As they become more common, many more people may glimpse them in the twilight. This alone may reignite a wonder and love for the natural world, something that has become so dimmed over the last few decades. As ambas-sadors for the natural world, badgers have few rivals.

Given these competing agendas, I asked Dominic Dyer, former CEO of the Badger Trust, if he could see any instance where it would be acceptable to cull badgers, for whatever reason. His answer was clear:

> 'In short – no. We have no certainty over the size of the badger population in Britain. Estimates range from around 350,000 to 500,000 at any one time. We know tens of thousands of badgers die on our roads every year (more than any other wild species), large numbers of badgers die as a result of illegal persecution and building development continues to pose a major threat to badgers and their habitats across Britain. On top of these threats, rapid climate change is also resulting in higher temperatures, heat waves and floods which also threaten badger populations. Culling for TB alone could be pushing the species to the verge of local extinction in parts of England, which badgers have inhabited since the Ice Age. Which is why we have lodged a complaint against the British Government in the Berne Convention. Taking this into account, there can be no justification for further human intervention to control badger numbers.'[31]

The badger conundrum goes deep into the heart of conservation. Encouraging people to love the natural world is vital, yet being realistic about the effect of wildlife in our hard-working landscapes is also part of good decision-making. The question is, if we cannot live with badgers, at present our largest predatory land mammal, how can we even imagine we can tolerate wildcats, lynx and wolves? Living with wildlife does require compromise, creative solutions and a desire to share. If we can gather together the love for badgers, engage positively and respectfully with those who want to control them, and present workable solutions to their specific issues, then we will be on the way to a wilder Britain.

Badgers, for me, are the test case that will truly stress-test our resolve.

*

On a sultry late summer evening, a few months before the COVID crisis, I drove the few miles from my home in Bristol to the outskirts of Portishead in North Somerset to meet local naturalist Chris Sperring. We headed into darkening woods that cling to a steep escarpment. The scouting trick of testing the direction of the wind with a wet finger indicated a sou'wester. After following tracks for twenty minutes, we settled downwind of a badgers' sett, our backs against the cracked bark of old beeches. The long shadows in failing light, the aroma of damp earth and the cawing of crows heading to roost is a combination of sight, smell and sound I struggle to put into words; an intense yearning for peace. A woodpigeon cooed its evening lullaby, a sound so gently soothing it flows like silk in a breeze. I wished I had thought to play it to my restless babies all those years ago. An agitated robin ticked in annoyance at our presence, but the midges were delighted to discover us in their neck of the woods.

Gradually, as night folded its wings over the trees, a hesitant, sniffing badger materialised at the entrance of the sett; as grainy as an old black-and-white film. This 'most ancient Briton of English beasts' could have been emerging from the past. It assessed the state of its universe with an upturn of its nose. Some deep-time fear of wolves no doubt stirred, but also a wariness of the dangerous humans that are always just metres away. On cue, two evening joggers with head torches lighting their way ran along the footpath close by, looking for all the world like racing beasts with burning eyes. The oval nose shrank back into the darkness. 'The problem with badger culling,' whispered Chris, 'is that it changes the atmosphere, it creates an air of permission to go back to the bad old days – to digging up setts and working with terriers. We are having problems around here now we haven't seen for many years.' Killing creates more killing. Always, the sound of traffic on the M5 motorway intrudes on this rural corridor, a droning reminder of the cheek-by-jowl nature of life in the west of England, and a constant underscore to the slow ticking of the clock. We settled back to wait.

This embattled old woodland has been made to work hard. Its scars are deep from centuries of chopping, coppicing, and now recreation, but it is still wildwood. The badger makes it so. Three hundred kilometres away in London, its fate is being decided in brightly lit offices. Plans are being discussed in Whitehall to increase the cull to up to fifty culling zones. There will be no end to the guns anytime soon.

The badger eventually re-emerged to the harsh, guttural cry of a raven over the valley and snuffled around the base of nearby trees. We watched the rotund form investigate the forest floor; its concerns are not with the pages of reports but with the scuttling of life in the undergrowth. I cannot think of a better word to describe the movement of a badger than 'trundle', a word with its origins in the rolling, revolving and bumpy way of a low and laden truck. At some time in the night, it would cross the fields below this wooded escarpment and pass through the herds of silent, breathy cows. After a while it disappeared into the heart of the wood, trailing in its wake the sweet odour of blackberries and mushroomy earth, tainted with a bitter miasma of our failings to embrace its world.

The darkness complete, Chris and I made our way back through the trees towards the orange glow of street lights below. Silver moonlight fell soft on grey fur and rich earth as we left the badgers to go about their business unperturbed.

A few months later no one wandered these woods as the spring 2020 lockdown kept us all away from the natural world. For a short time the badgers of Portishead found some semblance of peace. They emerged into quiet evenings and passed unseen through fields of cattle. They ambled down empty lanes while the world looked the other way. But it wasn't to last. By September 2021 the government announced further cull areas bringing the total to forty, meaning 76,000 badgers could be killed across England. The marksmen are now just a few miles away. The cow-covered, warm and wet grasslands of Somerset can be both home and battlefield for this rotund beast. It is up to us which it is destined to be.

5

Buzzards and Hen Harriers

Every time I see a buzzard, I want to give it a high-five; it is a bulky, noisy reminder of success. The buzzard bounce-back over the last forty years is proof that we don't have to live in a world of ecological failure, with the dull ache of despair at a homogenised and depleted world. And what's more, buzzards have come back on their own, without any fuss, money or micro-management. All it took was for us to reduce our persecution of them, and very quickly they sailed back into our lives and plonked themselves down on the nearest fence post. Short-necked and barrel-chested, they metaphorically rolled up their shirt sleeves and set about recolonising the old haunts from which they had been so ruthlessly extirpated. They didn't announce their arrival with a fanfare or an action plan, they simply came in through the back door and got on with it. Pondering the characterisation of the common buzzard, *Buteo buteo*, BTO scientist and artist, Rachel Taylor, mused, 'If buzzards were people, they would wear wellies and have a shed.'

Buzzards are birds of woodland edge rather than open land, so as long as they have trees (or sometimes cliff faces) to nest on, and small mammals, birds and invertebrates to eat, they will settle and breed. Today they are a common sight in the winter, plodding through fields searching for worms, or soaring and roller-coastering on spring and summer thermals. Their sturdy, nothing-fancy-but-does-the-job nests of sticks can now be found in woodland throughout Britain.

I clearly recall the first time I saw one up close. It was in the early 1980s in the Brecon Beacons in Wales, when there were only a few thousand pairs across the UK. I was driving down a small track in the late afternoon and spotted a large brown and cream-streaked bird of prey hunched on a fence post, looking for all the world like a stunted eagle. I stopped the car, captivated by the bird's size and presence. Yellow-legged, round-bodied, small-headed, yellow at the base of the beak with a vicious black hook, it glared back with a mixture of wariness and resentment. It didn't so much perch lightly, but rather rooted itself, staking its right not only to the post but also the trees and fields all around. I can't agree with Leslie Brown's 1986 book on raptors, which described buzzards as, 'sluggish and not very bold';[1] this one contained power and attitude in its stocky, feathered form, and it defiantly held my gaze. I felt an enormous surge of privilege. It took the universe ten billion years to produce the two living beings whose eyes now met for the briefest of moments, but the buzzard wasn't as thrilled as I was. Untouched by my metaphysical musings, it flashed a grumpy glare and launched itself skywards, its rounded and heavy wings languidly beating the cold air. Any serendipitous encounter with the wild is powerful and sears into the brain. I have never forgotten that first, face-to-face meeting with a buzzard, simple and brief as it was.

There are now an estimated 80,000 pairs in the UK (up from 10,000 in the 1960s) and they breed in every county, but are more common in the west. Half the size of an eagle, and for many people, possessing only half the charisma, they are neither really loved nor particularly disliked, except perhaps by some gamekeepers. Their plaintive, searching cry, like a sky-cat lost in a storm, can often be heard over mountains, farmland, greenbelt and coasts, even cities. Mewing and floating, spiralling and soaring, they draw our earth-bound eyes towards vastness. On a planet that feels as if it is losing wildness by the day, this chance to reconnect with nature is a vital service.

All in all, twenty-first-century Britain tolerates buzzards, but it hasn't always been so. The first records of them being considered a pest, and therefore presumably widespread across the land, is an Act from James II of Scotland in 1457, which describes them as one of the birds that should be destroyed for stealing poultry, rabbits and game. The familiar process of changing the fortunes of a creature by tarnishing its reputation and associating it with nega-tivity was set in motion. The word buzzard was used for people considered overweight and lazy, presumably because buzzards can spend hours sitting on a fence or branch, staring at the ground waiting for prey to pass by. The phrase 'You cannot make a hunting hawk out of a buzzard'[2] appeared, with a meaning roughly equivalent to the expression 'You can't make a silk purse out of a sow's ear.' In seventeenth-century Kent, records show that farmers killed thousands of buzzards in the period 1680–1690.[3] It was common practice for a church warden to pay 2d (two pence) for every buzzard head taken to him. In 1768, a certain R. Smith (who describes himself as the rat-catcher to Princess Amelia, the second daughter of George II) wrote about ways of catching 'winged vermin' to protect rabbit warrens and pheasantries (he also describes in detail how to kill foxes, badgers, sheep-killing dogs, wild cats and hedgehogs).[4] Even so, up until the 1800s buzzards probably bred in every county and were common.

Then, as for so many meat-eating creatures, the pressure on them was increased by the invention of the breech-loading gun in the mid nineteenth century. It spelled deep trouble as the decades of intensive game shooting began. Any creature, winged or not, that was considered a threat to gamebirds was removed in a whole host of brutal ways. 'Vermin', a word in my view which should be forever removed from the English language, were commonly shot, trapped, snared, poisoned, torn apart by dogs and beaten to death. Buzzards were just one of a suite of predators that were targeted for eating adult gamebirds and chicks, their demise made easier by their slow flight, their tolerance of people and their predilection for carrion, which was easily laced with poison. By the 1860s, they were considered 'by no means common and nearly exterminated in the eastern and midland counties of England',[5] which were the regions where pheasant and partridge shooting were most popular. By 1887, they were sufficiently rare that total extinction was considered a possibility. By 1915, they could only be found on higher ground in the west. They fared better than other birds of prey, though: the white-tailed eagle, honey buzzard, osprey, marsh harrier and the goshawk were hunted to extinction.

By the end of the Second World War the world had changed. There were fewer gamekeepers and the size of game estates was reduced. The hunting of wild creatures for taxidermy and eggs for collections also declined, sparking a buzzard revival. The clamouring, soaring 'poor man's eagle' once again appeared over parts of the lowlands. But then another blow was dealt. This time it was not direct persecution but the virtual destruction of a major food source.

Rabbits were a problem for farmers. Their numbers had expanded rapidly in the eighteenth and nineteenth centuries when winter crops were grown, ensuring them a food supply all year round. A large number of their natural predators had also been removed by gamekeepers, of which there were 23,000 in the UK in 1911.[6] By the 1950s, up to 100 million rabbits were costing the farming industry £50 million a year.[7] The solution was effective but cruel. In 1953 myxomatosis, a virus from South America, was deliberately introduced into Britain from France to curb rabbit numbers. The virus attacks their mucous membranes and causes swelling and discharge in the eyes. The suffering is immense and protracted, with infected animals taking over a week to die. Distressed, blind rabbits blundering along roadside verges were a common sight throughout the late 1950s and 1960s, their eyes bulging and weeping. It was an animal welfare catastrophe and 99 per cent of rabbits in the UK disappeared. This sudden mass cull had widespread effects, both good and bad. Over-grazed woodlands, grasslands and heaths began to regenerate, but in other areas rank vegetation and scrub shaded out rarer plants. The impact on the fortunes of the rabbits' predators was significant. Buzzards, foxes and stoats all declined, and buzzard numbers fell back once again, holding out mainly in the west and where rabbits were not as common.

In 1957, the journal *British Birds* published an article summarising the fortunes of buzzards before and immediately after myxomatosis and found 'a great decrease in breeding activity of Buzzards in all regions where Rabbits had become rare or extinct. Many, perhaps most, pairs did not breed at all. It was normal in local areas where the Rabbit-population was not affected, and where Rabbits had never been abundant.'[8]

Although rabbits slowly recovered as they gained immunity to the virus, and the ever-adaptable buzzard switched to other prey, buzzard numbers did not recover as they should. The reason given in the *British Birds* article has a chilling resonance: 'It has been widely assumed by poultry-farmers and shooting men that the Buzzards' depredations on poultry and game would increase when Rabbits became scarce. They have acted on this assumption by shooting more Buzzards.' Despite the fact they were theoretically protected by the Wild Birds Protection Act since 1880, it was a demonstration of the impotence of the law without the power of public backing. In short, where game rearing was popular, buzzards were rare. As N.W. Moore put it in the 1957 *British Birds* article:

Gamekeepers are more likely to be swayed by tradition and the occasional misdeed of a Buzzard – real or imaginary – than by ecological theory. It is likely that present conditions and attitudes will continue for some time. If they do, it is improbable that the species will become common in the east of the country however suitable the habitat remains in those parts … The future of the Buzzard in Britain will depend, like its past, on the opinions of those who preserve game.[9]

And if persecution wasn't enough, another wrecking ball, in the form of the widespread use of the organo-chloride pesticides DDT, Aldrin and Dieldrin in the late 1950s, destroyed any glimmer of hope for a revival. DDT was sprayed across crops to eliminate insects, transferring the poison from the insects into the bodies of small birds and thence into birds of prey, especially the bird-eating specialists like the peregrine, merlin and sparrowhawk. A build-up of DDT in the raptors' bodies affected their reproduction by thinning eggshells, which then broke in the nest. Buzzards were potentially vulnerable too, but already reduced to living mainly in the hilly west of Britain on a diet low in birds, they were not as badly affected as other species. American scientist and writer Rachel Carson described organo-chloride pesticides as 'as crude a weapon as the caveman's club', and they took a heavy toll. Her epoch-making book, *Silent Spring*, offered a devastating critique of these death-dealing chemicals and ultimately led to a ban on the use of DDT in the UK; but not until 1984, twenty-two years after the book was published, and twelve years after its use was banned in the USA. The coming into force of the 1981 Wildlife and Countryside Act gave added legal protection to all wild birds, and once more the plucky buzzard began to rebuild its life in Britain.

It requires skill and judgement to recognise moments of great change like this, and then to have the presence of mind to record it for posterity. Octogenarian ornithologist, artist and story-teller Robin Prytherch, who lives in Bristol, did just that.

Robin's top-floor flat in the Clifton district has a buzzard's-eye view over Georgian rooftops and across to the wooded cliffs of the Avon Gorge. Spread out on a coffee table are three maps of a 75-square-kilometre patch of farmland and woodland on the southern edge of the city. 'I first got interested in a buzzard survey in 1979,' says Robin. 'There seemed to be more around than people thought.' A few years later, Robin had set up his own research area and started the longest continuous study of buzzards ever undertaken, right at the point when they began their miraculous comeback. He has dedicated thousands of hours to ringing and monitoring, drawing and writing about them. Every Christmas he sends out hand-drawn cards of the local buzzards and each one tells a story gathered from hours of observation.

Sifting through a pile of these cards, I can only marvel at the obvious intimacy between man and bird, a relationship fostered over decades. Many have names, like Riv, Honey, Speckles, Gos and Spotty – individual characters in a forty-year buzzard soap-opera featuring episodes of loss and success, faithfulness, bigamy, incest and violence. One card shows a regal-looking buzzard on a branch with a couple of others perched on leafless winter trees in the background.

'This was Tess,' Robin tells me, 'the best breeder in my study area, she fledged over forty-three chicks in her lifetime. Her first mate, in 1984, was Tertials, and they had thirteen chicks together, but he died in 1991 after a few vicious fights with another male, Tuff, who took over as Tess's partner. I actually found the body of Tertials under a bush. Tess and Tuff went on to have thirty more chicks. She had some clutches of four, which is really remarkable. I last saw Tess in 2003 and she's now been replaced with another female. Tess would have been about twenty-two or three when she died.'

Tuff, Tess and Tertials, the three Ts of North Somerset, living out their long lives in the damp fields and woodlands of the Gordano valley, their intimate behaviour scrutinised and recorded by Robin. In 1984, when Tess first arrived, Margaret Thatcher was prime minister, the miners' strike began and I was a student linking arms around the perimeter of Greenham Common singing songs of peace. When Tess left us, Tony Blair was in Downing Street, two million people marched against the Iraq war and I had settled in Bristol to start my own family. Whatever events were playing out in the human sphere, the buzzards were in their parallel world, dealing with the ups and downs of their own event-filled lives.

My attention is now on the maps, spread out on Robin's coffee table. The first shows the territories he had mapped in 1988: nineteen large, amoeba-like shapes are drawn over the landscape, encasing both patches of woodland and farmland. They are all roughly the same size and show where each pair had a nest and the extent of the surrounding feeding grounds they defended. They avoided the greyed-out areas which represent the towns of Clevedon, Nailsea and Portishead. The next map, for 1997, just nine years later, shows far more blobs and they are more squashed together. There are now sixty buzzard territories on the southern outskirts of Bristol – a three-fold increase. The third map, for 2007, is even more densely populated. By Robin's reckoning, there were now ninety-two occupied territories, showing a near 400 per cent increase in thirty years. The buzzard recolonisation was well on track, but didn't stop there. 'This year [2019] it looks like we have 120 territories,' he said, 'and they have just about got to saturation point. They now defend much smaller areas; I think we are full up.' It is a pattern repeated across the UK as buzzards have increased by more than 600 per cent since the 1960s.

The buzzard colonisation continues eastwards where it has not yet reached capacity; there are still places where they could settle and breed once again. But there is not a unanimous welcome. Some landowners who run grouse, pheasant and partridge shoots are disconcerted by large birds of prey setting up on their patch.

The buzzard diet is varied and includes small birds and chicks, as well as mammals, reptiles and invertebrates. If game chicks are abundant, they will eat those too. Robin Prytherch recorded thirty-five different prey species in nests around Bristol, the most preyed-upon being rabbits and voles; but the number also includes plenty of crows, which is pleasing to the farmers. There is little game shooting in this mainly cattle-farming area and very little conflict with birds of prey. 'Everyone seems to love the buzzards around here,' says Robin. 'When I'm out buzzard-watching, lots of people ask me about them, including farmers, and the reception they get from people is very positive.' Going further afield, however, the reaction is more mixed. On my 500-mile walk for curlews in 2016, the keepers I met disliked buzzards and blamed them for the disappearance of wading birds, skylarks and plovers – as well as game. 'There are just too many these days,' was the common refrain. But the widespread belief that they take a lot of valuable gamebirds is not always backed up by the evidence.

In 2016, around a grouse moor in southern Scotland, thirty-two buzzard nests were monitored over three years.[10] Only 6 per cent of the prey remains found in or near the nest were red grouse, which is likely to be an over-estimate, as large prey is more likely to be found than smaller remains. Nest cameras, which record all prey being brought in rather than just what is found as remains, showed that in fact less than 1 per cent of the prey brought to the nest was game. Even in the winter months when other food is scarce, red grouse provided only 1–3 per cent of the prey. Professor Ian Newton, the UK's leading authority on birds of prey, commented, 'Clearly, on these figures, individual buzzards can have had no significant impact on this grouse population, especially as some of the grouse eaten may have been taken as carrion. It would take a lot of buzzards to have a significant effect.'

In 2015, a review paper was published which looked at the effect of buzzards on pheasants and concluded that: 'Historically, losses of poults (young pheasants) to raptor predation has been low, commonly (90% of shoots) ≤1% of birds released into pens, representing a small percentage of losses relative to all causes of mortality. A small number of shoots did suffer higher losses, estimated at >5% at one in 30 estates and >10% at some estates.'[11] It suggested further research was needed to see if these findings from twenty years ago still stand.

The British Association for Shooting and Conservation (BASC), an organisation set up 'To promote and protect sporting shooting and advocate the benefits it brings to the natural environment', agrees that at times the perception that buzzards are a problem is not matched by the evidence. Their estimate is that only 1–2 per cent of pheasant poults (young pheasants) released into woodlands are taken by buzzards each year. These are very small losses and the response is disproportionate. Much like a fox taking the occasional lamb, it is easy to blame the most visible culprit, and decry the now common sight of the buzzard in Britain.

With an increase of incidents of buzzard persecution by keepers, the BASC published a booklet which was endorsed by the RSPB, the Joint Nature Conservation Committee and Scottish Natural Heritage (NatureScot). It is constantly updated to give advice to pheasant gamekeepers:

The concentration of pheasant poults in and around release pens appears to offer an attractive source of food for birds of prey. The impact, however, may be lower than expected.

The daily food requirement of a sparrowhawk is some 40–70g, a tawny owl 75g and a buzzard 90g. Pheasant poults weigh some 600g at eight weeks, increasing rapidly to around

900g for females and 1200g for males at twelve weeks. For each bird of prey, therefore, which has a release pen in its territory, this equates to much less than one pheasant poult per day (even if fed entirely on pheasants). Furthermore, when feeding their young, birds of prey are hunting at a time of year when abundant alternative prey is available, including small mammals, birds and rabbits.[12]

The booklet lays out sensible measures to reduce losses such as not releasing pheasant poults until they are 7–8 weeks old (the age at which they are usually too large to be commonly attacked), putting reflective tape around pens to scare raptors away, reducing the number of perching posts near where the pheasants are kept, and leaving kills on the ground so that the birds can return to the same carcass rather than kill again. The booklet concludes:

It is unlikely that reducing the 1–2% loss to birds of prey in the release pen will significantly increase the number of birds available for shooting later in the season. Far more pheasants are lost to other predators, disease, accidents and starvation in the period after release.[13]

Some field sports magazines and online shooting forums are not convinced. They say that no deterrents work well, that buzzards are simply too numerous to keep away, and that their mere presence in a woodland is enough to spread fear among the poults, stopping them from venturing out into the open and feeding properly. They point to hot spots where predation rates are higher than the low percentage quoted. In 2016, pheasant gamekeeper Tom Boxall, who raises 10,000 birds a year for a commercial shoot in Gloucestershire, gave an interview to the *Guardian* newspaper.

'There's an old saying: where there's livestock, there's going to be deadstock. You accept the buzzards are always going to have some, but this year was horrendous. I lost 500 pheasants at £3.75 each.'[14] This is 5 per cent of his stock. Ian Danby, Head of Biodiversity for the BASC, told me recently that 'losses vary for sure, and there will be cases where there are some local impacts that are significant and there can be a case for licences. However, the general principle of working around protected predators is still entirely correct. A lot of birds of prey are doing quite nicely across the UK and so there are plenty of reasons to be optimistic.'

For some people, though, the change brought about by the increase in buzzard numbers has gone beyond what they consider acceptable and they want lethal control to be reintroduced as an option. At present, the only legal way is to apply for a licence to the national agencies, the bodies that advise governments on environmental matters, namely Natural England (NE), NatureScot (NS) and Natural Resources Wales (NRW). In 2012, in response to increasing complaints about buzzards, Natural England proposed a trial whereby adult birds could be captured and removed from a pheasant shooting area and their nests destroyed. The outcry was so great that the plan was dropped. In 2013, they did grant a licence for a gamekeeper to destroy four nests and their contents; but it took a Freedom of Information request for it to come to light, which infuriated conservationists. In July 2016, Natural England issued a licence, which came with strict guidelines attached, to a gamekeeper to shoot up to ten buzzards to protect pheasants.

The licence is time-limited with stringent conditions and is based on the law, policy and best available evidence. It follows rigorous assessment after other methods had been tried

unsuccessfully over a 5-year period. It is stipulated that the
licence must be used in combination with non-lethal measures
and only on buzzards in and immediately around the animal
pens – not on passing birds. These conditions are designed to
make the licensed activity both proportionate and effective and
we will continue to work with the applicant to assess this.
Killing wild birds without a licence from Natural England is
illegal.[15]

Once again, there was widespread condemnation. The number of
birds that can be legally killed under licence seems to be rising, and
so is the temperature surrounding buzzards and the game industry.
In 2016, Martin Harper, then the RSPB's Director of Conservation,
wrote a blog in response to the decision:

The killing of a recovering British bird of prey to protect an
introduced gamebird for the benefit of commercial interest is
wrong. The decision sets a worrying precedent. What will be
next? Red kites, peregrines, hen harriers? … Forty-five million
pheasants and six million red-legged partridge are released into
the countryside each year. We don't know what the ecological
consequences of this introduction are but it's hardly surprising
that it attracts predators. The loss of some of these gamebirds is
an inevitable consequence of doing business. Natural predators
should not be bearing the cost in this instance.
     A test of a modern society is one that tolerates predators and
finds ways to live in harmony with them. Reaching for the gun,
every time there is a perceived conflict, is the wrong response.[16]

Between 2016 and 2019, Natural England issued nine licences to control buzzards to protect pheasant shoots, which together permitted a maximum of sixty birds to be killed. The consternation around these decisions is not purely based on the individual cases. In the words of *Guardian* columnist Patrick Barkham, 'It is a precedent-setting, tone-setting action which reveals Britain's disastrously dysfunctional relationship with predators.'[17] Buzzards are finding themselves once again in the middle of gamebird trouble.

In their Asian homelands the common pheasant is revered. Its livery of burnished gold, emerald and red endows it with the majesty of a sun god; so much so that the pheasant may have been the inspiration for the legend of the phoenix rising out of the ashes. When it bursts into the air with loud cries and a clattering of wings it jolts our senses into the energy of the moment – especially so when over a kilogram of panicked flesh hits the car windscreen. Sixty-five pheasant-related car accidents per year were reported in the UK between 1999 and 2003, 6 per cent of these resulting in people being seriously injured or killed.[18]

Pheasant releases in the UK have increased by approximately 900 per cent since the 1960s, as more efficient rearing methods have been developed.[19] Even though tens of millions of pheasants are released each year, only 50 per cent are recorded as shot,[20] leaving the rest to disperse into the wider countryside. Some succumb to disease and predation, but a lot die on the roads. Devon-based conservationist Derek Gow called them 'a standard road surface in the west of England'. Pheasants seem particularly susceptible to being hit by cars as they are cumbersome during take-off, have short flight distances and spend most of their time on the ground, commonly near roadside verges. An increasing number, though, are surviving the hazards of modern Britain and are establishing themselves as wild birds. British Trust for Ornithology (BTO) data indicate a nearly 100 per cent increase in the population of feral pheasants since the 1960s.[21] The knock-on effect of this is still under review, but further BTO research indicates that pheasant releases do sustain high numbers of predators,[22] and data from the Game and Wildlife Conservation Trust (GWCT), among others, suggest that high pheasant densities might be altering hedgerows,[23] changing the community composition of woodland invertebrates,[24] and may be having long-term negative impacts on the diversity of woodland species.[25]

As pheasant shooting is an ancient sport in the UK and goes back several centuries, the increase in the numbers of pheasants raised for sport has crept up on us and largely gone under the radar. Pheasants may have originally been introduced by the Romans, but they have fallen in and out of favour over the centuries. The most common type of pheasant seen in the UK today, the ring-necked pheasant, was reintroduced in the nineteenth century, when their popularity for shooting took off in a big way. Cock birds provide enough meat for up to three people, and their curling flight in strong autumnal winds is a test of the shooter's skill. In 1910, Winston Churchill, alongside MPs and ministers, was part of a three-day, eight-gun shoot at Warter Priory in Yorkshire.[26] Records show they bagged 4,926 pheasants, 1,385 hares, 396 rabbits, 34 partridges, six woodcock and a duck. Nowadays, thankfully, bag rates are lower and people pay for the number of pheasants they want to shoot per day, usually between 200 and 500 birds. To accommodate this, many estates produce a surplus of pheasants to put on a good show of numbers.

It was an uncharacteristically warm October day when I met the head gamekeeper of a pheasant shooting estate, who wishes to remain anonymous, at a stunning mansion sitting within over

5,000 hectares of downland in the west of England. Driving through the ornate front gates, which opened automatically at an unseen signal, I admit to being in awe of the grandeur of the house and the vastness of the grounds. They speak of an accumulation of wealth beyond imagining, a legacy of empire that we British carry in our social structures and our psyche.

If visiting a grouse moor is like stepping into a brooding moorland painting by George Lambert, then on that sunny day in the green heart of England, I felt I had taken on the persona of Gainsborough's Mrs Andrews in his famous portrait of the said Mrs Andrews and her husband. To my mind – that of a city-living non-shooter – grouse and pheasant shooting were similar sports, just different birds. In some ways this is true, in that they both involve guns and game, but the experience of place is vastly different. Windswept, open moors for one give way to rolling, cultivated fields dotted with copses and defined by hedgerows for the other. Instead of crouching behind butts and firing at wheeling, wild, native birds careering close overhead, a pheasant-shooting party stands in a line out in the open. Large numbers of captive-reared, non-native birds are driven over the top of woodland towards the guns so that they curl and twist high in the sky. Describing this part of England in 2007, the magazine *Shooting Gazette* wrote, 'The shoots in this golden crescent of countryside … reside in every shooting man's wish-list of the most desirable venues. Collectively, they have carved out a remarkable reputation for showing sporting birds of the best kind … Mother Nature and the good Lord have produced valleys that promise class action.'[27]

We drove to a patch of broadleaved woodland surrounded by an electric fence where young birds (poults) are kept after they are bought from a dealer at six or seven weeks old. The eggs are procured from abroad, the chicks raised in cages and then sold on to estates. Their first home is usually in a woodland pen, which provides a secure place for them to acclimatise and discover the out-of-doors. For three weeks they are fed and kept safe from predators by keepers. Once they are large enough, the gate is opened and the birds are free to range into the surrounding fields where they find acres of food crops, shelter and supplementary feed from hoppers. Predator numbers continue to be kept low to help them survive until the shooting season.

This particular shoot is not intensive. It is open only on twenty days a year, and eight guns will expect to bag 200 birds a day. Even so, to provide these 4,000 birds, a minimum of 10,000 are reared and released each year. I asked what predators cause the most problems for young birds – buzzards? 'No, not here, they maybe take a few, but not enough to worry me. Foxes and badgers sometimes, and there are more and more kites around nowadays. One year, otters got into the pen and killed sixty birds in one night. They do a lot of damage to the stocked rivers too.' I didn't, though, get the impression that predator control was a big part of this keeper's job, unlike on grouse moors, 'but there are a lot of shooting estates round about, so predator numbers are low anyway.' I asked if he thought the high numbers of birds released each year help support unnaturally large numbers of predators, and if so, was that a problem for the wider countryside? 'I don't know, I'd have to see the science, but they probably do feed foxes.'

This is a vexed question, and one that is receiving more attention. In 2019, the British Trust for Ornithology paper quoted earlier shed some light onto the relationship between gamebirds and avian predators. The authors assessed a wide sweep of data sets and found positive associations between gamebird release areas and increased numbers of generalist avian predators such as buzzards and crows. This in turn, they suggest, might alter the predator–prey balance of an area and have negative implications for other wildlife. Lead author, Dr Henrietta Pringle, stated:

> The idea that gamebird releases might enhance populations of generalist predators is not new, but our results are the first to indicate this may actually be happening on a national scale. While gamebirds are only one of the factors that could shape predator populations, our work emphasises the need to better understand the impacts of releasing roughly 46,000 tonnes of gamebird biomass into the countryside annually. For context, the estimated total biomass for all native UK breeding bird species is just 19,500 tonnes.[28]

If game is increasing avian predator numbers then it is likely that they are also boosting mammalian predator numbers, though here too, more research is needed before general conclusions are made.

Everywhere on the estate there were cronking and clattering pheasants and scuttling French partridges (also reared here for shooting), running along the tracks, feeding in small flocks in the fields and emerging from copses and hedges. Driving around, I was amazed at the amount of land that was dedicated to the birds. On top of a rise we looked out over vast, open fields of crops, all of it dedicated to game. Maize provides cover, kale is nutritious food, large, linear patches of cover crops like triticale, linseed sorghum and millet provide seeds, refuge and shelter. In the centre of many fields, ridges of beetle-banks composed of various grasses and wild-flowers allow insects and spiders to thrive, while all around the edges are miles of specially planted hedgerows. Much of this work is subsidised by the agricultural grants that are available to every farmer for the benefit and support of wildlife on their land, and wildlife includes pheasants. It is one of the quirks of British law that a pheasant is livestock when in a pen, but becomes a wild bird when released. Crops like maize are not used for any other purpose; once they are no longer needed, they are simply ploughed back into the soil and the area is replanted.

Keeping all this going makes the role of a lowland gamekeeper more like that of a cereal farmer. 'Lots of other birds love this too,' said my guide, gesturing to the cultivated vista that stretched into the distance. 'The food crops and cover help all kinds of species and the air is alive with songbirds in the spring, it's my favourite time of the year. The number of butterflies in the summer is astonishing, so the woodland and the farmland benefit lots of wildlife, not just game.' Research by the Game and Wildlife Conservation Trust does indicate higher songbird numbers in woodlands managed for pheasants.[29] Its authors write that they recorded 'approximately 40% more birds in woods in southern England and between 22% and 32% more birds were observed in pheasant-managed woods than control woods'.

Natural England estimates that around 1.2 million hectares of lowland farmland are managed for pheasant and partridge shooting. In a research paper published in 2009 they list the pros and cons of shooting. For the former they are in agreement with GWCT and conclude:

In general terms, sport shooting in the lowlands has had a positive effect on the landscape. Many hedgerows, field margins and small woodlands are maintained more for their sporting value than for their biodiversity interest, although the practice can be beneficial in both aspects. Many land managers with shooting interests plant small areas of game cover to provide food and shelter for partridges and pheasant. These crops provide a useful food source for farmland birds such as sparrows, finches and buntings when winter cropping regimes may have reduced other feeding opportunities.[30]

This assessment, though, is surrounded by caveats. Among them are warnings of the detrimental effects of lead shot, poisons laid down for rats (who proliferate in the maize fields), an unnatural distortion of predator numbers, illegal persecution of birds of prey, food competition between native and non-native birds and the disturbance caused in rural areas by the shooting itself. The ethics of intensive sport shooting isn't part of the list. The big questions surrounding the rights and wrongs of causing so many bird deaths for entertainment and using so much land for bird food are left to the conscience of individuals.

On that warm October day, mixed flocks of chattering tits and finches rushed around the hedgerows, stout corn buntings flitted about, as well as nervy squadrons of fieldfares. A kestrel hovered motionless above a ride. There was obviously much more life in the estate than just pheasants. But I still had a problem with numbers. If only 4,000 birds are shot in a season, why the need to cater for 10,000? 'We have to have a good show of birds, but bear in mind we are small. There are estates around here that shoot for 200 days a year and bag 200 to 400 birds a day, so the number of pheasants they put down is far greater.'

The need to 'show' birds and the pressure to provide large numbers inevitably leads to many unaccounted bodies. On the bigger estates thousands of carcasses that are not taken home end up being collected and buried, although the keeper I met was adamant this did not happen on this shoot. Some incapacitated birds suffer lingering deaths. Half-dead pheasants left on the ground raise important animal welfare questions. If all were eaten, it would provide one justification, but the sheer number of pheasant and partridges raised today means there is a glut in the market and their monetary value is low. Former head gamekeeper of Holkham Estate in Norfolk, Simon Lester, is concerned. 'I do feel the industry has gone over the top. What really gets to me is when you can't sell the end product, it's gone too far.'

Jake Fiennes, the present General Manager of Conservation for the Holkham Estate in Norfolk, agrees that small shoots may have general benefits for wildlife, but that larger ones are a problem. 'Most big commercial pheasant shoots have limited environmental value. The smaller shoots that have entered into agri-environment schemes adjacent to their maize crops, they have greater abundance of farmland birds, that is undoubtedly true. But on the big shoots, shooting four days a week, hundreds of birds a day, releasing between 10,000 and 60,000 birds, there is limited value in that. And most people don't eat what they shoot. Many birds are buried or burned. There has been an increase in applications for incinerators on shooting estates in the last three years.' There are other worries too. Lead shot is scattered around the landscape and lodged in the birds' bodies, so much so that the Food Standards Agency recommends pregnant women and young children limit the amount of game-meat they consume.

No other country provides such intensive shooting – it is uniquely British. The fiery sun gods of Asia are simply a sporting commodity in much of the UK. As we ended the tour, I asked the keeper if he liked pheasants. 'Yes, I do, but they are pretty stupid. Most of my job is keeping them alive, they seem intent on killing themselves.'

On the drive back home, I pulled over and walked along a track to the top of Salisbury Plain to look out over the rolling landscape, a soft and beautiful vista in the evening light. By now shadows were beginning to lengthen, giving a depth to the contours and a sensuality to the hard realities of agricultural Britain. Nothing, but nothing is straightforward here. Red flags and a line of tanks trundling down a distant hill added another, unsettling, dimension to a challenging visit, a day which had raised more questions than answers. I felt troubled. There is not a hunting, shooting or fishing bone in my body, I have never shot anything (other than a paper target) and don't eat meat. But I have never believed the world has to be like me, and my family are not vegetarians. There is room for us all if we practise restraint, have respect for each other and for non-human life and we treasure this wondrous planet. Stretched out before me was an agricultural and shooting landscape managed with steel blades, chemicals and financial spreadsheets. Somehow, wild creatures with ancient instincts have to find a home in this industrial space. If low-level shooting is helping wild birds under pressure, then I can live with that – but what about the negatives of illegal predator control, lead poisoning, the use of valuable land just for gamebirds, and the unnecessary suffering to the birds?

I wondered if there were other ideas not yet on the table that could make the estates work harder for a wider range of wildlife. Could any of the game estates also be managed for endangered ground-nesting birds like curlew and lapwing, both of which are plummeting in number? A question I put to Jake Fiennes. 'I can't see any reason why land couldn't be made available. Especially if direct agricultural support goes after Brexit and public goods are the new income stream. My belief is that we need multi-functional habitats and there would be no reason why they couldn't be made suitable for lapwing and curlew reintroductions. And who knows where game shooting will be in ten years' time?' It is hard to read the future, but change of some kind is most certainly on the way.

*

According to stereotype, if pheasant shooting has the air of picnic hampers and prosecco, grouse shooting is scratchy tweed and a hip flask of whisky. It has been a pastime of the aristocracy since the seventeenth century. Red grouse are native birds that live on heather moorland, nest on the ground and have a low, erratic flight which makes them highly attractive as a target. Plump and succulent, their roasted bodies furnish the tables of fine restaurants and reassure diners that all is well with the wild meat of the uplands. Their guttural call and rather comical red eye-shadow must stir the heart of shooters as the twelfth of August approaches, the official start of the grouse shooting season.

Originally, birds were shot on the ground as they perched on tussocks, or were taken by trained hawks. In the eighteenth century, as guns improved, grouse were shot in flight as they were flushed from the heather by lines of men and dogs walking across the land – so-called 'walked-up shooting'. It was available only to the fit and wealthy with plenty of leisure time. With the introduction of the double-barrelled breech-loading gun in the mid-nineteenth century, alongside the spread of railways giving easier access to the uplands, more people could take part in this country sport. Now, instead of walking, the shooters stood in a line and the birds were driven towards the guns by 'beaters' and dogs in what is known as 'driven grouse shooting' or DGS. It became so popular that shooting schools developed, jobs became dependent on it and the range of guns and equipment expanded greatly. But it was still available only to the well off and landed gentry.

This continued, with some wartime interruptions, until the structure of society and the distribution of money began to change in the latter part of the twentieth century, particularly from the 1980s onwards. In this modern era, DGS shooters are no longer confined to the traditional upper classes but encompass anyone with a desire for expensive country leisure, such as big-salaried, city corporates. Now the emphasis is often (but certainly not always) on lavish shooting weekends and large bag sizes. This has been a damaging development as the large numbers of birds these clients demand has driven the intensity of grouse management. This transition from aristocratic pastime to high-end field sport has demanded greater numbers of red grouse and has also put pressure on any predators that threaten this lucrative business. It is now thought, by the industry's own study,[31] to provide 1,520 full-time equivalent jobs (in the form of keepers, hospitality, beaters, loaders etc.) and to be worth nearly £100 million to the UK economy, although others dispute these figures. Not all DGS is this intensive. Some moors are run by families or small business consortia, often at a loss, and are more akin to passion projects and have lower bag sizes. But it is true to say that the majority of DGS moors are centred on making money. Since the middle of the twentieth century, therefore, grouse shooting has fundamentally changed in character, with a knock-on effect for predators.

Certain heartbreak species come to represent the tragedy of grouse moor conflict; creatures so persecuted they cannot find a foothold on the steep climb to recovery. The hen harrier is so stark an example that for people living in England even catching a glimpse of one is very rare indeed. Named after its predilection for taking domestic chickens, it was once a common bird of prey in the UK. Only a handful of pairs now breed successfully on English moors, despite there being enough suitable habitat for a few hundred. Whereas the buzzard is recolonising Britain after the cessation of widespread and relentless persecution, hen harriers have not rallied in the same way. Smaller than a buzzard (the male hen harrier weighs in at 400 grams, a male buzzard can be 1 kilogram), males are altogether more ostentatious. With striking, ash-grey, black-tipped wings and piercing yellow eyes, they frolic and swoop on spring winds, performing breath-taking manoeuvres for their mate, earning them the name 'sky-dancers'. As with most raptors, females are larger, up to 600 grams, mostly brown with a round face and with distinctive pale stripes across the tail, hence their common name, 'ringtail'. They nest on the ground and have a liking for the conditions produced by managed heather moorland, which supplies lots of small birds, mammals and chicks to feed their young. A bird-eating raptor living under the same conditions as, and in close proximity to, commercially valuable game like red grouse does not make for a fairy-tale ending.

Although hen harriers are still common across mainland Europe, and categorised as being of Least Concern by the IUCN Red List, they are failing badly in Britain, where only around 500 pairs remain. The situation is particularly bad in England, which now has fewer than twenty breeding pairs, mainly found in or around the 150 grouse moor estates on the northern moors. There are a number of reasons for low numbers, including the usual habitat loss and afforestation, but by far the biggest threat is persecution.

In 2019, a multi-author study published in the journal *Nature Communications*[32] showed that a hen harrier is ten times more likely to disappear in areas with driven grouse moors than over the wider landscape. Data were analysed from fifty-eight birds that were satellite-tagged between 2007 and 2017. The findings were incontrovertible. Of those fifty-eight harriers, only seven were still alive at the end of the study period. Five birds were found to have died a natural death and there were only four cases of known satellite tag malfunction. Therefore, the shocking conclusion reached by the report is that 72 per cent of the hen harriers were confirmed, or considered very likely, to have been illegally killed. Steve

Redpath, then professor of conservation science at the University of Aberdeen, and one of the report's lead authors, concluded, 'Our analysis points the finger at continued illegal killing on grouse moors across the north of England.'

Hen harriers are locked in a dysfunctional relationship with grouse moors. If left alone, they breed very successfully on them, but the same moors are also the site of their persecution. As ground-nesting birds, harriers benefit from the same management as red grouse, namely intense control of predators like foxes, stoats and crows, and the patch burning of heather to encourage staggered growth. A patch-burned moor provides expanses of long heather that act as cover for nests and more open areas with an abundance of food in the form of the chicks of grouse, skylarks, meadow pipits, curlews and lapwings, as well as voles and shrews. In addition, harriers are sociable. Unlike most birds of prey, they will tolerate other birds of their own species nearby, and they can form loose nesting colonies. Numbers can build rapidly, and in just a few years a moor can find itself hosting a dozen or more hen harrier pairs. As each pair can have up to six chicks, there are many hungry harrier mouths waiting for meat. As hen harriers feed their young at exactly the same time that their grouse chick neighbours reach a perfect size for a meal, the scene is set for conflict.

For a six-week period from when the harrier eggs hatch, the male will do most of the hunting and will take small chicks – the adult birds are too large for him to tackle. Once the harrier chicks are bigger, the female also hunts, and she is powerful enough to take adults. It is a bizarre situation. For the harriers, it is like living in a free supermarket, but keepers are paid to produce and protect red grouse – not harriers. For many generations, this situation has fuelled the illegal killing of hen harriers on grouse moors. In recent decades, there have been numerous attempts to resolve this problem and to find a way for both raptors and grouse to co-exist.

The now well-known Langholm Moor, a grouse moor in southern Scotland, became an experimental site in the 1990s for a grouse and hen harrier project called the Joint Raptor Study. The plan was to see what effect, if any, raptors had on grouse numbers. It found that hen harriers, when protected from any persecution and benefiting from grouse moor management, quickly built up to twenty pairs within a few years. They ate up to 40 per cent of the grouse chicks and 30 per cent of adult grouse.[33] These large losses meant there were not enough grouse to shoot when the season opened, and eventually grouse shooting was abandoned. Other factors were thought to come into play to explain the rapid build-up of harrier pairs, such as the particular grass and heather mix present on Langholm. Grass encourages large vole populations, a key food for harriers, especially for the males which predate smaller prey. Moors with more grass attract more harriers. But taking all factors into account, it was concluded that the presence of harriers could affect the viability of a moor.

Between 2008 and 2018, a different trial was undertaken to explore how the two species could co-exist – the Langholm Moor Demonstration Project.[34] A technique called 'diversionary feeding' was used, which involved a routine of laying out of dead cockerel chicks and rats on feeding posts or on the top of walls near a harrier nest to make alternative food easily available. The result was startling; the predation of red grouse chicks was reduced by up to 86 per cent. It was, in effect, the same as having food delivered to the door, rather than having to go shopping. Instead of a harrier bringing 4.5 red grouse chicks per hundred hours to the nest, they only brought 0.5 chicks per hundred hours; the rest of their food was supplied by the rats and cockerel chicks. This seemed like the basis for a workable compromise, backed up by good science. Keepers, however, were not convinced. If the number of harrier pairs stayed low, at around one or two pairs, then diversionary feeding is feasible; but if numbers start to increase rapidly, as had been shown in the Joint Raptor Study, it becomes prohibitively expensive, time-consuming and impractical. This was likely to happen, as the newly fledged harriers return to their natal moor. So, although diversionary feeding was acknowledged as a possible way forward under some circumstances, the impasse continued.

In the spring of 2014, the year when only four pairs of harriers attempted to breed in England and the diversionary feeding trial was well underway, I went to Langholm Moor to interview the then head game keeper, Simon Lester. At the time I was producing the BBC Natural History Radio series, *Shared Planet*. I wanted to record a harrier nest and see diversionary feeding in action for myself; but most importantly, I wanted to get a keeper's view.

It was an eye-wateringly cold and blustery day, with scudding clouds and the constant threat of squalls. The high energy of the weather was matched by the constant, agitated klack-klacking of a female harrier swooping above us, fearful of our being too close to her brood. Her feathers were a dapple of rich brown and cream and her face as round and peering as an owl. At times she was so close I felt I could reach out and touch her wings.

Simon laid out twenty-four chicks and eight rats on top of a stone wall in the bottom of a valley, just a few metres from the nest. We then retreated to let the female settle and to watch her swoop down and take the free food. From the high vantage point above the valley the grouse moor stretched into the distance, treeless as tundra. A mile ahead it stopped abruptly in an unnatural straight line. The heather and sphagnum moss were truncated by the green wall of a vast Sitka spruce plantation, an introduced conifer from North America planted as a cash crop. I wondered what the wind felt like in that dark, forbidding place, a forest with no light and little life. Up on the bluff, it tugged at our coats and whistled through the stands of heather before rushing off across the open land. But even in a storm, the inside of a plantation is deadened, as the wind is sliced into thin streams of dulled air by the packed stands of trees. Sitka plantations suck the life out of landscapes.

The upland plateau, with its hummocks, deep riverine crevasses and muted palette of muddy greens and browns, makes perfect habitat for the harrier's nest. As we watched the female provision her brood (with one eye constantly on us), I tried to make sense of the complexity that has brought us to this sorry point. Harriers on some driven grouse moors are eliminated secretly and silently – under the radar and beneath the law – to such an extent that English birds are all but extinct; and they are badly persecuted in upland shooting areas of Scotland too. This is the twenty-first century; we are supposed to be enlightened and informed, to be a nation that cares for its wildlife heritage, not cleaving to a long-gone past with its dubious Victorian attitudes. But only more questions and intractable issues came to mind.

If society turns against driven grouse shooting and it becomes unprofitable, perhaps even banned, what will happen to this landscape and to the other creatures that thrive here? The management of grouse moors includes rotational burning to encourage new heather growth. Predators like foxes and crows are efficiently controlled. This creates a predator-free mosaic of varied sward that is rich in small mammals, insects and covered areas for nesting. This intensive management also benefits other species, apart from red grouse and hen harriers. Grouse moors provide food and habitat for golden eagle, peregrine, merlin, short-eared owl, as well as lapwing, golden plover, curlew, meadow pipit and skylark. If heather moorland disappeared, these species, already in trouble elsewhere, may also decline. There are a few possible post-shooting scenarios for what may happen to the land, depending on the owner. It may be rewilded and become natural woodland, if the money can be found to allow it to do so, which is an increasingly likely scenario in the new environmental landscape of the twenty-first century. If that fails, though, the landowner may well give it over to Sitka plantations, windfarms or sheep grazing as a way to make up for the lost revenue from shooting. If any of these happen, the breeding and feeding areas for a number of species would be compromised.

Perhaps some of these species (with the exception of golden plovers or red grouse) could nest in lowland farmland, as they do across Europe, but hen harriers have no recent tradition of nesting in the lowlands and would have to be introduced to those areas artificially. This is on the cards as part of Natural England's Hen Harrier Joint Recovery Plan,[35] but this is not yet enacted and is mired in controversy. At present, most lowland farmland is poor habitat for ground-nesting birds. Grasslands are cut frequently for silage, the land is drained to make it better for crops or livestock, and stocking density of sheep and cattle is often high, increasing the chance of nest trampling. As discussed in previous chapters, generalist predator numbers are also unnaturally elevated. For all these reasons, lowland farmland is dangerous and unsuitable for many species. In addition, if harriers were to become established, they may well become a predator of pheasants and partridges, and the conflicts with the game industry would continue. Only a large-scale redesigning and reimagining of our landscapes, in both the uplands and the lowlands, will turn Britain into a country that provides both healthy food and abundant wildlife. Farming could

become more sustainable and wildlife-friendly through the introduction of a different system of subsidies, underpinned by
consumer demand. Driven grouse moors could be more balanced
if the expectations of shooters for large bag sizes could be reduced,
even if that means more predators are allowed to thrive and some
species like curlew and lapwing don't do so well in these areas.
Changes like these could greatly improve the nature of Britain as
a whole, with species more widespread and integrated into daily
life. But while we produce high numbers of gamebirds and intensively produced food, the present situation is unlikely to change
quickly.

How to unravel the different agendas driven by food production,
tradition, money, sport, culture and community vision? The hen
harriers and waders find themselves tossed around on stormy
waters, unable to find a place to settle that is not dictated by human
wants and needs. Simon Lester and I watched a wild bird of prey
grab slaughtered chicks from an intensive poultry farm to feed its
young, which in turn, if they should fledge successfully, have a high
likelihood of being killed by custodians of a sport steeped in a
British class system founded on the riches of Empire. The travails
visited on bird by man – and it is mainly men – felt as raw as the
wind and unfathomably complicated.

Simon, now retired from his role as a gamekeeper on both
pheasant and grouse estates, was one of those who worked hard to
find a way forward. 'If we want these uplands subsidised by driven
grouse shooting,' he told me, indicating the open moor around us,
'then there has to be a mechanism to allow that to happen. I for
one wouldn't like to see a countryside devoid of raptors, but I think
there has to be a measure of when enough is enough?' But I don't
know who decides that – there is no wildlife handbook with the

answers laid out. We live in such a human-made environment, no one knows what a 'natural' number of any species is, and agreeing it is very difficult. Simon also wasn't too encouraging about the efficacy of the many meetings that had taken place over the decades. 'There was a lot of conversation, but I think the frustrations began after the meetings. Perhaps part of the problem stems from the fact that it was always the same people sitting facing each other over the table for years and years. We need fresh thinking and new ideas.' Simon would favour a whole toolbox of options to be available to keepers of driven grouse moors to enable them both to do their job and to allow hen harriers to share the habitat. But it is a wish-list that many conservationists won't accept. It includes diversionary feeding, but also the option for the lethal control of common raptors like buzzards, and Simon also supports what is called 'brood management'.

Brood management, or brood meddling as opponents call it, is a controversial way of limiting the number of hen harriers on a grouse moor. It is part of DEFRA's Hen Harrier Action Plan, an attempt to rescue this beleaguered bird from national extinction. It was proposed as a trial based in northern England and time limited to two years, 2019 and 2020, and was (and is) being administered by Natural England. The idea was that once an agreed quota of harrier pairs for a moor has been reached (usually one pair per 10 square kilometres), eggs and or chicks from 'excess' nests are removed under licence and reared in captivity. The fledglings are then released in the same area, but away from the moor. The hope is that the harriers will begin to occupy the wider landscape and establish themselves across the UK, becoming a common raptor once again. Natural England want brood management to 'lead to a self-sustaining and well-dispersed breeding population of these beautiful birds across England'.[36]

There are some forceful and dissenting voices, however. Mark Avery, a prominent campaigner for hen harriers and fierce opponent of driven grouse shooting, wrote about brood management in his blog:

> Yesterday, Natural England announced that it had issued licences for Defra's highly controversial Hen Harrier brood management scheme … This is a taxpayer-funded scheme that gives the criminals what they want, without them running the risk of getting prosecuted. Defra is soft on crime, and not so much soft on the causes of crime but more like completely in bed with the criminals. Natural England's job is to plump up the pillows, smooth the sheets and supply hot-water bottles.[37]

Brood management is seen by many conservationists as a sop to the grouse shooting industry – a recognition that the law has failed to protect the birds because prosecutions are so rare and difficult to obtain. Instead of strengthening laws and introducing other measures like licensing and vicarious liability (which prosecutes moor owners if crimes are committed against birds of prey on their land), brood management is seen as shifting the battle lines in favour of driven grouse shooting. Opponents, which include the RSPB, also believe that there should be no such trials until all persecution has stopped. In 2019, Mark Avery, along with the RSPB, took Natural England to court to try to ban the trial. The challenge was defeated. Mrs Justice Lang, the presiding judge, deemed that the trial was a scientific project and could therefore go ahead. There was bitter disappointment and an appeal was lodged, but as of March 2021 no decision had yet been made. Meanwhile, the Brood Management trial went ahead.

In all, five harrier chicks were removed from a grouse moor and reared in captivity. They were released in the late summer of 2019 on land adjacent to the moor. However, by mid-October three tags had already stopped working, raising concerns of illegal killing yet again. A few days later, a fourth tag stopped. It was a dire situation, prompting one gamekeeper to despair, 'If this is someone mucking around, it makes me ashamed to be associated with shooting.' Twitter and Facebook were awash with recriminations and 'told-you-so' posts that deepened and hardened positions. I called the owner of the land where the birds had been released and asked him his thoughts. 'Don't assume they've been shot,' he said. 'When the tags were first put on none of them worked for a week. They are not that reliable. I reckon they have run out of juice as it's been so overcast and rainy recently. I wouldn't be surprised if they start working again, once the sun is out. There is a naturally high death rate among young raptors, that might be part of it too.'

Meanwhile, the two remaining harriers sent back data confirming they are great travellers, with one male trekking almost 3,000 kilometres to Ireland, Southampton, Greater London and Wales before returning to Yorkshire, an average of 89 kilometres per day. Then, in November, two tags sprang back to life and once again started transmitting. A Natural England blog, written in May 2020 by Dave Slater, Head of Species Recovery for Natural England, stated: 'That is a strong success rate compared to the 2018 nesting data which show that five of the 14 wild nests failed entirely and only two of the 14 wild nests were able to fledge five chicks.'[38]

By the summer of 2020, however, all five chicks had once again stopped transmitting and are still missing. One is highly likely to have died crossing the sea, but the others have simply disappeared from view, and three out of the four stopped sending signals over driven grouse moor areas. It is true that some tags used on the chicks don't work well, and it is true that many young raptors die in their first year, but it is still a disheartening, and some reckon suspicious, set of statistics.

In 2020, another nine chicks were hand reared and eight were released (one died in captivity), and we await news of their journey into adulthood. The Natural England blog ends on an optimistic note: 'Numbers of successful nests in England continue to rise over recent years since the launch of the Defra Recovery Plan in 2016. Numbers are still well below where they could be, but there have been over 20 successful nests recorded in England so far this year (2020).'

Although the figures for the persecution of hen harriers make for immensely depressing reading, the increasing numbers of wild nests are glimmers of hope. From their darkest hour in 2013, when no birds successfully fledged any chicks in England, recent years have seen welcome and surprising changes. Over eighty chicks have been raised to fledging since 2018, outstripping the total for the previous five years combined. The area over which the birds are breeding has also expanded, and includes grounds managed for grouse shooting. This about-turn took many people by surprise, but it remains to be seen if this does indicate a sustained hen harrier revival.

In 2018, I visited one such successful nest in the Peak District with a young grouse moor keeper. After a steep climb, we sat on a hillside looking out over the brooding hills of heather, not yet in bloom, and talked about how the trend towards more intense shooting over the last few decades may be coming to an end, and about the change to the fortunes of hen harriers that may just be happening. 'I love this place and I care about those birds in the nest over there, I think this is the future,' said my companion. The moor has a population of breeding curlew as well as lapwings and golden plovers. The air was filled with piping song. Through binoculars, we observed a female harrier sitting tight, well aware that we were watching her. While so many ground-nesting birds disappear into the background, this large raptor seemed proud and proprietorial. Suddenly, a flash of white caught my eye in the far distance. A male harrier twisted into view and circled above the nest, a pale, soft glow of a bird – ghostly and beautiful – adding a shard of light to a sky threatening rain. There is nothing more evocative than a white sky-dancer floating over moorland. Words fail to convey the mixture of joy, wonder and relief.

The sense of being on the cusp of change was powerful, but was tempered by the reality that a handful of harrier nests doesn't make a comeback. There are so many intertwined threads of life in upland Britain that it will take years to tease them apart and address each concern with understanding and respect. Competing agendas and entrenched views have hardened, and are inflamed by mistrust and anger. Many of the people I approached for this book did not want to be named or their locations made public for fear of intimidation. The heartening fledging figures, and successful hen harrier nests on grouse moors, may indicate that some level of reconciliation and reorientation is underway, that perhaps even a tipping point has been reached. Yet even writing these words, I can feel the scepticism from those who are less optimistic than I am, fuelled by the seemingly constant reports of raptor persecution over grouse moors.

The key to bird-of-prey revival, and the hen harrier in particular, is to repair the fractured relationships between conservation and the shooting industry, a relationship which is at present characterised by the trading of insults, intimidation and a head-butting diplomacy. In the twenty-first century, simple arguments around good guys and bad guys are no longer helpful. As Isla Hodgson, an expert in wildlife conflict at the University of Stirling summarises:

This was a war waged between humans about something else entirely; deep-seated issues about land ownership, governance and power, disguised simply as a dispute between talons and tweed. While this may not be a revelation, we still lack understanding of the true complexity of these arguments – the social and political elements that have caused a dispute over a protected species to become so intractable.[39]

The demand that driven grouse moors be banned is a popular war cry that rings true for many, and it is human nature to take sides and become adversarial. Far harder is the path to finding shared ground and to building consensus. Some grouse moors and pheasant woodlands do valuable wildlife conservation – there are positives that can be built upon as well as problems to be solved. While illegal persecution of birds of prey is undoubtedly still taking place, this is an issue that must be confronted by the industry itself as well as by a strengthening of the law. If this fails to happen quickly, it is only right that the sport be banned. But, as with every abrupt cessation of human activity, be that political or social, there must be a well-thought-out exit plan, otherwise the consequences could be worse than the status quo. Many people struggle with a pastime that is socially exclusive and kills birds for entertainment, but rather than ban completely, another approach is to build on successes and establish a better-regulated and more humane shooting ethic that values wildlife, not just bag numbers. Low-intensity walked-up shooting is a good example. Otherwise, without a sound, well-funded exit strategy, we could be abandoning many species to an uncertain future in a country deemed to be one of the most nature-depleted in the world.

As glimmers of hope appear in this desolate, poisonous war-zone, in the form of increasing numbers of fledging hen harriers, now is the time to build upon a shared vision of richer wildlife landscapes.

Driven grouse shooting, though, has a public-perception mountain to climb. It has the effect of focusing anger and it brings to the fore much of the angst many people feel about a range of issues, from how we treat the natural world to class privilege. In 2020, the COVID-19 pandemic saw people's outdoor activities curtailed. It was illegal to meet more than six people out of doors, in order to restrict the spread of the virus. DGS, however, was excluded from the 'rule of six' as it was deemed a sport alongside football and cricket, a decision which fuelled resentment and much negative media comment. Driven grouse shooting is also under scrutiny as society becomes ever more alarmed by climate change and the increase in heavy rainfall and flooding. The burning of heather moorland, opponents say, produces bare ground which increases rainwater runoff, as do drainage ditches. Others decry the lead shot in meat and the intensity of predator control simply for a sport. The fate of raptors and other breeding birds on driven grouse moors has quickly morphed into a wider debate about the general management of our uplands in challenging times. It is no longer the more simplified rift between grouse shooters and conservationists. As we all search for a better way to live on this earth, all non-essential activities must justify their place on a planet under ecological stress, grouse moors included.

Lasting change for the good is possible, and it comes from a realignment of hearts and an acceptance of new ways to live. It is reinforced by success stories which build confidence and inject hope and energy. Perhaps the tentative and faltering change we see in the survival of hen harriers on moors in England is one sign that deeper concerns for the natural world are beginning to gain traction; that the old ways of thinking about 'vermin' are being replaced by a new vision for British natural history.

*

The buzzard comeback is also a beacon of hope. As it slowly beats its powerful presence into free air, somehow our guns, traps and poisons seem a little less destructive. Hearing a buzzard mew over Bristol places my heart in some ancestral place; it is a portal to a mountain top and free, fresh winds, and gratitude washes over me. But the hen harrier? Do enough sport shooters want these wild predators to come home?

At only 250,000 square kilometres, Britain still provides 66 million people with places to live, industrial complexes, farmland, forestry, 'wilderness areas', ports, energy production, sporting estates and parklands. All these amenities sit cheek by jowl, and many areas are highly populated. Heard over a mountain, the evocative cry of a buzzard is the joyous sound of the wild, but over a grouse moor or pheasant shoot, it is a threat. These places could be just a kilometre or so apart.

Hatred caused the birds to disappear from the skies. Stopping their persecution will bring them back. But it is only mutual respect, compromise and compassion that will keep them there.

Predators can overwhelm us with their intensity, their singularity of purpose. Embodied in the form of a small hobby (around 200 grams), swooping and swerving to catch dragonflies, it is a marvel of aerobatics. Scaled up to the size of a hen harrier or a buzzard, even more so a kite or eagle, and we struggle with the impact on our lives. Birds of prey have been, and still are, a target for frustration and anger. As we plan the world we want to see in the future, it will be a test of our commitment to nature whether we allow the full suite of raptors to once again fully overlap with our world.

6

Red Kites and White-Tailed Eagles

Protecting wild creatures and the places they live is driven by passionate hearts with an emotional connection to the natural world. People who work with wildlife love this planet and want to see it bursting with life in all its riot of form, colour and sound. A pity then, that so much of conservation terminology is deadening to the soul. The phrase 'cultural carrying capacity' (ccc) is not exactly sexy, but it is a vital concept to understand when planning how we can live with predators. The 'ccc' of a species is not the same as its biological carrying capacity – the maximum population size that can live in a specific environment – rather, it refers to the number of a particular species people can tolerate in any given place. American journalist and author Jon

Mooallem believes that 'ccc' is the key to revival of wildlife. 'It's the one thing that really matters right now in terms of what species are going to stick around on the planet or not.' In a podcast about his book, *Wild Ones*,[1] he speculates that the future of wildlife will depend on how much people know about a species, care about it, like the look of it and how unobtrusively it integrates into our lifestyles:

> How many deer are we going to have? Well, we are going to have as many as we have before they start pissing people off. We are making decisions about what lives and dies, and what we want where, all the time. The fact that black bears in America are now considered a nuisance is a measure of the success of their conservation. You see it a lot with species that do rebound, where all our hard work pays off. Suddenly we are not sure why we wanted them back. There is always a tension between romanticising certain animals and wanting to make sure they survive, and then not being sure how to co-exist with them.[2]

In the UK, the reintroduction of two magnificent birds of prey is now testing their 'ccc' for a wilder Britain. One is the red kite, the other the white-tailed eagle.

Larger, less tidy-looking and richer in colour than a buzzard, the red kite has long wings, a grey head and a deeply forked tail. Senior scientist for the British Trust for Ornithology, Rachel Taylor, describes them as soaring on 'conker-brown wings lit with a sweep of pale spangles from wrist to wrist, and a bright chestnut tail twisting and angling across the wind.'

The white-tailed eagle, also known as the sea eagle, is even bigger, one of the largest birds of prey, related to the American bald eagle. It has the longest wingspan of any European eagle – over two metres – and the females can weigh as much as seven kilograms. Both sexes are grey/brown in colour, except for that startling white tail, yellow legs and a thick, yellow, meat-cleaver beak.

Both of these magnificent raptors were once common right across the UK; they were our neighbours and daily companions. Both succumbed to centuries of sustained persecution, habitat loss and accidental poisoning, but both are now being returned to the skies through deliberate reintroductions. The red kite is further ahead on the road of recovery, but success will depend on our willingness to adapt and accept them as close neighbours. In fact, the red kite can be considered an urbanite.

Shakespeare commonly saw a London sky full of red kites soaring over stinking piles of city waste, much like black kites over the waste dumps on the outskirts of some cities in India today. The Bard declared the capital to be 'the city of kites and crows'. The early sixteenth-century botanist, Carolus Clusius, reported seeing as many kites in London as in Cairo. Consummate scavengers and hunters, they offered a much-needed avian street-cleaning service. Raw sewage flowed down gutters and piles of rubbish were left out to rot. So valuable were red kites for tackling the accumulation of filth that killing one was punishable by death. Even so, they were a nuisance. In 1544, William Turner published *Avium Praecipuarum*, thought to be the first printed bird book. He recorded that kites took bread from the hands of children and fish from women,[3] earning them a reputation for cowardly thieving. Worse still, they would descend from the sky en masse after a battle and devour dead bodies. Falconer George Turberville, in his *The Booke of Faulconrie or Hawking* (1575), described kites as 'base, bastardly, refuse, hawks'.[4] It is a harsh judgement on a bird of supreme versatility and capable of breathtaking aerial acrobatics. Locking talons in mid-air, a courting pair can cartwheel towards the ground as a roiling swirl of feathers and fury.

Red kites were as maddening as they were useful. They preyed on the chicks of game and domestic fowl, and would pinch hats off people's heads. The Greek poet, Homer, called them 'snatchers'. And they had an eye for the fancier stuff of human life. In *A Winter's Tale*, Shakespeare warned, 'When the kite builds, look to your lesser linen', a reference to their stealing washing left out to dry, which they would then use to decorate their own nest. Today, kites' nests can sometimes be as gaudy as a Playboy mansion, lined with tea towels, frilly pants, England flags, gloves, sponge balls, socks and magazines. Each time a female lays a clutch they often redecorate, producing a riot of sticks, colour and chintz that builds up year on year. A showy message that this plot in the suburbs is taken.

Only for as long as they were useful to us would kites remain in our favour. Once city officials took over the removal of refuse after the plague of 1665–66, kites had outstayed their welcome and centuries of persecution began. Large bounties were paid and numbers fell dramatically. Their increasing scarcity made their eggs and bodies more valuable to egg collectors and taxidermists, adding to the pressure. John Knapp, in his *Journal of a Naturalist* written in 1829, recalls fifteen kites being captured in Gloucestershire in 1767, but noted it was already being driven to lonelier woods and less visited spots and was 'greatly on the decline'. At the end of the nineteenth century, John Henry Salter, an ornithologist and botanist at the University of Wales, noted in his diaries that almost every known nest had been pillaged and the birds shot. By 1932, only two nests were known in central Wales and those two females were related. It looked like the endgame.

The story of their return from the brink was dogged with twists and turns and dead ends. As early as 1903, concerned ornithologists set up the Kite Committee, who organised nest surveillance and protection from the hordes of egg and skin collectors. Measures to protect the red kites were partially successful, but it became clear that the slow breeding rate of the Welsh birds was not going to allow for their expansion out of Wales. Especially as those that weren't deliberately targeted succumbed to the extensive poisoned bait laid out in fields to kill foxes and crows. By the 1980s, the population was still only around thirty pairs. In the mid-1980s, one farmer in West Wales managed to kill eight adult kites at one bait site, taking out over ten per cent of the breeding population.

The astonishing number of red kites flying in Britain today is due to good luck and good people taking on the challenge at the right time. For five years in the 1980s, Peter Davis and Tony Cross took red kite eggs from the Welsh nests, incubated them in captivity and released seventy fledglings back into the wild, in a process called 'headstarting'. By contrast, the wild population produced only nineteen fledglings at most. As two-thirds of juvenile kites survive to adulthood, headstarting was an effective boost. Other events worked in their favour too. A transition to indoor lambing to protect lambs from foxes and crows, the establishment of the Wildlife and Countryside Act in 1981 and stronger sentences for poisoning and egg collecting (imprisonment for up to six months) allowed the kites to bounce back. Legal protection, however, was more of a threat than a reality and a source of deep frustration for Tony Cross, who told me: 'Not that anyone was actually jailed for stealing kite eggs locally. Obtaining the evidence to secure a prosecution is extremely difficult. Despite seeing men going into a nest wood, finding spike marks up the nest tree, a pair of tree-spikes hidden in a rabbit burrow nearby and an empty nest, we still couldn't nail it. It was very frustrating. But at least the threat was there and it definitely helped.'

At the same time, moves were underway to reintroduce kites into England and Scotland. As recovery for the Welsh birds was only just underway, kites were sourced from Europe.

Beginning in 1989 and for the following five years, ninety-three nestlings from Spain and Sweden were released at each of two locations, the Chilterns in the south of England and the Black Isle in Scotland. Since then, release sites have been established in the East Midlands, Yorkshire and northeast England. The last birds were released in 1993 in Scotland and 1994 in England. The newly fledged birds continued to be fed animal carrion, staving off the starvation which so often kills young raptors. No longer was meat put out to poison them, but to nurture them back to abundance.

The UK population has now risen to over 4,400 breeding pairs and the Bard's bird is spreading to many regions where it has not been seen for a century. Any train journey from Bristol to London is always leavened by the sight of red kites soaring and turning in the wind, mainly over built-up areas in Berkshire. Up to sixty birds have been seen sitting on a multi-storey car park near Reading. Kites are people-birds, commuter-belt scavengers, bringing wildness to manicured, urbanised southern England.

But this welcome recovery is not without problems. Kites are still the adapters and chancers they have always been. Their reputation as a menace is re-emerging as age-old resentments rise once more to the surface. The fact that the red kite reintroduction in the Black Isle has not been as successful as in the Chilterns is put down to the surrounding game estates, which refuse to tolerate yet another meat-eater threatening their livelihoods. Every year there are confirmed reports of shootings and poisonings and the body count is rising. A blog by the Zoological Society of London, ZSL, summarised the crimes committed against red kites:[5]

As of February 2019, 27 of 335 red kites that underwent post-mortem examination by DRAHS (Disease Risk Analysis and Health Surveillance Programme)[6] between 1994 and 2019, were found to have shotgun pellets when radiographed which illustrates the persecution red kites experience in the UK. The RSPB's Raptor Persecution Map[7] shows that 258 raptor persecution cases were confirmed shooting incidents. Shot red kites have been found to have fractures, external trauma, and internal bleeding.

Red kites feed on the carcasses of rodents that have died from consuming anticoagulant rodenticide. This secondary poisoning causes internal bleeding; the effects are gradual, developing over several days. In the final phase of the intoxication, the poisoned animal dies from haemorrhagic shock, and the haemorrhage can be observed at gross post-mortem examination. Further testing of the tissues means the concentration and type of poison can also be determined. [...] A paper by Molenaar et al (2017)[8] demonstrated that of 110 birds analysed for toxicological analysis, poisoning was diagnosed in 32 red kites, with 19 from second-generation anticoagulant rodenticides, 9 from other pesticides and 6 from lead poisoning.

In April 2020, three red kites were shot in Powys in what was described as a 'horrific attack'.[9] The battle to win the hearts and minds of some sectors of rural society has still not been won. In urban areas, it is, so far, generally a happier tale. Feathery shadows gliding across the mown lawns of the suburbs add a frisson to daily life. So much so that in Reading, one in twenty households put food out in their gardens to feed the kites – a slab of meat next to peanuts for the blue tits. Upwards of 300 kites visit Reading every day, swooping onto back lawns and snatching meat in their talons and providing an urban spectacle that can raise the hair on the back of the neck.

In a blog on her PhD, ecologist Melanie Orros highlighted the extent of people's new-found enthusiasm for kites:

> Kites were being offered food in well over 4,000 gardens across Reading and the surrounding suburban area … On average a kite would need to visit between 4 and 9 gardens offering food each day in order to get a full day's meal … so many people feed kites in Reading that this means somewhere between around 140 and 320 kites could get all of the food they need each day.[10]

Unease, though, is growing. Non kite-feeders complain that they are now so habituated they intimidate people into dropping food, threaten small dogs and cats, and make a mess of cars. Red kites are becoming the new urban gull, only much bigger. In 2018, a local paper reported that a red kite had scratched two toddlers on a picnic,[11] and in 2019, the *Oxford Mail* quoted an alarmed day tripper:[12] 'People say they can't hurt you but that just isn't true. They are big birds with sharp claws and a wingspan of around six feet. A couple of years ago I was with friends for a birthday tea at Watlington Hill and my friend had his head quite badly scratched by one who took his sandwich.'

After only a few years, red kites are transitioning from rare spectacle to suburban pest. Stopping supplementary feeding is recommended by the RSPB, but living cheek by jowl with a sociable predator may require more demanding changes, such as where and how we eat out of doors, which will certainly be a test of our resolve to see them thrive and expand.

In the early days of recovery, some Welsh farms began to spread buckets of offal onto fields and then charge a fee to visitors to see the spectacle of tens (today it can be hundreds) of raptors putting on a display that wouldn't look out of place in a Harry Potter film. Once the sworn enemy of sheep farmers, now they are an income stream. Twenty years ago, I went to see it for myself. Blustery winds and empty skies were soon filled with kites performing dramatic fly-pasts and grabbing at offal with their talons. A buzzard waddling among the flesh was relentlessly dive-bombed. It was a chaotic, even gory scene, but infused with wonder. Was this a glimpse of what sixteenth-century Londoners regularly saw and took for granted, a feathered beauty-and-a-beast of a bird that weaved wildness into the city filth? To what extent this spectacle influenced the mind of the greatest wordsmith on earth we cannot know, but the kite was there, playing its part in the creation of words of such great potency that they tied our souls to his pen.

Kites are still inspiring us. 'Red wings of passion, Keep swooping and rising, Dipping and gliding,' writes the composer Adrian Williams in his song 'Red Kite Flying', which captures a wild raptor on the wing in a single female voice and minimalist piano accompaniment. Kites are also captured in glass and exhibited on bright, white walls. Rachel Taylor is both a scientist with the British Trust for Ornithology and a glass artist. Her 'Red Kite' floats on powerful, feathered wings; focused and vital. I went to see it displayed in the Oriel Môn arts centre in Anglesey. It is uncanny that a material so glinting and brittle can produce a warm, muscle-taut bird that seemed to glide down the stark corridor. In a personal communication, she wrote:

One of the dimensions to making birds (of all possible animals!) in stained glass is its near-parallel with alchemy. I'm taking glass – made using fire to transmute earth into something that plays with light – and using lead (of all things!) to make birds out of it. Birds, ephemeral creatures of water and air, made of lead and earth; and the most brittle, heavy, static materials made to look like moving feathers, air and light. The kite is a celebration of the power, grace and beauty of the bird, but also an expression of fragility; needing care and attention. He is one-dimensional in a three-dimensional world, and looks different to the person standing on his other side – much like the differing viewpoints of humans about the bird he represents. And all this beauty, all this fire and light, is completely dependent for survival on a strong supporting hook.

I love the glorious colours of the kite, and their loose-winged, athletic flight; but most of all I love them for having forgiven us our history, for accepting our repentance and taking back their birthright in the tumbling skies of Wales.[13]

Glass is a fitting material. Fragility is inbuilt into the precarious position of the red kite in the UK. Its presence could still be shattered and swept away; we have the power to let them live or die. In many places over Britain today you can see them writing their story in invisible script across the sky, a tale of love then loathing – and perhaps love once more?

I asked Tony Cross what he thought about the success of red kites after his decades of working to bring them back. 'With the benefit of years of hindsight, I wish we had allowed them to repopulate England naturally from Wales, without having to import birds from Europe. It gives ammunition to those who say the birds have been "imposed" on them from abroad, and some people think the

Welsh birds are introduced as well. Given time and protection, they would have spread out from Wales on their own, especially as the population suddenly took off, but we couldn't know that then. There are lessons to learn, though. If we tell people they only eat carrion and don't kill anything, it is misleading. Kites are mainly scavengers but they do take live prey and they will take chicks, not discriminating between endangered chicks and common species. I've found the remains of a young curlew in a kite nest – a species in serious trouble. We have to be honest, and then the road to recovery is easier; people feel kept in the picture, don't have false expectations and they don't feel hoodwinked.'

It is a wise point. An openness about the reality of living with predators may have benefited the still turbulent recovery of the largest birds ever to fly over Britain.

*

As a huge eagle appears over a field of lambs, it changes the mood music of the skies. A menacing tone creeps in as it peers down from its bed of air, its gaze fixed on livestock on the ground. No matter how real or imagined the threat to livelihoods, the sheer presence of this predator is enough to concentrate emotions into a critical focal point. So much so, that in the past the extirpation of the white-tailed or sea eagle was so thorough that not a single British bird remained after 1918. The last one was shot in Shetland after the same sorry saga of intense persecution by land managers and farmers. This time, to put right past wrongs, we had to rely solely on birds donated by Norway to return them to our skies.

If you could take to the air and fly 480 kilometres east from Orkney you would arrive in Stavanger, the so-called oil capital of Norway, a watery, rocky coastal city of pastel-coloured wooden houses, skyscrapers and bobbing boats. Tucked away in a less affluent area, just off a roundabout, British wildlife street artist, Mark Anthony (street name, ATM) has captured in paint a super-sized white-tailed eagle straight out of the air and placed it on an outside wall at the end of a factory. It is a full four metres tall and so full of life, so visceral, it looks as though it could peel itself away from the brick and wheel out over the ocean. Painted in acrylic, it holds its immense, golden brown wings aloft, the feathers ruffled and rippled by the wind. The sinuous legs hang down, dangling yellow clenched feet with black hooked talons. The white tail fan is spread out and the pale head strains forwards, its far-seeing eyes locked on prey. The intimidatingly huge, yellow, hooked bill is held in readiness. The glory and the tragedy, the hope and the increasing fear surrounding white-tailed eagles are captured on a bland, windowless wall. This is a powerful piece of street art by the master of bringing the wild into the heart of cities. I asked Mark why he had chosen to paint this bird in a Norwegian city:

The white-tailed eagle was a natural choice for Stavanger, as the birds reintroduced to the Scottish Isles in the 1970s came from Norway. I wanted to celebrate that international co-operation and forward thinking, as an example of what can be achieved to reverse the disasters of the past and create a richer modern Britain.

When I started on the design I wanted to capture and communicate something of the bird's awe-inspiring size and presence. I have many special memories of seeing them; once watching the giant bird, like a huge black rectangle, banking through a flock of panicked greylag geese, against a backdrop of dark hills and shimmering sea. Or lying on my back in the purple and pink flower-rich machair of Harris, looking up to see an eagle circling and gaining height over the hill of

Ceapabhal, until it set off on a long deep glide across the water to the islands, finally disappearing in the dazzle of sea and sky. It was such a primal experience, just land, sea, sky and the great bird.

In my painting I wanted to communicate that sense of space and sea air, its mastery of the wind, its majesty.[14]

White-tailed eagles dominate. Their huge wingspan, up to 2.5 metres for females, makes the common description of them as a flying barn door very apt. Like buzzards and kites, they are relatively tolerant of people, and it is this trust and approachability, combined with their large size, which led to their complete eradication. Across Britain, from the Isle of Wight to the Northern Isles, the skies were emptied of one of the largest birds of prey on earth.

Until, that is, eaglets from Norway arrived in the far northwest of Scotland in 1975. For the next decade, a government-sponsored programme released eighty-five on the island of Rhum. They acclimatised well and began to spread. The first reintroduced birds built a nest and laid an egg in 1983, and the first wild chick fledged in 1985. Success, though, was not guaranteed. The survival rate of young eagles is low. They don't normally start breeding until they are at least five years old, and even then, a pair may only fledge one chick every two years. To keep the numbers viable, in the 1990s a further fifty-eight Norwegian eaglets were released. A third phase of reintroduction took place on the east coast of Scotland between 2007 and 2012, with the release of a further eighty-five young birds. In 2013 the first pair from the east-coast project bred successfully, fledging a single chick.

The population is certainly growing, and it is estimated there could be 700 pairs in Scotland by 2040. We came across one pair in 2013, on a family holiday on the island of Ronay in the Outer

Hebrides. Each day a huge shadow crossed the sun. The Anglo-Saxon name for them, *erne*, means 'soarer'. I admit to feeling concerned as we walked the heathery slopes, our small white terrier bouncing ahead, looking for all the world like a mountain hare.

Today, the white-tailed revival continues south of the border. Using eaglets from Scotland, the Roy Dennis Wildlife Foundation is in the process of releasing sixty eaglets on the Isle of Wight. In 2019, the first six birds were released, and in 2020 a further seven, with the hope that the eagles will now slowly spread and become re-established throughout the whole of the UK; and so far, these birds are faring well.

Old attitudes, though, are showing signs of reviving. In Scotland, at least eight white-tailed eagles have been killed and four clutches of eggs stolen since the start of the reintroduction project, most recently in 2020, when a poisoned adult was discovered in Donside, in Aberdeenshire. The National Wildlife Crime Unit keeps detailed reports of all incidents:

> This list of shame even included the very first white-tailed
> eagle chick fledged in the east of Scotland. This 2013 chick
> mysteriously disappeared in early 2014, with its last sighting on
> a grouse moor within the Cairngorms National Park where
> other birds of prey have been found dead in suspicious
> circumstances. In 2013 in Tayside, a tree with a newly-built
> white-tailed eagle nest was felled.[15]

Twenty-two pairs are settled on the tourist Hebridean honey-pot island of Mull, and I was promised the sighting of a nest.

Some days lift off the page of our memory and seem hyper-real. It was mid-April, not long after dawn on the Ardnamurchan peninsula, heading for the Mull ferry. I stood in a layby and drank in a scene too beautiful for words. Loch Linnhe sparkled in clear light. A gentle mist rose from the surface of the water, as though the lake were gently exhaling; a shifting boundary between cold air and dark depths. It drifted across the surface, wrapping the feet of the islands in silk. Distant hills layered to another realm. Nothing disturbed this watercolour vision; the earth was quiet and breathing softly. Everything and everywhere wore pearly blue, grey and white. My nineteenth-century Scottish hero, John Muir, who was induced to transcendence by wild places such as this, wrote: 'Oh, these vast, calm, measureless mountain days, inciting at once to work and rest! Days in whose light everything seems equally divine, opening a thousand windows to show us God.' Muir must have once stood on this spot, before going to America to establish a series of national parks. And then a muted splash from an otter in the rocks below broke the reverie. Jolted back to reality, the day hardened and became real. We don't live in heaven; here on earth there are appointments to keep and eagles to see.

I had envisaged the trek to see a white-tailed eagle nest would require a long walk over moor and crag. On this bright day I imagined the views of the island would be magnificent, and perhaps a descendant of Landseer's stag would stare from a rocky outcrop. I was looking forward to an immersion in wildness and sharp air. It would also be a chance to reconnect with Muir; it had been a while since I had felt him at my shoulder. Although most of his life was in America, he never lost his Scottish heart and described himself as having 'tinctures of bog juice' oozing through his veins. Famed for his hardiness, Muir took to the high mountains for days on end with just some tea, a loaf of bread and a copy of Robert Burns's poetry. My rucksack had pounds of chocolate, sandwiches, coffee, thermals … we could be out for hours. It was somewhat deflating, then, to arrive at our destination on this famously rugged island by parking next to a golf course and walking a few hundred metres along tarmac to the edge of a green.

My guide to all-things-eagle was David Sexton, an old friend and RSPB officer for Mull. He has been monitoring them for over thirty-five years; if anyone is their champion, it is David. We joined a group of eagle-tourists halfway through a tour and looked through binoculars over the manicured greens to a copse. Was this pared, clipped, rule-bound place really the haunt of the bird the Gaels called 'the eagle with the sunlit eye'; a predator so huge it is accused of carrying away pet cats and dogs, and even livestock?

High in a tree a small head with a huge beak poked out over the rim of a vast thatch of sticks. It looked a little comical and pin-headed, altogether not the eyrie of giants I was expecting. There was no blustering wind or haughty stag, just well-dressed golfers teeing off and ambling around the putting greens. We eagle-watchers strained to get a better look at this fabled goliath, hoping for some eagle-action. But there it sat, the bird-god that was once so revered its skulls decorated Neolithic tombs, incubating its eggs to the quiet clack of metal on dimpled ball. Its reputation for cosying up to humans is not misplaced, as David confirmed:

'White-tailed eagles have been following us around since Neanderthals, no doubt earlier, making the most of whatever we left around. They are far more like scavengers than hunters so it paid to hang around us and eat our kills. They are just doing what they've always done. It shows how different they are to golden eagles – they wouldn't nest on a golf course – goldies are far too wary of people. If I went up to that nest now, the bird would fly around making a lot of noise, but it wouldn't be scared off – it's one of the reasons they were so easy to eradicate.'

White-tailed eagles once fed on the remains of the wild creatures we hunted down and left strewn across the landscape. Today,
their diet can sometimes include our livestock, especially lambs.
The majority of these will be carcasses, but Scottish sheep farmers
accuse them of taking large numbers of healthy live ones too. The
farmers are angry at what they see as a huge predator being
imposed on them with almost no consultation or compensation
written into the plan. From a sheep farmer's perspective, these
eagles make a hard life even harder, compounding other current
concerns such as climate change, the future of farm payments and
even veganism.

Yet eye-witness accounts of an actual killing of a lamb are
extremely scarce. The most compelling evidence is often in the
aftermath, the bones found in the bottom of nests, injured lambs
in fields – damning indictments produced by the prosecution when
the eagles are on trial for damaging sheep farming. It is too easy,
though, to be dismissive of the farmers' fears. These are real
concerns from people who are facing increasing threats to their
long-term communities, cultures and traditions. Sheep numbers
are declining as farms are abandoned and the younger generation
opt for less arduous, more lucrative lives. The future for upland
sheep farmers is looking more uncertain as the political map of the
UK and Europe shifts, and the farm payments they have relied on
for so long are not guaranteed. When people feel powerless in the
face of enormous change, it can have the effect of focusing energy
on what can be done to keep the world stable. White-tailed eagles
are an imposing, physical reality and an easily accessible, controllable factor in a largely intangible array of threats. This eagle has
become the focus of a more general sense of fear and angst. Exactly
how much they contribute to the many woes of hill farmers has
been the subject of much research.

In 2004, a report for the Scottish government, *The Impact of White-tailed Eagles on Sheep Farming on Mull*,[16] drew together all the available evidence at the time and found a nuanced picture. By studying the carcasses of 114 lambs found near eight nests of white-tailed eagles, the researchers were able to give a picture of the activity of the breeding eagles at lambing time. The crucial distinction to be made is between those lambs that have been killed by eagles and those that have been scavenged after death. Lambs that are alive when attacked by an eagle show puncture wounds from the talons, with bruising and blood pooling around those wounds. Scavenged lambs, however, only show the puncture marks with no bruising. Between the years 1999 and 2002, the total number of lambs where evidence suggested killing rather than scavenging was 29 lambs, with 85 carcasses believed to have been scavenged. This means that, on average, each pair was taking fewer than four lambs per season. In fact, it seemed that most lambs were taken by only one or two pairs, with the rest predating them opportunistically rather than systematically. This suggests there may be 'problem' eagles that specialise in predating lambs rather than this being a widespread behaviour. These figures were obtained by studying just eight nests; extrapolated to the twenty pairs on Mull at the time, the researchers concluded that, over the three years of the study, white-tailed eagles were probably the cause of death for fewer than forty lambs per year (compared to thousands from other causes).

The size and weight of the lambs that were killed indicated that they may have died anyway from poor nutrition or exposure, as they were comparable in size and condition to the hundreds of lambs found dead across the mountain each year. Only the largest and heaviest lambs survive their early weeks in environments as harsh as on Mull. In a bad year, and on poor grazing, there can be up to 30 per cent mortality of lambs,[17] which nationally translates to 4–6 million deaths. The 2004 report concluded that losses due to white-tailed eagle predation are very low, especially compared to the 18,500 livestock (many of which are sheep)[18] that are allegedly killed or injured by loose dogs each year in the UK.[19]

Ten years later, in 2014, a camera in Oban recorded 117 prey items being brought back to a white-tailed eagle's nest between January and July; 21 small mammals, 14 birds, 7 fish and 66 unidentifiable bodies were captured on film – and the remains of nine lambs, indicating a continuing problem. David Sexton regularly surveys nests and certainly finds some lambs, but many other creatures too, like gulls, auks, lots of geese and corvids, herons and even the occasional hedgehog. In one nest, he saw the tentacle of an octopus wriggling over the rim, then the whole body appeared as it tried to escape. I asked David for his opinion on eagles actively predating lambs:

'I've personally never seen them killing. I've tried very hard in many different locations in lambing areas where they are accused of killing lambs. I sit and watch, thirteen hours a day on one occasion, just to see what they were doing and how they use the landscape, and they were not killing those lambs. I saw them go for greylag geese feeding among the lambs in the middle of the field. It doesn't look good, all you see is the eagle going in and the sheep running, but it was after a greylag goose sitting on a nest. But they're big birds of prey, they are perfectly capable of it and we fully accept they are going to kill some lambs, even though the eye-witness accounts are few and far between, but it's the scale of the killing that's always disputed.'

For the farmers, though, this is not how it appears. There is a well-circulated photograph taken by a tourist of a white-tailed eagle flying across the hills clutching a dead lamb (which may well have been scavenged after death). Farmers find injured lambs with wounds they believe can only have been caused by something as big and powerful as a white-tailed eagle. The only large predators on Mull are white-tailed and golden eagles – badgers and foxes were eradicated long ago. The Scottish Crofting Federation spells out the worry for many farmers trying to make a living in white-tailed eagle territory:

> We have had too many cases already of crofters having to abandon their use of valuable hill grazing, increasing pressure on their scarce in-bye and leading to greatly increased feed bills. Yet this method of extensive, low-input sheep husbandry is at the heart of the High Nature Value Farming model which is so beneficial for both upland biodiversity and reducing the carbon footprint of sheep farming in Scotland. The Scottish Crofting Federation is also concerned that an increase in sea eagle numbers and the further expansion of their range may result in ever more crofters' flock predation across the Highlands and Islands.[20]

Derek Gow, a Devon-based conservationist, rewilding consultant and farmer, has little truck with this attitude. It's time, he says, to call a halt on subsidising a lifestyle choice. 'When you see that picture of an eagle with a lamb dangling from its talons, go through the economics of it. This lamb is a subsidised lamb anyway – without the money that comes from the tax payer's purse you couldn't farm sheep in those environments, it would be simply impossible. And it's declining anyway. Down here in Devon we had one and a half thousand breeding ewes, and there were three of us working on it. At best it broke even, normally it lost money. These small flocks of fifty or a hundred sheep in the west of Scotland, it's utterly unviable, it's simply a cultural hobby, funded by the tax payer, and it's driving the landscape further into the ground. That lamb will be a black-faced lamb. If it lives long enough to go to market it will only be worth at most thirty pounds. It then goes down south to be fattened, as you can't fatten it in the hills. It might then be worth sixty pounds at tops. If an eagle takes four of those, that is all you have lost. Now if your business is critically reliant on the loss of those four sheep, on a couple of hundred pounds, you're finished anyway.' Relationships on Mull hit a new low when one farm accused the white-tailed eagles of taking a lamb a day, forty in total, over lambing time, but David Sexton doesn't agree with the conclusion:

'It was the coldest wettest spring anyone can remember; no grass grew and the ewes had no milk. The lambs were dying out on the hill from starvation, and then being eaten. They weren't being killed. That difference was lost in all the emotion. We need something to blame and white-tailed eagles are so big and obvious they are easy scapegoats.'

Further fuel for the fire came in 2020, when a report in the *Herald* suggested that white-tailed eagles cause so much stress to ewes they can't get pregnant.[21] It was illustrated by a dramatic picture of an eagle tearing at a lamb carcass with the caption: 'White-tailed sea eagle (*Haliaeetus albicilla*), feeding from a caught lamb, United Kingdom, Scotland, Argyll, Mull.' In the comments below the article, the photographer who took the shot of the eagle and the lamb, Peter Cairns, wrote, 'Just for clarity, the image used in this feature does not represent a wild eagle predating a viable lamb. I took the photo many years ago as part of a book project and for illustrative purposes only. This sea eagle is captive and the lamb was already dead. The image is in the public domain but in this case has been used in a misleading context.' Despite this obvious twisting of the truth, the photograph continues to be used, and provides another example of the false claims and counter-claims that have dogged the presence of these raptors for over forty years.

White-tailed eagles are as native to Scotland as golden eagles, yet their presence was airbrushed out of history. When they suddenly reappeared, huge and unmistakable, it was a shock to many who found adjusting to a 'new' predator in their midst very challenging. It is a cliché but it is also true that we are what we remember, and it is a tragedy that we so rapidly forget the past.

I asked David Sexton why golden eagles weren't in the spotlight; they are far more active hunters than white-tailed eagles, only slightly smaller, and there are twenty pairs on Mull.

'Farmers won't have a bad word said about golden eagles because they have always been here, they weren't wiped out. White-tailed eagles were got rid of, but goldies survived in remote crags and glens away from people. They are seen as part of the heritage of the land. But these new birds, they are viewed as interlopers that shouldn't be here, and that we conservationists have dumped them on the farmers. I've seen golden eagles kill full-grown sheep, and we find lamb remains in their nests every year, but the farmers say they know them and have always lived with them, they like them. Golden eagles fly around with a halo; white-tailed eagles have horns sticking out of their head.'

The language used to describe white-tailed eagles is harsh. They are accused of causing 'killing fields' and 'devastating losses', these beliefs reinforced by a Scottish Natural Heritage (now NatureScot) report published in 2019. Farms in Argyll and Skye, chosen because of reported high losses due to eagles, were monitored between 2012 and 2018. The results fanned the flames as one farm alone claimed to have lost 181 lambs to the white-tailed eagles in those six years. The National Farmers' Union of Scotland saw this as a justification for their hard-line stance, as their president, Andrew McCornick, commented in a press release at the time:

> For a long time, the impression has been given that only weak or dead lambs are subject to White-tailed Eagle (WTE) predation. Recognition that predation includes healthy sheep and lambs vindicates what many farmers and crofters affected by WTEs have been saying for some considerable time.
>
> With one WTE monitor farm able to clearly demonstrate the loss of an extra 181 lambs in the period 2012–2018, it is clear to me that WTE predation could have a serious impact on the sustainability of hefted hill flocks on some farms and crofts.
>
> The papers also recognise that, in areas where there is a lack of alternative prey, the predation period extends beyond lambing time in the spring and presents a threat to lambs and adult sheep throughout the year.[22]

David's work-life is immersed in managing this conflict between hill farmers struggling on the edge of financial survival and the return of a native eagle that is seen as a giant threat. He often comes face to face with angry farmers, determined to vent their frustrations. 'At times,' he said, 'it feels that when I'm in a room of farmers, there is a frenzy of hate towards the birds, but when I speak privately to individuals, people are more reasonable.'

Perhaps some of that softening of attitude is due to the increasing benefits farmers see from tourists coming to Mull to see the eagles. A study commissioned by the RSPB found that eagle-lovers boosted Mull's economy by £5 million each year and provided jobs for over 100 people. In fact, many of the same farms and estates who say they have problems with livestock predation also let farm cottages to eagle-watching tourists, and allow wildlife tours on their land. It is a complex, convoluted and evolving situation where emotions and practicalities wrestle uneasily on an island where only the sea and the weather seem eternal.

In recent correspondence, David told me that he had had two encouraging conversations with farmers. He wrote: 'One farmer said, "Not all Sea Eagles are bad", the other, who was noticing most of his tourists were there to see the eagles, said, "Maybe we have to change ..." So maybe, just maybe, we are inching forward.' All farmers are having to adapt to a changing world, and many hill sheep-farmers in particular are facing a difficult future. Those I have met are intelligent and good-hearted people who are being asked to make huge shifts in their world view. It is not surprising it is not always done easily or with a light heart.

Eco-tourism is helping Mull's farmers and land managers to become reconciled to the reintroduction, but other measures are also being tried. NatureScot's Sea Eagle Management Scheme gives financial aid to farmers in eagle areas, as well as providing practical advice. Farmers can try both audio and visual devices, to scare the birds away, as well as diversionary feeding (as tested on hen harriers), which involves putting out alternative food sources to distract the attention of the eagles away from the lambs. In some places, licences have been granted to fell the trees where eagles regularly nest. Not everyone wants any part of these compromises; they simply want to get rid of problem birds. Licences are available to kill ravens and crows, which are implicated in the deaths of many lambs, and so the more intransigent crofters want these licences extended to eagles.

One of the lessons learned from the reintroduction of white-tailed eagles to Scotland was that more consultation with the farming communities would have been beneficial prior to the first release. It was not clear at the time, though, that it was needed. Continental white-tailed eagles eat mainly seabirds, small mammals and fish; taking lambs is almost exclusively a Scottish phenomenon and probably due to the coincidence of hungry eaglets appearing at the same time as lambs are born on the hills. With the benefit of this hindsight, much more was done to prepare the ground for later releases of white-tailed eagles on the Isle of Wight by the Roy Dennis Wildlife Foundation.

Overwhelmingly, around 80 per cent of the public on the island who completed questionnaires and who went to public meetings were in favour. Some farmers, though, were far from happy. David Sexton went to a very difficult meeting organised by the National Farmers' Union: 'Buzzards are hated there, and so a white-tailed eagle – bigger and badder – that got everyone going. They didn't quite throw things at us, but not far off. People were lashing out and shouting, "Go home, we don't want you here!" It was one of the worst meetings I've ever been to.'

Despite the farming opposition, a five-year reintroduction programme is now underway and in August 2019 the first six eagles were released, with a further seven in 2020. The tracking devices show they travel widely, even as far as the Scottish Borders. So far, one bird has been found dead and another is missing, fate unknown (presumed dead), but juvenile deaths for the species are notoriously high. The other eagles are still alive and may breed in a few years, helping return this magnificent predator to an island where they haven't been resident since the eighteenth century. The bigger vision is that eagles will also spread their wings and colonise the mainland too. Only time will tell if we allow this to happen.

It would be wrong to give the impression that it is only farmers who oppose the return of the white-tailed eagle to British skies. Some conservationists I spoke to in Scotland are worried about the effect a seabird-eating eagle could have on declining species like fulmars, a point I put to David in our later correspondence. There is a touch of weariness in the way he answers these queries, borne from many years of explaining and justifying their presence:

'Sea eagles certainly eat fulmars, quite a few of them, so in that sense you could say they are a 'problem', especially if you're the unlucky individual fulmar which is eaten! But to claim sea eagles are a 'problem' for the species as a whole is inaccurate. In Scandinavian countries with a lot more sea eagles than the UK, fulmars are stable or increasing. And don't forget, fulmars were a scarce breeding bird in the UK until the twentieth century when their numbers were boosted for a while by the white fish industry that provided discarded fish offal from boats, a practice which has now stopped, so the numbers are going down again. I'm sure small, isolated colonies of fulmars might be affected, if there's a pair of sea eagles nesting nearby, but generally it's the change in fishing practices and climate change which is affecting the population as a whole. Equally, fulmars have caused the deaths of young, inexperienced eagles which approach them face on and get vomited over. They lose the waterproofing of their feathers, leading to hypothermia and death – it's what has happened to young sea eagles released on Fair Isle in 1968. Experienced adults catch fulmars from behind. But if someone is anti-sea eagle, they'll tell you they're responsible for the decline of everything. I've heard them being blamed for the decline or extinction of hares, ptarmigan, herons, goats, skylarks … the list goes on! None of it is true.'[23]

As my day with the eagles ended on Mull, David and I sat in a car looking out over a rocky bay, the rain now hitting the windscreen as it swept in from the sea. The early brightness had succumbed to the softness of grey, sodden, low cloud. A curlew probed the mud and a few gulls floated across the skyline. We chatted about compromise, truth and reconciliation, and David's constant battle to keep presenting the good side of the eagles to a farming world that doesn't always want to listen. 'We need to keep giving the positive stories,' he said, 'even though it is frustrating sometimes, otherwise politicians would only hear the negative press.'

I asked if it was worth it – all this effort and emotion for one species. Perhaps time and energy would be better spent on more general conservation initiatives. He disagreed. 'There's an argument for a symbolic gesture, something attention-grabbing that draws people into the importance of nature. From a big predator like a white-tailed eagle lots of other things fall into place. They might even be a farmer's friend in a way – eating crows, ravens, geese, rabbits, and they can keep mink numbers down. I think it is worth every minute of every day getting positive messages across.' We sat in silence for a while listening to the rain and the waves. The ancientness of the land seemed to yearn for this bird, a living, breathing symbol of continuity between the past and its future. And then, as if on cue, a huge dark shape appeared on the horizon and sailed over the restless sea.

Seals

'Septimus is lush – lush! And he's the best example we have of cumulative impacts!' Sue Sayer and I are sitting in her cosy cottage in Cornwall discussing grey seals. She has been studying them for over twenty years, and her passion for them led her to found and run the Cornwall Seal Group. Septimus is a 2.4-metre-long male, or the skeleton of one to be exact, and the third longest ever to be washed up in Cornwall. To help with her charity's outreach and education work, she had his carcass buried, then his bones dug up, cleaned up and reassembled. Today, instead of swimming wild around the coast, he trundles around the country in wooden boxes as an exhibit. The unlovely phrase, 'cumulative impacts' hides a whole host of horrors. Septimus is the embodiment of the reality of life for a seal in British seas.

As we sipped tea, Sue reeled off what the skeleton of Septimus had revealed about his pain-filled life. His oldest injury was a bent sacrum, the 'tail bone' at the base of the spine. This area is very strong, formed by fused vertebrae, so only a powerful impact could have caused that kind of damage, perhaps a boat strike. It was evident on the outside of his body by a pink scar, which was obvious on the photographs of his limp form lying on a beach. Two years prior to his death he also nursed two broken ribs, which may have been the result of crashing violently into the water after being disturbed off rocks. Seals panic easily and launch themselves onto the surface of the sea, a heavy belly-flop that can damage their bones. People, dogs, loud noises, boats, canoeists, paddle-boarders – all manner of human-based activities can spook them. Unlike our ribs, which mend if they are kept as still as possible, a seal's chest cavity needs to be mobile for it to survive. As they dive up to 300 metres for food, their chest collapses under the pressure, and then expands again as it surfaces. Septimus's ribs had no time or space to heal. It is hard to imagine the pain he must have endured hunting for food, or when hauling himself onto beaches. Then, just before he died, he suffered another broken vertebra, perhaps again caused by a collision with a boat. Septimus was as battered and broken as a cage fighter.

His other conditions were just as painful but more systemic. Septimus suffered from serial illnesses. His flippers showed missing claws with infection damage present on the bone. He had also had such a severe sinus infection that it had eaten away at his cheekbone, another agonising condition. It is known that long-lasting marine pollutants such as polychlorinated biphenyls (PCBs) and heavy metals from industrial processes suppress the immune system of marine mammals, and hence compromise their ability to combat infections. Although PCBs were banned in Europe in 1981,

300,000 tonnes were produced in the previous thirty years for a variety of industrial products.[1] Through incineration, runoff and leakage from landfill, large quantities made their way into the marine environment where they remain, accumulating in the fatty tissues of animals like seals. Sue doesn't know what role, if any, they played in Septimus's death as no full post-mortem was carried out, but he obviously succumbed to illnesses he couldn't fight. He may well have been so poorly with his sinus condition he could have been semi-conscious, resulting in him accidentally bashing his head, the final blow that killed him. It was hard to fathom how much this one animal had suffered, and it seemed that much of it was at our hands.

Sue then clicked on her computer screen and produced the most shocking photograph of all. It took me a while to spot it. 'There, can you see?' she pointed to a close-up of his ribs. 'He had been shot! The worst thing is, he was shot illegally because that's a shotgun pellet. It must have been fired at close range, otherwise it wouldn't have got through his skin and blubber. Fifty to seventy pellets would have sprayed out, hitting him all over. Whoever fired the gun was right next to him. This pellet seems to have lodged against the bone when he was young and the bone then grew around it.' She held her hands a metre apart, to demonstrate how close someone must have been when they pulled the trigger. It took me a while to process the information and what it conveyed about humanity.

Sue reached under the desk, dragged out a large box containing his skull, and heaved it onto the desk. There it sat, an anonymous finality of bone. All traces of the personality and physical traits of this once magnificent beast had long since rotted away, leaving only a sterile structure. The enormous sockets once held dark, limpid eyes that saw the mystery of an underwater world, or the curious spectacle of two-legged animals clambering over many of the places where he wanted to go. His ear cavities (they have no external earlobes) heard the cries of pups and the plaintive wailing of females, as well as the cacophony of clicks made by schools of fish. He may even have been deafened by the thunderous blasts of the sub-aqua industrial landscape; pile driving, sonar booms, hammering and roaring engines. The huge cavity for his nose, misshapen by disease, would once have contained the complex olfactory nerves that helped him smell out food, friends and enemies. Sue thinks a seal's sense of smell is their most useful sense, so good in fact that they can identify individual beaches by the odours of different bacterial assemblages in the sand. Blind seals are known to cope well in the wild, depending on smell to track down prey and aided by their whiskers, which can detect the tiniest vibrations.

We both took a quiet moment to reflect on the sullen skull of Septimus sitting between us. I couldn't help stroking it gently, imagining the beast he once was. I wanted to apologise, but also to explain as much as I could why we had caused him so much suffering. In my mind, I reeled off some excuses. Accidents happen at sea, so the cliché goes, and maybe seals are not always easy to spot in choppy waters. The skippers of the boats probably didn't see him in time, they might not have realised there had been a collision. Septimus was probably an unfortunate maritime road accident, collateral damage in the busy highways of our seas. The industrial pollutants that poisoned his system weren't understood to be harmful to sea mammals at the time we manufactured them; and we didn't know they would be 'persistent contaminants' that would last for years in the environment without breaking down. At least in the UK we no longer produce those particular chemicals, albeit too late for Septimus. It is true though, I had to admit, the sea is still a rubbish dump where out of sight is out of mind, and policing global oceans is almost impossible.

But most of all I wanted to explain why some people are cruel; why they would get so close to him they could look him in the eye, then raise a gun and fire with a weapon that they must have known couldn't kill him outright but would cause terrible injury. Weak justifications swirled around my brain, but I couldn't form them into coherent thoughts, because some things are just too hard to understand. The undertow of the human psyche can drag us to depths that are cold and dark. For some, it is easier to give in to that bitter tide than to fight it and stay in the light. Arrogance, malice, deferred anger, revenge, insecurity, a desire for power and domination, all of these lurk within, emitting siren calls to tempt us, but there can never be any excuses for abuse.

Septimus did escape one horror, though – he didn't appear to have wounds caused by net entanglement. Photographs of his carcass on the beach showed no signs of cuts or constrictions from fishing lines or nets. Plenty of other seals are not so lucky. Sue has found over a hundred net-entangled seals each year for the last three years. I saw it for myself.

I first met Sue back in 2012, to record a radio programme on her passion for seals.[2] We stood on a cliff and looked down at a beach covered in mainly female seals and pups. One small seal seemed to have a bright red necklace. 'Oh yes, one of the golden-brown juveniles. We have over a hundred net-entangled seals, this one has blood all round its neck, it really needs rescuing or it won't survive to adulthood.' It was a shocking sight, a red, raw ring with a necklace of webbing still in place that was digging ever deeper into the growing pup's flesh. It looked excruciating, even more so splashed by salty waves.

'Net entanglement is a huge welfare issue for our seals. If seals interact with an operational fishing net and get stuck, they drown. But if they play with a discarded net at the surface – we've watched them do it – they swim over it, around it, under it and the next thing you know, they've swum through it. And it's not just Cornish marine litter we get here, we've had at least four items we can trace back to Maine on the east coast of America.'

Our world is bound by invisible rivers, the global currents and air flows that swirl around the creatures of this earth, carrying them to distant places, bringing them food, distributing rain and storms – and they transport our rubbish into their homes, no matter how remote or inaccessible. There on the beach below us was the embodiment of months of agony which may have been caused by an act of carelessness thousands of miles away.

The seals Sue finds and can rescue are the lucky ones. She showed me a series of photographs of a young female seal that had a net cutting into her neck so tightly the whole area was bloodied and infected. She was skinny and distressed and although it took a while, the team managed to catch her, cut the net away and treat the wound. Twelve months later, the indentation of the scar was very visible, but she was now round, sleek and had a mate, and she went on to be a mother.

The Convention on Biological Diversity report from 2013[3] shows fatal entanglement in, and ingestion of, marine debris by marine animals has increased by 40 per cent in the last decade and estimates that over 100,000 marine animals, such as turtles, dolphins, seals and whales, die each year from interaction with plastic debris. Prior to 1950, fishing nets were made from natural rope which eventually broke down, but the world-wide adoption of plastics has condemned millions of sea creatures to horrible deaths for centuries to come. Today, 40 per cent of all ocean debris is plastic fishing gear. In fact, research for the United Nations Food and Agriculture Organisation estimates that 640,000 tonnes of fishing equipment are abandoned each year into the ocean.[4] The twenty-first century is increasingly aware of plastic pollution, but the debris continues to build, choking the life out of the seas. The exposure risk to plastic is greatest within thirty kilometres of the coast, the zone where most fishing takes place and where Britain's two species of seals spend the majority of their time.

The grey seal (*Halichoerus grypus*, meaning 'hooked-nose pig of the sea') and the harbour seal, sometimes called the common seal (*Phoca vitulina*, meaning 'calf or dog of the sea'), are, in some ways, misnomers. The harbour or common seal is rarely found in harbours and is not very common in the UK, while the grey seal is far more common, quite often seen in harbours and is rarely just grey. For both, though, the islands of Britain and Ireland provide the fish stocks, inlets, rocky outcrops and beaches that both species need for their half-in-half-out-of-the-sea lives.

The grey seal is a UK speciality, and British waters house 40 per cent of the world population and 95 per cent of the European population, around 135,000 animals. These bulky, blubbery, glistening predators are great ocean travellers and range widely away from the coast. Excluding the fully aquatic whales and dolphins, grey seals are the largest surviving native British mammal, weighing up to 400 kilograms and reaching 3.5 metres in length. Horse-faced, Roman-nosed and sporting a dappled coat of subtle hues from black to light grey, it is a beautiful, deep-diving, water-dog that delights us with its bobbing inquisitiveness. Like floating Russian dolls, grey seals pop up vertically and peer into our lives. They seem to find us to be the most fascinating creatures on earth. Found all around the coast, but more numerous in the north, they are expanding in number, especially down the east coast. As grey seals become ever more abundant, their smaller relatives are struggling.

Harbour or common seals are snub-nosed, giving them a cute, human-like face. They are more human-sized too, weighing up to 100 kilograms and growing to a maximum length of 1.6 metres. The UK has only 5 per cent of the global population, around 40,000 seals, and they can be found right around the northern hemisphere. In the UK they reside mainly in Scotland, although there are populations in the Thames Estuary and the Wash, but not as far south as Cornwall. In contrast to greys, these are stay-at-home coast-huggers; 'mud-puppies', as zoologist Mark Simmonds described them to me. They rarely travel beyond fifty kilometres from where they were born and are of a different character. Grey seals often haul out in large, snorting, wailing gangs – rather like a squabbling football crowd. Harbour seals prefer smaller groups with more personal space, and they are not so rowdy – although they do huff, puff and snarl if disturbed. More akin to opera goers, perhaps.

Harbour seal numbers are falling dramatically in some areas, but no one knows why. It is one of the great ocean mysteries and it's happening on our doorstep. Orkney, a former stronghold of harbour seals, has lost 90 per cent of its population in the last fifteen years. Around the Tay estuary it is a jaw-dropping 95 per cent decline in the same timeframe. Even in Shetland they have declined by 45 per cent. The Scottish west coast, though, is bucking the trend and seeing an increase in their numbers. It is all very odd. I met John Baxter, an honorary professor at both St Andrews and Heriot Watt Universities as well as former Principal Marine Advisor to Scottish Natural Heritage, to discuss the strange case of the UK's vanishing harbour seals.

'With such huge and sudden losses, we should expect to find piles of bodies, but no dead ones are pitching up along the coastlines. There is also no evidence of mass culling, and shooting on that scale would surely be noticed by locals.'

Thinking of Septimus, I postulated whether PCBs or pollution could be killing them, or reducing their fecundity?

'It is hard to believe, especially as some populations are increasing, and in many areas where they are disappearing there is no heavy industry or excessive pollution.'

Are fish stocks moving due to climate change? If harbour seals remain faithful to one area, perhaps they are falling foul of a shift in their food supply?

'We have no evidence of emaciated seals, and other fish-reliant species in the same areas seem to be doing fine; the pattern of fish movement just doesn't match.'

Predation then? Orcas (killer whales) live around the UK coasts and they eat harbour seals?

'This can't be the cause; only a few tens of orcas at most live in British waters; there are simply not enough of them to account for what is happening. Greys can eat harbour seals, sometimes in gruesome ways, and grey seals are certainly increasing. Big male greys have been seen pinning down smaller harbours with a flipper, biting through the skin and then rolling it over and over, unpeeling its flesh from its body like we peel an orange. Scientists once thought these "corkscrew" injuries were caused by boat propellers, but it seems the larger, stronger greys can use the smaller harbours as an occasional snack that they unwrap on the rocks. But this inter-species predation cannot explain the huge losses in only a few places. None of the models we have tried fit the pattern.'

John believes that this order of decline can only be caused by a fall in the breeding success of the harbour seals in some specific areas, 'but why that is we cannot, as yet, say.'

Both grey and harbour seals draw us in with their endearingly plump form, large, round eyes and calm gaze; they are aquatic oversized baby-like creatures. As seals float near the shore their moans and wails reverberate in caves and inlets, eerie laments that rise up cliffs and spread over the land to inhabit our dreams. Their pups cry like our babies – urgent, plaintive sobs – sounds that have always torn at our hearts. For generations these sea-people have been our marine alter-egos, embodied in our legends and tales of mermaids and mermen.

Ancient folklore of 'selkies' tells of seals coming ashore at night to cast off their skins and dance naked, transformed into beautiful people bathed in moonlight. It is said that men have crept to the shore at midnight to watch them, becoming so entranced they captured seal-women for their wives, hiding their skins so they could not go back to the sea. The seal-wives proved to be maternal, strong and faithful companions, but they constantly turn their heads to listen to the waves, yearning for their own. Some escape their kidnappers, find their skins and return to their seal-world, leaving their human husbands heartbroken on the shore. In other tales, young girls are seduced by large male seals. The progeny of a human and a seal have webbing on their feet and hands, and they slip in and out of the water with ease. These seal-children carry sea salt and waves in their ocean-eyes, and see the world differently to their earth-bound friends.

Selkie legends declare that the largest, strongest males are crowned the King of the Seals. These giants can swim against the strongest of tides. The King Seal summons mass gatherings; thousands of seal-subjects from all the oceans arrive to listen and pay homage. Maybe Septimus once joined the mighty throngs. It is the responsibility of the ruler of the seals to warn his citizens of the dangers of getting too close to humans, but it is often to no avail. In selkie tales people sail out to meet seal folk and converse with them as they lie on rocks or float in the sea, sharing with them their woes and dreams. The seals tell us about their underwater kingdoms of waving kelp, coral and pearls, and we tell them our secrets and relate stories of grand palaces and of crowns glistening with crystals taken from deep within the earth. At times the seal-people help us out of danger, allowing us to climb on their backs so they can take us to the safety of the shore, where we shower them with gratitude. Then, when all the talking is done, we take out a bludgeon and kill them.

Violence is woven into selkie stories, perhaps as a way of making sense of our relationship with animals that we are both drawn to but ruthlessly exploit. In the tough, pre-industrial world of fishing folk, seal skins were prized for waterproof clothing and shoes, their flesh was food and their blubber could be squeezed for oil. Sealers were hardened men who sailed to the pupping caves to take mothers and newborns where they lay. They stunned them with a blow to the head, then skinned them alive before they came round. For centuries we interacted with seals this way. They inspired our stories, but we treated them as mobile convenience stores for everyday essentials.

As the great wheels of industrialisation gathered pace in the nineteenth century, providing us with new products and sources of fuel, they lost their cloak of mystery as well as their monetary value. Sealskin was eventually phased out to be replaced by other materials, and petroleum and gas was used instead of their oil. The fishing industry for salmon, mackerel, herring, sardine and white fish burgeoned, and seals underwent a new transformation – from companions in a subsistence world to pure competitors in a commercial one.

Killing seals to protect fish stocks was so prolific that by 1900 it was estimated there were only 500 grey seals left throughout the

UK, although later estimates have revised that up to a few thousand. Whatever the actual figure, it was dangerously low and they became the first mammal to be protected by law through the Grey Seals Protection Act of 1914, which forbade killing any grey seals in their breeding season in the autumn. Outside of that time slot they could still be shot or poisoned by lacing salmon bait with strychnine. To add to the incentive to kill, in parts of Scotland a bounty was offered by the Fishery Board for the tail of a grey seal if it had been seen near fishing nets. Despite this, the partial protection worked, and by the 1930s numbers had risen to 9,000. Further protection was afforded in 1932 with the Conservation of Seals Act, which extended the closed season and stopped the hunting of grey seals on the island of Haskeir, off the Outer Hebrides, where hunting had been unrestrained. Even so, the government could alter the dates and agree to some culling if deemed necessary. All the while, the harbour seal remained unprotected.

By the 1960s grey seal numbers were at 34,000, but harbour seal numbers were in steep decline. The rise in greys brought with it ever louder demands to manage the threat of 'marauding seals', which were blamed for damaging the east-coast fishing industry and for eating the migrating salmon as they made their way from the sea to the rivers to reach their spawning grounds. The seals were accused of killing and maiming at will, and of destroying the tradition of fly fishing on the great Scottish rivers. The increase in the number of seals breeding on the Orkney and Farne Islands became a focus for all these ills, and in 1958 culls of breeding seals were sanctioned. Seals and their pups were shot, clubbed and poisoned as licences were issued to manage what was seen as a plague of seals eating valuable fish. Thousands were killed in the 1960s, but the government were unprepared for the backlash.

Society was changing. There was more awareness of what was happening to wildlife through radio, TV and newspapers than in previous decades, and the general population felt betrayed. 'Murder in the Nursery!' headlines gave voice to the growing number who opposed the slaughter. The National Trust, who managed the Farne Islands, came in for particular criticism. 'Never again can anyone interested in British wildlife regard the National Trust as anything but a bitter joke,' wrote one angry correspondent to the *Newcastle Evening Chronicle*.[5] Organised groups were joined by weekend walkers and day trippers, amalgamating wildlife concern as never before. Emotion was rife on both sides. By the late 1960s the cull had to be stopped. The seal killing spree had produced outraged conservationists and incensed fishermen; something had to be done to bring the sides together.

In 1969, a debate on a new Conservation of Seals bill was held in the House of Commons, led by John Temple MP. His two-pronged approach wanted to bring unprotected harbour seals under the same protection as greys, but also to make sure fisheries could tackle a problem if they saw it. 'The Bill is extraordinarily delicately balanced. It is the first Bill to deal directly with conservation. Its object is to conserve – I emphasise "conserve" – a healthy seal population and what I will term a sensible level of population. We must recognise the rightful interests – the economic interests – of the fishing industry.' He declared his own interests as both a conservationist and as President of the Fisheries Organisation Society, President of the National Council of Salmon Netsmen of England and Wales, and Life Vice-President of the Salmon and Trout Association.

He began by asserting that, apart from people, seals have few if any natural predators in British waters, and then set out his case for a management strategy. It is worth quoting much of the debate in full from the official Parliamentary record in Hansard as so many arguments have moved very little in the intervening fifty years.

Of course, it is basic and fundamental to the Bill that seals eat fish. This is the other side of the seal problem – the fact that they are considerable predators of our fish population. If total protection were given to seals, the balance of nature itself would be upset.

Early this century the grey seal was in danger of extinction. Hence the protection Acts. Since that time the increase in the grey seal population has been extraordinarily dramatic. The converse has happened with the common seal. Without protection, the common seal population is declining to an alarming extent, and that is one of the major reasons why the Bill is urgent.

The increase in those [Scottish] seal colonies has been quite dramatic, so much so that the Secretary of State for Scotland … has authorised an annual cull in Orkney of about 800 seals. I am informed that that annual cull goes on extraordinarily satisfactorily. These Orcadian hunters, as they are called, have to carry out their hunting under licence because they are hunting for the grey seal during the close [breeding] season.

The situation in the Farne Islands is different. The total seal population in the 1930s was 400 or 500 seals and the population has grown to 5,000 or 6,000 seals, a tenfold increase. Between 1952 and 1967 the pups born increased from 600 per annum to 1,800 per annum. If this situation continues uncontrolled, the seal population will double every nine years.[6]

Temple acknowledged that a cull was not necessary for harbour/ common seals; with no protection, they were still heavily hunted.

In the Shetland area, 800 pups per annum are being taken, and the slaughter of adult seals is increasing. In some areas around Shetland very few pups are surviving at present. To give an example, here are some figures from the coast north of Fitful Head. In 1954, the common seal population was about 300 adults and 91 pups. This year, there are a mere 38 adults and two pups. It is thought that the common seal population has fallen to about one-tenth of what it was 15 years ago. My Bill is urgently needed as a safeguard against the deteriorating situation for the common seal.

Now, I come to the position of fish and fishermen. So far as I know, it has never been controverted that seals are exclusively fish eaters. They consume about two tons per annum per head. United Kingdom seals eat approximately 100,000 tons of fish a year, a considerable mouthful, and the damage which they do to those which they do not necessarily kill is considerable, too. The most affected in the fish world are the salmon and the cod. On the east coast of Scotland, the damage to net fisheries is severe and is, without doubt, increasing. Today, 10 per cent of salmon taken in the coastal nets are found to be damaged by seals, and that proportion has been rising relentlessly in the past few years.[7]

Not everyone, though, bought into the logic of the argument. Peter Jackson MP called the title of the bill 'a misnomer. It should be described as a Bill for the protection of the salmon fisheries.' He questioned the evidence presented:

The balance hinges on the extent to which seals are regarded as a threat to the fishing industry …

I understand that in the period 1952–58, 231,000 salmon and 191,000 grilse were taken. In the period 1959–65, the figures are 233,000 salmon and 218,000 grilse. As I am sure the hon. Gentleman recognises, this represents a marginal increase in salmon landings, and yet over this period there has been a considerable increase in the seal population.

Jackson went on to give more facts and figures, showing that he agreed that grey seal numbers were indeed rising, but so too were the numbers of fish, so how could this be justification for culling?

I agree that seals are predators, and acknowledge that they cause damage to the fishing industry. The question at issue is whether the damage is on such a scale as to be thought insufferable. In my view, the losses which could be attributed to seals are minimal and should be borne by the industry.[8]

Despite these objections, the Bill became law in 1970. At the time the Conservation of Seals Bill was hailed as a good compromise between blanket protection and management under licence. The legislation allows fisheries to kill seals throughout the year to prevent damage to their fishing nets, tackle or catch, including the breeding seasons, and even to cull seals in Special Areas of Conservation, but only with a rifle – poisoning and clubbing are no longer allowed. And there is no requirement to report the species or the number killed. This is still the law in England and Wales today. One seal scientist I spoke to described the Conservation of Seals Bill as the most mis-named piece of conservation legislation on the planet, being far more in favour of the fisheries than the seals. Only one person has been prosecuted in the fifty years of the Bill's existence.

Scotland rescinded the 1970 Conservation of Seals Act and established the Marine Scotland Act in 2010. It is now illegal to kill any seal at any time in Scotland, except under licence, and any seals that are shot have to be recorded and the numbers published. Official government figures show that nearly 2,000 seals have been shot in Scotland since 2011,[9] a number deemed necessary to balance the rise in seal numbers with the decrease in ocean fish, the dwindling numbers of wild salmon, and the dramatic increase in salmon farming. The fishing industry points to land-based interests like forestry and farming, which can cull wildlife that damages their stock (deer browsing trees and foxes attacking lambs for example), and they demand the same powers to protect their businesses.

For inshore fishing and salmon farms, the conspicuousness of seals picks them out as the main threat. For many, they are marine vermin, foxes of the high seas, and a danger to the creatures we want to take for ourselves. Trawler fishermen complain that their nets have been torn and vast numbers of fish damaged and partially eaten, salmon farmers say they attack cages, biting and wounding fish indiscriminately and that no deterrents can keep them away. Fly fishermen see them as increasing competition for the traditional sport of fly fishing for wild salmon.

Seals draw to themselves all our anxiety about the state of fish in British waters. They concentrate the issues caused by decades of overfishing and by the more recent establishment of intensive salmon farming, finding themselves caught in the confusion and contradictions of our relationship with the sea. We persecuted seals to virtual extinction, and now decry their recovery. We trap large numbers of their prey species in nets and cages, then resent them for being attracted to the bounty. We even remove vast amounts of their preferred food, especially small fish like herring and sand eels, and feed it to captive farmed salmon, where the fish often live in overcrowded and lice-infested conditions. From the outside looking in, it is hard to make sense of it all. And meanwhile, all around, the oceans are in crisis.

The words of the Director General of the FAO (UN Food and Agriculture Organisation), José Graziano da Silva, are stark. Since 1961 the annual global growth in fish consumption has been twice as high as population growth, demonstrating that the fisheries and aquaculture sector is crucial in meeting the goal of the FAO of 'a world without hunger and malnutrition'. The result is that, worldwide, fish stocks are under immense pressure. According to a 2018 FAO report, two-thirds are either fully or over-exploited,[10] and human population is still rising. The oceans are the best example of the 'tragedy of the commons', where a shared resource is everybody's right but no one's responsibility.

The once mighty cod, mackerel and herring fisheries of the North Sea collapsed in the 1970s and 1980s due to centuries of overfishing. Through strict management they are now slowly but patchily recovering. Fishing for sand eels, on the other hand, continues to intensify. Sand eels are abundant fish which form large shoals and for most of the year live buried in the sandy substrate of shallow waters (they are the thin, silver fish seen hanging out of the bills of puffins, a sight beloved by wildlife photographers). Sand eels are a vital part of the diet of a range of seabirds, whales, dolphins and seals. Of the five species that inhabit the North Sea, the lesser sand eel, *Ammodytes marinus*, comprises over 90 per cent of the catch.

The sand eel fishery is huge, by far the largest in the North Sea. In the last decade, around a million tons have been taken annually,

Denmark alone catches 458,000 tons of sand eels in EU waters every year. None of this is for human consumption. As an exceptionally oily fish they provide food for fish farms, other animal feeds and the fish oils in health supplements. At one time, sand eels even fuelled Danish power stations. Demand is set to increase. The FAO indicates that, as wild fish come under increasing pressure, aquaculture and its associated demand for fish oils will dominate world fish supplies by 2030. The Scottish salmon farming industry alone is set to triple by 2030, to produce 300,000–400,000 tonnes a year. As it takes 4 kilograms of wild-caught sand eels to produce 1 kilogram of farmed salmon, intensive, industrial-scale, sand-eel fishing is inevitable. The knock-on effects for ocean health are yet to be seen.

As wild salmon are declining alarmingly (see Chapter 9), the Scottish farmed salmon industry has boomed and is now one of the UK's biggest food exporters. It is said to be worth more than £1 billion a year to the economy. It has seen a rapid rise to dominance. Within a few decades, salmon transitioned from a luxury food to a commonplace item in supermarkets. More than 200 fish farms now operate in Scotland, and almost all of them are owned by just five Norwegian companies. The shift from small-scale, locally owned businesses to large, international, intensive industries may, however, benefit seals. Fish farming is monied and growing in value, bringing investment in stronger cages and nets and a whole array of technical aids, such as acoustic and laser deterrents, to protect the fish from predators. Scottish Sea Farms records that culling of seals was down by nearly a third in 2018 in areas where these new measures were in place. The welfare of seals may be one of the reasons for these improvements, but even stronger drivers come from the public demand for seal-friendly fish, and, surprisingly, much of this comes from America.

In 2016, the US National Oceanic and Atmospheric Administration agreed new rules to stop the import of salmon from countries that kill seals. To comply with US standards, they must have a programme that, 'prohibits the intentional killing or serious injury of marine mammals in all fisheries.'[11] America is the leading importer of Scottish salmon, with exports worth over £200 million per year. The Scottish government attempted to argue for an exemption, claiming 500,000 fish a year are lost due to seals and breaching of nets, but they failed. In June 2020, the shooting of seals to protect salmon farms in Scotland was made illegal.

Official regulation goes a long way, but policing illegal activity along remote coastlines and out at sea is difficult. A trawl of the internet reveals many news stories of illegally killed seals every year. In January 2019, two pregnant harbour seals were found in Essex, presumed, but not proven, to have been shot by anglers.[12] It is thought two more were killed at the same time, but their bodies have not been recovered. Photographs show a bloodied hole in the chest of a sleek, grey-coated harbour seal, its body as smooth and torpedo-shaped as the bullet that killed it and its three-month old foetus. They died at the hands of an experienced marksman. The activist group Sea Shepherd ('Sea Shepherd fights to defend, conserve and protect our oceans') offered a £3,000 reward for information which could lead to arrests, but to date it remains unclaimed. Videos on Sea Shepherd's website show their activists recovering the bodies of shot seals washed onto rocks, the position of the bullet holes indicating that death was not instant. 'We target the worst offenders first,' Sea Shepherd's Rob Read told me, 'and our main weapon is the camera.'

The video library has distressing footage of men shooting seals from boats, cliffs and beaches from all around Scotland. 'It is very frustrating,' said Rob. 'Some of the fishermen see seals purely as competition, not as an indication of healthy fish numbers. If there are a lot of seals, then there are a lot of fish. But they have a different mindset. We see the same story in Canada – where they club seals to death to protect fish. It is simply the wrong way to think about things. It doesn't work. And anyway, seals don't eat much salmon, they are really bad at catching them. Salmon are strong, fast swimmers. Many of the shot seals we have found haven't had salmon in their stomachs. Seals will, though, have a go at a bag of salmon hanging in the water or caught in a net – of course they will.'

One film on Sea Shepherd's website, taken in 2015, shows a group from a local business, the Scottish Wild Salmon Company (also known as Usan Salmon) based on the east coast of Scotland, surrounding a marksman lying on the ground, his gun aimed at the water. They had a licence to protect their nets from the seals, which they claimed were destroying their livelihood, but there was some suspicion that this was a cover for a bigger operation. When wild salmon arrive from the open ocean, they spend time in coastal waters before heading inland to navigate the rivers that lead to their spawning grounds. 'The problem is,' said Rob, 'three times as many dead seals with bullet holes in them were washing up around their remote house and processing sheds than they had claimed they were shooting.'

Newspaper stories from the time report distressed locals and holidaymakers finding dead seals on the beach and seeing men with guns along the shore. One elderly German couple, who had just arrived for a holiday, witnessed a seal being shot, then packed their bags and left that day. The men were purportedly aggressive when challenged.[13] 'They even shot over our heads to get a seal, which is illegal in itself,' said Rob. 'So, we had some of our team go to film them.'

At first, the video is chillingly surreal. Environmental activists are filming the fishermen filming them, slowly moving round each other, keeping a short distance apart. Few words are spoken in this sea-shore dance of restrained aggression, while in the background a man with a gun ignores the video-off just a few feet away. Suddenly, a dull thud indicates a shot has been fired and the camera pans quickly to the roiling sea as it turns red. Unseen, just below the surface, a seal thrashes and twists in panic, and presumably pain. For a macabre few moments, a fountain of blood spurts in the air like a nightmare water feature. The cameraman and companions gasp and keep the film focused on the seal's death throes while the marksman fires another couple of shots, packs up his things and the group walk defiantly away.[14] It is a ruthless exhibition, and the atmosphere is as cold as the wind buffeting the microphone.

Switching to the Scottish Wild Salmon Company promo film, posted in 2010, there is a different perspective.[15] Against haunting Celtic music, hardy men process wild salmon caught in nets hanging in the water from poles just offshore, or they manually haul fishing nets over the side of small boats. The salmon are dispatched with blows to the head. There is no commentary, just shots of traditional fishermen at work. The website reads, 'We catch prime condition wild salmon and seatrout in environmentally friendly traditional Scottish bag nets (traps), ensuring our product is of the highest quality. The wild salmon and seatrout we catch are the harvest of some of Scotland's finest East and North Coast rivers.' Compared to the horrors of an intensive salmon farm, it looks, from the video, to be infinitely preferable.

Some salmon in intensive fish farms are so infested with sealice that they are eaten alive. The fish pens can hold up to 200,000 fish, and they are doused in chemicals and antibiotics. Their waste pollutes the surrounding waters, and sand eels, anchovies, herring and sardines are scooped out of the sea in their millions to be ground into pellets to feed them. Don Staniford runs a small organisation, Global Alliance Against Industrial Aquaculture, and has spent twenty years highlighting the issues. In 2017, he gave an interview to the *Guardian* newspaper. 'What we are seeing now is a chemical arms race in the seas, just like on the land farms, where the resistance of plants to chemicals is growing. In fish farms, the parasites are increasingly resistant to chemicals and antibiotics. There has been a tenfold increase in the use of some chemicals in the past 18 months.' The same arguments that rage over intensive farming on the land have arrived out at sea.

The Scottish Wild Salmon Company, the last business based on netting salmon in the sea, was found guilty of breaching a number of terms of its licence, including fishing beyond its designated season, and it was fined. The government also halted the whole sector: in fact, there are no companies left that net migrating salmon; there simply aren't enough fish in the sea. But the whole saga has left a legacy of bitterness and resentment. As so often in the media, the sides appear simplified into good versus bad, which is rarely the case. To get behind the headlines, I went to see the Scottish Wild Salmon Company for myself.

The day I visited the Pullar family near Montrose on the northeast coast of Scotland, it had been raining hard for the first time after a prolonged dry spell. I pulled over on a small lane leading to the farm to gather my thoughts. It had been a long and tedious drive and my mind was filled with what it would be like to meet reputed seal killers. As the grey clouds quickly disappeared, the fresh, rain-washed breeze and brilliant sunlight lifted my spirits. It was difficult to believe such hostility could be played out in this otherwise peaceful and remote part of Scotland. Looking beyond the fields and out to sea, the atmosphere felt ripe with life-enhancing petrichor, the smell of the earth after rain. From the Latin *petri* for rocks and *ichor*, the substance that flowed through the veins of ancient Greek gods, it is a wildly over-the-top reference to the sense of joy that is enlivened by the passing of storms and the rich odour of wet earth that follows. Fortified, I drove into the farmyard stacked with large, empty trailers, which had 'Scottish Wild Salmon Company' written on the side.

David Pullar, the elderly father of the family, was very kind. He fussed over how far I had come, told me I should have put my campervan in their yard and not paid for a campsite, and made me a large plate of scrambled eggs on toast with endless mugs of tea. He told me that he knew salmon were declining, he had seen the difference from when he was a young man, but they could have kept going as a business if they could just have been allowed to 'keep the seals down a bit, they haul out right where we fish'. He told me that animal-rights activists were aggressive, wearing balaclavas and coming around the house at night, shining torches through the windows. He knew that seals were doing what they have evolved to do, which is eat fish, but there had been a big increase in numbers of grey seals in his time and the salmon stocks can't sustain it.

He said it was fair enough that they were asked to stop fishing for a while, at first for three years, later extended to seven and now indefinitely; 'everyone has to think of the bigger picture', but they wanted compensation for loss of income, which they are now arguing about with the government. 'They keep shifting the goalposts and we have bills and wages to pay.'

I asked if he understood why people got upset about their killing seals. He did, likening it to how some people react when deer are shot to protect forests, but it comes down to numbers – too few fish and lots of seals. 'People get upset because they think of deer as Bambi, and they are nice animals. Well, seals are nice-looking creatures too, especially the pups, but they eat our fish.'

Was it only seals that he thought were a problem for salmon stocks? Around 260 bottlenose dolphins return to the Scottish east coast each year in time to feed off the salmon run, eating up to 23 kilograms of salmon a day each. David's son George, who had just come in, nodded. 'I didn't believe that was true until I saw it for myself, a dolphin throwing large fish into the air, but no one would suggest controlling them.'

George had come into the kitchen for a snack with another of David's middle-aged sons, whom I recognised as the defiant marksman from the Sea Shepherd video. They made me more tea and were welcoming but cagey. We were sitting at a kitchen table with a panoramic view of the shore and flat rocks below. It is a lovely spot, which I commented on, especially in bright sunshine with white waves breaking against the slabs of red sandstone. 'Aye, and a good place to watch for seals, it's a favourite place for them to haul out – right there – and it's not too far for a shot.'

Court cases, battles for compensation, a sullied reputation – it all weighed heavy in the air. George showed me photographs of salmon that had been attacked by seals in their nets. They had missing heads or tails, or part of their sides bitten off. 'We can lose a lot of a catch in one day,' he said, 'and people get upset when I try to protect what is ours. What we take is tiny compared to up there.' He nodded his head towards the sea, in the direction of the immense factory trawlers that daily head out from further up the coast to hoover countless millions of fish out of the oceans, including bycatch of seals, dolphins, seabirds and even whales. In a European Union report from 2018, the UK declared that up to

3,000 harbour porpoises and around 1,000 common dolphins and seals of both species had been killed in active fishing nets. This is an average estimate; it could be twice that figure. In 2016, on the island of Tiree in the Hebrides, a killer whale washed up on a beach. It had died from entanglement in fishing gear. The cost to marine life from our demand for fish is very high.

Before I left, David Pullar took me to a large room full of piano accordions, which he collects as a hobby. He played me some traditional tunes and proudly told me stories of legendary accordionists he had known. It all seemed so homely, yet incongruous and surreal, considering the rancour that permeates references to this family's business and their role as a lightning rod for opposing views.

I left the farm with a heavy heart. Once again, as on so many occasions when researching this book, I found myself painfully aware of the inconsistencies in our attitude to the natural world. It is abhorrent to recklessly and illegally kill seals, yet in terms of sheer numbers, the Pullars' activities pale into insignificance compared to the slaughter further out at sea. A thousand marine mammals die every day as bycatch in commercial fishing nets, from seals to whales, but they are considered inevitable collateral damage. As long as there is a high demand for fish, this will continue. All abuse of sea life, large or small scale, is utterly wrong and it is up to us to protest, to demand change and to reflect our concern in what we buy.

The industrialisation of fishing during the twentieth century has done terrible damage to people and to the sea. It is not uncommon for hired fishermen to live in near slave-like conditions on some fishing boats, and such large-scale fishing all over the world is driving fish stocks to the brink of extinction. Immense suffering is imposed on the millions of tonnes of fish that are hauled to the surface and left to suffocate in the holds of trawlers. And despite recently being made illegal, hundreds of thousands of tonnes of edible fish are thrown back into the ocean dead or dying if they are not the target species. As their swim bladders are so damaged by the sudden changes in pressure, most cannot survive the trauma.[16] Large-scale fishing is changing whole ecosystems by shifting the natural balance between predator and prey. The smaller fishing businesses are then left to glean whatever remains in whatever way they can. And what is seen as competition from seals can be a tipping point. Recent reports from the west coast of Ireland show seals with bullet holes washed ashore on beaches, a result of local fishermen taking matters into their own hands.[17] Despite research from Queen's University Belfast, which showed that seals have negligible impact on commercial fish, and that seals may help fishermen by eating the predatory fish that the fishing boats are targeting, the perception that there are too many seals persists.[18]

The stress on ocean systems, from river to sea, ripples outwards. Our attitude to the wildlife that is viewed as competitors for this valuable resource – the seals, dolphins, sharks, whales and even fish-eating birds like cormorants, mergansers and goosanders – is also under strain. The pressure to supply cheap fish to an increasingly expanding market can result in the local conflicts that took place on the rocks below where I sipped tea with the Pullars; where masked men square up to fishermen with high-powered rifles. Around the world, seals are blamed for taking 'our' fish, and are shot or clubbed to death. It is yet another example of our blaming wildlife for problems of our own making. The issue is not that there are too many seals but that fish have been so over-exploited that there are too few left in the sea to meet our demands. And if seals are expanding in number, that can only be a good sign that fish are still present.

And there in the middle of it all, wailing and crying among the waves are the seals themselves, the tangible link between the land and the sea and the focus of so much angst.

The human journey with seals has come a long way from the time we told our selkie tales charged with power and mystery, when our imaginations shifted easily between turf and surf. Back then, says Seamus Heaney in his introduction to *The People of the Sea*, by David Thompson,[19] we had, 'eye-to-eye and breath-to-breath closeness between living things'. Thompson travelled the coasts of Scotland and Ireland in the 1940s and 1950s, documenting this intimacy in the form of Celtic selkie folklore; timeless and poignant stories that still speak to our ancient souls. In that old, inner place it is not unusual to converse with a seal on a wave-washed rock.

One such story tells of an Irish seal shooter, Sean, who surreptitiously killed a fine old male seal because he needed new clothes. Sean was once famed throughout the west coast of Ireland as a great hunter of seals, but was now an old man with his sealing days behind him. In any case, the new landlord forbade anyone from shooting seals on his property. The landlord dearly loved each and every one of the seals that lived along his shore and he claimed he knew them as individuals. Sean, however, was desperate for a new waistcoat. One day he dusted off his old gun, slipped out in the early morning and did the deed. He skinned the seal and hung the pelt to dry out of sight. A week later the landlord appeared at his house.

'Sean, I have lost one of my seals, I think it is one of the bulls, and I'm beginning to think he has come to some harm.'

'I'm not sure, but you might be mistaken, sir, for no man can count the seals in the sea.'

The landlord insisted he knew them as well as his own brothers and sisters, and the one that had gone missing was a particular favourite. 'He was the one that had a mark on him, Sean. He had a white mark like three links of a chain by the side of his neck,' which was exactly the pattern on the skin that hung in Sean's outhouse. Thus was Sean's crime uncovered.

It was an astonishing story to read: I had suddenly and wondrously discovered a golden thread that linked a world now lost in Celtic mists to the modern age of computers, memory cards and pattern recognition programmes.

'When I started trying to recognise individual seals in 2000, I would sit on the cliff top drawing their fur patterns seen through my binoculars. Today, digital cameras and eight-gigabyte memory cards are essential. Each seal has its own unique pattern, a bit like our fingerprints. Me and the team – we have seal spotters all over the coast – take photos, identify and collate 117,000 in one year. You have to be blessed with a good imagination and memory! I can personally identify around thirty per cent of them without having to look them up.'

This seal aficionado is Sue Sayer again, founder of the Cornwall Seal Group, the lady who talked me through the turbulent life of Septimus, and who can reel off the names of seals as if they were old friends.

'Some of my favourite girls are called Lucky Bunting, Man with a Horse and Cart, Carousel, Hearts, Butterfly Shadow Puppet, Rabbit, Ghost, and some of my old boy-friends are Hook, Chairlift, White Back Z, Twenty-three, Kettle, Hearts Bum Bites. We had one female marked but then had to change her name when she got famous. She was originally called Gun-Tongue because she had a pattern like a backwards-facing gun on one side of her neck and on the other what looked like a little mouth with a tongue sticking out. I know, not an attractive name! Then, she hit celebrity-dom, so we had to change it to Tulip Bell, which is much nicer. The mouth-and-tongue pattern look a bit like a tulip and if you look carefully [pointing], you'll see a little bell next to it.' (I couldn't). 'She is famous because we now know, from sharing her photo with our extended group, that she regularly travels between here and the Isle of Man.'

And this is the crux. By following individuals, Sue can track seals over years and build up their life histories. She knows their illnesses, accidents, fights, fecundity and preferences. She knows that all the grey seals of the southwest visit Cornwall's beaches and are part of a wider, mobile Celtic sea population that travels from the Isle of Man to the Scillies, France, the Netherlands, Belgium, Ireland, Cornwall, Dorset and Devon. She knows that social interactions are not as simple as once thought, that individuals are just that, individuals, with complex lives, friendships and mating partners. Her work informs the science being carried out in a number of universities. Through all this information she can lobby for protection for key areas and build up evidence if abuse is suspected.

On the human side, her team of observers transmit their passion for seals to the wider communities where they live, helping to reconnect people with wildlife and the sea through individual stories, helping us all make the connection between the creatures we see before us and the ocean. Sue's work draws out the individual from the crowd and allows each animal to tell us their story about the challenges they face in a rapidly changing world. From all this work we can build a more complete picture – a more subtle picture – of the issues the living world (ourselves included) faces, especially in a time of unpredictable climate.

Sue has two skeletons in the cupboard. If Septimus is big and battered, Augusta is small, less than a metre long, and perfect. She was the first pup they found from the 2017 breeding season, but she had died within days of being born, despite being healthy. This time it was her flesh, not her bones, that told the cautionary tale.

Augusta's fore flippers showed sore, red patches that had worn through the fur and skin to the flesh beneath, indicating she had been moving around the beach for a long time. Her nose was also red-raw from attempting to suckle anything she could find, like knobbly rocks or barnacles; she had been rubbing her snout hard against them in a desperate attempt to elicit milk. Augusta carried the hallmarks of a pup who had lost her mother and had died of starvation. It is not unusual for young pups to die; a mortality rate of 35 per cent or more is recorded,[20] but 2017 was a very bad year. Storm Brian battered Britain in October 2017, right at the start of the grey seal breeding season. Brian combined strong winds with big spring tides and the ensuing chaos can easily separate mothers from pups: storm surges can literally carry small pups away to sea. The result was that 50 per cent of the pups on the beaches of Skomer Island off the coast of Pembrokeshire were washed away, and 75 per cent of pups off the Isle of Man. The number from the Scilly Isles is unknown, but likely to be high. More seals were recovered in Cornwall that year than were born there, their bodies rolling in on raging waves. Augusta could have been born in the Scillies.

Technical language has a way of flattening reality and removing emotion. Storm Brian and many others in the last few decades have produced what is called 'compound flooding,' where big waves, high winds and large tides combine with heavy rainfall to overwhelm coastal areas. It is a deadly mix, and as the climate warms, Europe can expect more such flooding more frequently.[21]

Powerful waves undermine the bases of cliffs, winds erode loose rock faces and water seeping down from saturated ground above loosens cracks. In 2011, dramatic footage of 100,000 tons of rocks falling into the sea in North Cornwall was captured by tourists and posted on YouTube.[22] What their video didn't show was that the debris blocked two pupping caves used by many females and their pups, seals well known to Sue Sayer and her seal-watching group. Bloomer was one of them, a female Sue had known since 2004. She was one of a number of nursing mothers Sue has not seen since, and the last time she saw her, Bloomer was swimming around the cave. From the roll-call of names now missing from the beaches, they have a good idea of which seals were trapped.

Our ability to grieve for one mother, Bloomer, and her new pup, illustrates the way in which we now have individual portals to the magnitude of global issues. Warming oceans, storms, overfishing, shifting fish stocks and the increasing demands on ocean resources all come ashore in the round, smooth bodies of the predatory seals of Britain.

In days of old, seals spoke to us through selkie folklore, stories that reminded us of our interconnectedness with all that exists beyond the shore. But that changed, as it did with so many creatures, with the dawn of the industrial exploitation of both the oceans and the land. Seals transitioned from fellow beings surviving in a complex world to that catch-all term, 'vermin'. The fish of the sea became 'ours' and seals were thieves that had to be eradicated. We had severed our ties with the people of the sea. But what of the future? Does this story continue in an age of mass extinction? We need new, enlightened selkie tales to repair these broken relationships. A wiser, more creative connection to the wild world of the oceans is essential in the decades ahead, as we navigate the huge challenges of the twenty-first century.

It is now more important than ever that we confront the calamity that we have visited upon the oceans. In many ways, seals, our watery alter-egos, hold up a mirror to our nature. What we see there should shock us to the core. From the wracked body of Septimus to the bloodied nose and flippers of Augusta, from all the carcasses with the bullet holes and smashed skulls, from the seals trapped in caves and killed by storms and to those with ever deepening wounds from entanglement with fishing nets, it's a deeply troubling picture. Putting right the wrongs that have been inflicted upon seals must be among the first steps to restoring the health of the oceans. It is vital for the seals themselves, for our human minds and our hearts – and because the world's salt water, the vast oceans and seas, are awash with wonders. We live on a salty blue planet and it sustains all of life on earth.

8

Wild Plans

February 2020, Aigas Field Centre

I don't know if I'm looking backwards into the past or forwards into a wilder future – it is a strange, out-of-time feeling, hovering above history. Through a slot in a panelled wooden fence, I see a wildcat lying on a branch of a Scots pine, about three metres above the ground. It knows I am here, and its eyes stare back into mine. The gaze of wild things has no simpering expectation of food, no cupboard love; I can give it nothing and feel inadequate and soft-bodied in its presence. The cat lounges among the sharp needles and ragged bark of old trees, its razor-sharp senses on alert.

Rain spatters and spits, pushed on by a cold wind, but the wild-cat is unconcerned. Few people can muster the pure sense of self that emanates from a feline predator. We may physically restrain these creatures inside cages, but they carry the tough terrain of the wildwood in every hard muscle of their beautifully furred bodies, and their eyes shine like stars. I know I have no place in their hearts, although they do in mine. But they are not admired by everyone, as Portia Simpson explains in her memoir, *The Gamekeeper*.

> The primary job of gamekeepers in previous eras was to eliminate any potential predators of the game, and in the days when the diets of most carnivores and raptors were little understood, most took it as carte blanche to kill anything and everything. The meticulous records kept by one Scottish sporting estate show that in a three-year period during the nineteenth century, its keepers killed: 246 pine martens, 106 polecats, 67 badgers, 46 otters, 301 stoats and weasels, 198 wildcats, 15 golden eagles, 27 sea eagles, 198 ospreys, 63 goshawks, 98 peregrine falcons, 285 common buzzards, 371 rough-legged buzzards, 83 hen harriers, 275 kites, 462 kestrels, 78 merlin hawks and over 100 owls, together with 1,431 hooded crows and 475 ravens. With carnage on that scale, it is not hard to understand why so many species were pushed up to – or over – the brink of extinction.[1]

Our attitude to predators over the centuries unfolded one dead body at a time, the pile growing ever higher. Meat-eating creatures were competitors, and today, wildcats teeter on the edge of oblivion.

People rarely tolerate these feisty felines in their midst, but often they secretly admire them. Even those who relentlessly hunted them down had a grudging respect for their 'devil's strength'. Writer David Stephen called them 'one of the lords of life', and described their wail through the lonely corries of a Scottish mountain as 'the devil's black laughter: hiss and crackle, scream and sob. The wildcat's skelloch is of the lonely places, of mountain and high forest. Beside him the caterwauling alley cat is a cartoon clown.' [2]

Kenneth Richmond, in his book *Highland Gathering*, recalls an anecdote describing a wildcat:

Pound for pound the wild cat [sic] is probably the most efficient fighting machine in the world, and the most vicious. When faced with a dog it holds on with its teeth and tears away with the claws of all four feet. Dougald (the keeper) had once seen a sheep dog mauled in this way, an ugly sight and one he had never forgotten.[3]

No doubt the cat felt trapped and threatened, but the sheer force of nature of wildcats gave rise to many exaggerated tales. One story even has one leaping for a man's throat, like the killer rabbit in the film *Monty Python and the Holy Grail*.

It is a bitter paradox that we eradicate the creatures we don't want while simultaneously desiring their attributes. As thousands died in gin traps, the image of a wildcat was put on the crest of a federation of Scottish tribes, the Highland Clan Chattan,[4] as a symbol of ferocity. Dating back to the thirteenth century, the federation has the motto 'Touch not the cat without a glove', to warn the world to treat them with respect. It is a sentiment that rang true for Benjamin Jones, then the staff naturalist at Aigas Field Centre near Inverness, run by the naturalist and author Sir John Lister-Kaye.

Each cat is intrinsically fierce to the core. Even if you think you might be able to build up a rapport with one, it definitely isn't the case, they will just turn around and hiss and spit at you. It is so deceiving because at a glance they look similar to domestic cats, but they don't behave like them; they have been described as mini leopards. They spit and jump and they can charge you as well. Some days I've had to leave changing their water because they won't tolerate me being there – and it can be intimidating inside a pen! John was attacked once by a big tom cat called Hamish. It slashed his corduroy trousers at the knee and drew blood and would have ripped right down his leg if he hadn't been wearing wellies. For me, though, they encapsulate everything that we are lacking in the British countryside, a real wildness. They have the characteristics of a lost landscape of big predators, all rolled up into a small mammal. They are a predator that we could quite easily accommodate back into the countryside, and because they stay out of our way, I think we can live alongside them without any altercations. It is really exciting to work with them and towards releasing them into the wild in the future.[5]

Wildcats never colonised Ireland or many of the Scottish islands, but they would once have had a wide distribution on the British mainland. As the ice-age glaciers retreated 7,000–9,000 years ago and woodland spread across the land, wildcats moved here from Europe using land bridges to the continent that had not yet been submerged by the rising sea. As nocturnal hunters, theirs was the world of the moonlit forest and the glide of soft-winged owls. They relied on ambush and stealth rather than speed. A barely discernible rustle, an explosion of force, and their mammalian prey was killed by that characteristic big-cat bite to the neck. Mice, voles, amphibians, weasels, polecats, insects, fish and birds formed their prey base, but their diet consisted mainly of small mammals. Once rabbits arrived with the Romans, they took the top spot on the menu. As late as the 1970s, when wildcats still stalked the rough-hewn corners of Scotland, a PhD study of their scats and stomach contents by L.K. Corbett at the University of Aberdeen showed that rabbits and hares formed the majority of their food:

> Wildcats in Scotland prey extensively on rabbits, with shrews and birds being minor prey items in the diet. Lagomorph remains were found in 92 percent of 546 scat samples. The cats preyed heavily on young rabbits when they were available in the spring and summer.[6]

More recently, European surveys confirm the importance of young rabbits, but later in the year wildcats switch to whatever is abundant in their territory, which at times might include some gamebirds.[7]

When it comes to a question of past population density, Roo Campbell (formerly of Scottish Wildcat Action, now of Saving Wildcats) estimates that approximately one wildcat per three square kilometres would have been possible, depending on habitat. This gives a rough estimate of 60,000 animals that could have once prowled the landscapes of Britain. With a gentler climate and large areas of woodland and grassland, wildcats would have been more common in the south than the north; most wildcats were soft southerners. But no more. By the sixteenth century they had been eradicated from the south, and the last wildcat was shot in northern England in the mid nineteenth century. Only the Scottish cats remained to run the gauntlet of hill farmers and gaming estates, where relentless persecution drove them to ever more remote refuges. The Highland forests and hidden valleys of northern Scotland are the only places today where a handful still exist in the wild.

As wildcat numbers dwindled, domestic cats were increasing in the Highlands. Prior to the nineteenth century, pet cats were rare in tough, northern reaches, but new railway connections brought the fashions and accompaniments of the south to even the most remote places, where local communities were expanding to accommodate the growing sport of shooting both gamebirds and deer. With so few of its own left, the beleaguered wildcat turned to its domestic cousins to breed. British wildcats originated from European animals but domestic cats stem from the Near East and North Africa; they are related but not the same. This criss-crossing of separate genetic strands created a 'hybrid swarm', where the original hybrid generations survived and interbred again with pure wildcats. The famed Highland Tiger began its crossfade into a creature of complex mixed genes.

In 2019, after an intensive study of the DNA of 295 wildcats from both museum specimens and free-living wildcats from Europe, the true Scottish wildcat was declared functionally extinct. It is thought that as few as thirty animals are left in remote parts of the north of Scotland, and most (likely all) are hybridised to some extent.[8] There is no viable Scottish wildcat population left. This stark reality means that if we want true wildcats back in our lives then only years of selective breeding will hone them into what is considered an acceptable genetic shape.

The cat in front of me in a pen in Aigas is part of this herculean effort to bring back the wildcat and to maintain the integrity of ancient genes. The air at Aigas is infused with a determination that wildlife mustn't lose its authenticity, its defining individuality, in an age of mass homogenisation and globalisation. Uniqueness matters. The diversity of life matters. The wildcat is a connecting rod to the ancient past, to a time when Britain held a rich assemblage of native wildlife. Lose it and we lose more than simply another species of Felidae, we slice away a part of our biological heritage.

There are thirty breeding centres holding around a hundred wildcats with the desirable combination of physical appearance and genes. All have been carefully selected from private collections or were taken directly from the wild in Scotland and Europe, and they form a bedrock for a future reintroduction programme. If all goes to plan, the first release site will be in the Cairngorms, perhaps as early as 2025. Hopes that this target can be met are rising; the number of 'pure' captive wildcats is slowly increasing as the genetic signature of hybridisation with domestic cats is steadily eradicated.

'Just by looking at a wildcat we can start to score them,' says Charlotte Robertson, a young field-assistant at Aigas. We huddle together against the squally rain, perched on a wooden bench looking at the captive. 'Domestic cats are smaller and they have a thinner, more tapered tail. But a wildcat is chunky with longer legs and its tail is really fat at the end and has a black tip, like it's been dipped in paint. It has around three or four strong black rings around it. The black line down the spine mustn't go down the tail. The coat is bit like a domestic tabby, but on a wildcat the stripes that run from the spine down the sides are thick and bold and there is no spotting. They can't have white on their feet, but it is okay to have some white on the muzzle. There are a number of features that a wildcat has to have, or not have, to be considered pure. This male scores well, but he's not quite a hundred per cent.'

I look carefully, trying to tick off the range of characteristics, and he certainly looks like the real thing, especially framed by gnarled pines and the vast, grey Scottish sky. I begin to feel stirring the power of rewilding; that disparate, ill-defined movement to bring wildlife back to Britain. It is still half-glimpsed out of the corner of the eye, but it is a building presence. Here and there pockets of nature are burgeoning as wildlife is given priority over profit, a result of more people yearning to reconnect with the natural world. There are some prominent public examples, like the Knepp Castle Estate in Sussex. This once intensive cereal and dairy farm now brims with woodland and wildlife. After generations of damaging agriculture, the down-trodden soils are left to gather their resources and release the wildness that lies within. Dormant seeds are sprouting, new bird and insect life is finding its way to the trees and flowers, and mammals of all sizes are thriving. Old breeds of pigs, cattle and horses have been brought in to keep parts of the land free of tree cover, replicating as much as possible a post-glacial Britain of wildwood and open pasture maintained by large herbivores and wild boar. It is still mildly managed, it is not a truly wild landscape, but it is giving nature the breathing space for free expression, within the constraints of the modern world.

To varying degrees, in different guises and at different scales this movement to share the land with nature is being repeated around the UK. Maybe, sometime soon, its many fruits will unleash their energy onto the wider landscape and into our psyche to produce transformational change. It is hoped that wildcats will form part of a scintillating, sinewed future, but for now the edges of the wooden pen in front of me define the limits of the world for the Scottish wildcat.

The dozen wildcats at Aigas are breeding stock and not destined for freedom. It will be their future descendants and yet-to-be-born cats from elsewhere that will – hopefully – form a viable population of feline predators in Britain. Whether or not this happens will not only depend on generating a large number of quality cats

– which could be considered the easy bit – but also on getting conditions right on the ground.

Since wildcats last prowled through post-glacial Britain, the land has become urbanised, farmed and managed. Wildcats will have to fit into already existing agendas. In addition, their own natural predators and competitors, such as lynx, wolves and eagles, have either been extirpated or reduced to small numbers in restricted places. But new threats have taken their place, ones which are alien to their innate instincts – collisions with cars, disease, high-technology-aided persecution, and perhaps most devastatingly, hybridisation. This primeval cat will walk through a fundamentally different world of dangers with similar yet different cats around every corner.

Britain swarms with domestic cats. A staggering eleven million pet cats and one and a half million feral cats now provide a reservoir of undesirable genes, as far as the wildcat is concerned. A quarter of British adults own at least one cat;[9] they are the nation's most numerous pet, and they evoke a ferocious loyalty and love in their owners. Even Leonardo da Vinci called them living masterpieces. The wildcat *Felis silvestris* is an ancient relic in an ocean of the domestic *Felis catus*. If wildcats are to succeed then domestic cats will have to be managed, and that puts the project on a collision course with our dearly held concept of individual freedoms. In the areas designated for the release of wildcats the local feral and stray cat population would have to be neutered or culled, and local cat owners asked to microchip and neuter their animals, and preferably to observe a night-time curfew by locking them indoors. In Scotland, Saving Wildcats has a programme of sterilising at least three-quarters of feral cats in areas where wildcats still exist to try to reduce further hybridisation, the minimum necessary to be effective. Nevertheless, you would be forgiven for thinking that a large-scale reintroduction programme would be nigh impossible because of the sheer number of domestic cats in the system. Not necessarily, believes Roo Campbell, but it won't be easy:

> As a project we use sterilisation to reduce the risk of domestic and obviously hybridised cats interbreeding with our remaining 'wildcats' (noting that probably all wild-living cats remaining in Scotland have some history of hybridisation). Both lethal and non-lethal methods take a huge amount of resources and so, ultimately, we need to stop recruitment into the feral population by changing the behaviour of cat owners so that they act responsibly by ensuring their pets are neutered, vaccinated and microchipped. The killing of feral cats by a publicly funded project would cause concern among some sections of society and impact support for our work. Without that public support, removing the risk of further hybridisation will be difficult to achieve.[10]

If, and it is a big if, enough people do agree to the return of the wildcat, then evidence from Europe points to hybridisation not being as big a problem once the wildcats become established and their numbers build up. With enough of their own species, wildcats preferentially breed with their own species, rather than domestic or hybrid cats. In Europe, where wildcats still persist in the wild in decent numbers, hybridisation rates are less than 10 per cent compared with around 100 per cent in Britain. It seems that only when the population falls below a threshold, as it has in Scotland, do wildcats interbreed. With a strong and healthy population, wildcats can intimidate domestic cats, they can even kill them in a violent struggle over ownership and access to territory and prey. As Roo Campbell told me, 'I used to be able to tell when a particular male hybrid wildcat was in one area of where I was studying them in Scotland because a local householder would tell me her neutered male pet was peeing on her bed instead of outside.'

At present, the needs of this ancient feline and the realities of modern Britain are at odds. Our twenty-first-century lifestyles have organised the world around our needs, but the wildcat is challenging us to move aside and make room. The wildcat reintroduction project is laying bare the realities of bringing back predators close to home. Ordinary citizens will be asked to make changes on behalf of a wild creature they have forgotten existed. This is new territory. The return of a once extinct butterfly, for example, asks very little of us; even the wilding of 1,500 hectares of Knepp has not demanded behavioural change in society. The wildcat, however, stalks around the very core of who we think we are and our belief that we are the centre of the world. It pads quietly to the heart of the matter, sits down and pierces our sense of self with its clear, sharp eyes. It asks a simple question – will we do what it takes to allow it to return?

For wildcats to roam free again we must actively want to see their starlit fur weaving along a hedgerow, fierce eyes burning, and their 'cackle, scream and sob' piercing the night, even if there is a price to pay for us. At present, the majority of Britain is settled into the comfort of convenient urbanisation and removed from the intensity of the wild. There are no scratches on the bark of local trees, no wildcat graffiti stating its presence: 'I am here, this is me and this is home.'

No one remembers wildcats, so no one expects them to live with us. Many will be amazed Britain had its own mini-tiger, and it will come as a shock to our tame existence. Only a concerted programme of inspiring public education will make wildcat re-introduction acceptable; many simply won't see the point of prioritising one cat (wildcat) over another (domestic). Even if this is possible to achieve in the Highlands of Scotland, will it be welcomed in the populated, crowded and leafy suburbs of the south? It may take some persuasion. Considering that the majority of cat owners don't even put bells on their pets to protect wild birds, accepting stricter constraints may well be a bridge too far.

Into the fray steps the independent and feisty Scottish-exile-in-Devon farmer and conservationist, Derek Gow. Well known for his direct action, Derek believes established conservation is 'small-scale, incredibly cautious and very slow,' and doesn't think there is time for much deliberation. He has built six pens on his farm that already house wildcat kittens, the seed stock for his own captive breeding programme for the south of England. If all goes well, and in collaboration with others, he will breed and acclimatise 150 kittens a year. I visited him on an autumn day and we drank tea as a downpour battered the roof of his outhouse office. It had rained for weeks and the road to his farm, the farm tracks and the fields were sodden. His spirit, though, was not.

'The best release sites today are likely to be the last sites wildcats were found while they were still being heavily persecuted. To give them the best chance they will need access to food, in the form of small mammals, and interconnected cover in the form of edging, scrub and woodland margins. Wildcats, being solitary, have a different social structure from feral cats, which tend to live in colonies. So, if they are not persecuted, they do not necessarily need a large area to survive but a patchwork of fields, scrub and woodland. But they must be linked. We mostly have that in the south. There is work to do to connect habitats but let's get on and get these cats back where they belong. There is a crisis in biodiversity which requires action, not meetings and talk.'

The kittens are kept away from people and allowed to hunt live prey to keep them 'mentally alert'. He is just at the start of his project and it will take many years and cooperation with other enthusiasts to get enough cats for a reintroduction programme into areas like the Weald and the more remote parts of Devon, but his vision is clear and dynamic. 'We just have to get going – we have to do something; Britain is so nature-depleted. In 2020, when Knepp had its first breeding white storks, the first in Britain for six hundred years, thousands of people commented on how much hope it gave them for the future. That is what we have to do, fill this country with hope by bringing back the incredible array of wildlife we used to have. We can do it.'

George Monbiot, author and commentator, agrees it has to be done for the sake of the ecological health of Britain, but also because we have a moral duty to live by the standards we demand from others.

> We expect people in much poorer countries than ours to live alongside tigers, lions, elephants, hippos, crocodiles, and other large and dangerous animals. We get upset when people kill or exclude these animals, and campaign for it to stop. So, are we really to decide that we can't tolerate wildcats in our own nation? If so, what does this say about our proclaimed love of wildlife? People in other nations could reasonably accuse us of double standards.[11]

Derek Gow believes there is general support for his bold, bright dream, but also acknowledges some concern among sheep farmers who worry for their lambs, conservationists who are apprehensive about woodland ground-nesting birds, and gamekeepers, whose job it is to protect pheasants on shooting estates. In time, he feels fears can be allayed and that public support will grow. How exactly a crowded south of England will cope with a miniature tiger is yet to be tested, but Derek explains his plan to me:

'We have to create a rolling programme of groups of cats going ahead of other groups, in effect saturating areas so that dispersing cats don't breed with domestic ones. England is a great place to release them, it has a richer warmer environment than Scotland by far; this is possible. Hybridisation is the biggest problem they face, and it will happen sometimes, you can't completely control that, and if that means every so often one has a ginger spot on its fore-head or a white paw, does that really matter? If it looks like a wildcat and behaves like a wildcat, then for me it is a wildcat.

'A territorial felid living at low density right across the landscape will have widespread effects and help balance out our lack of top predators. They will have an effect on the population of grey squir-rels, for example, and that is welcome.

'I'm not saying it will be easy, but we have got to do something. My worry though, is that our national thinking about predators is not where we need it to be. That is where we have most work to do – to get ourselves up to speed on accepting wildness back into Britain. The Americans are far ahead of us on this one.'

Derek is the personification of energy and commitment, and has the personality to push through, but getting Britain predator-ready can only be achieved if the will permeates through every layer, from the general public to ground-level conservation to top-level politics and economics. Unlike America, there are no vast national parks for predators to disappear into; wildcats, maybe even lynx and wolves, all predators on the reintroduction list in the UK, will have to live with us. And that can be dangerous.

In the 1980s, 129 wildcats were reintroduced to three German forests,[12] and although some of the cats settled well and began reproducing, a large percentage were killed by cars in the first few weeks and less than 30 per cent survived. They are still shot and trapped by farmers and hunters as well. It is legal to kill feral cats, and many are shot at night using night vision or infra-red weapons. Is it really possible to tell if the cat is a true wildcat or a feral when glimpsed through a grainy, indistinct viewfinder? There is no guarantee the world will be kind to wildcats. Roo Campbell believes all the issues have to be overcome because time is running out: 'We are almost certainly the last generation who has a realistic chance of saving this iconic species from extinction.'[13]

*

If wildcats are presenting us with problems, then a cat that is twice the size poses more. The lynx persisted in the deepest woodlands throughout Britain until 1,300 years ago when it finally succumbed to widespread deforestation and hunting. Lynx are on the discreet and enigmatic end of secretive – they can retreat into the mottled canvas of a forest and vanish, which staved off their extinction for a long time, but eventually they joined the list of post ice-age victims. Powerful, solitary, angular, square-headed, spike-eared and beautiful, their pelt was highly desirable for use in clothing to portray wealth and status. Titian, the grand master of sixteenth-century Venetian portraiture, draped the spotted black, brown and cream fur over the shoulders of important Italians to convey their place in society.

Small deer like roe are their favourite prey, but they will kill a wide range of creatures such as rabbit, fox, badger, pine marten, wildcat, squirrel, grouse and red deer. They will, on occasion, take domestic pets and sheep if they wander close to the woodland edge. There are no reports of lynx attacking people, and indeed they are incredibly difficult to see. Given their secretive habits and specific prey, dare we welcome them back as a safe addition to our depleted suite of predators? Not without a lot of education. When Lillith, an eighteen-month-old escapee from a zoo in Wales, peeked around the fence of a caravan park in 2017, she was immediately shot dead as a danger to life and limb.

Plans to reintroduce them (maybe within ten years) to the larger forests of Northumberland and the growing Caledonian forests of Scotland are constantly raised and they provide a tantalising glimpse of back to the future. Lynx enthusiasts believe they must take their rightful place among an array of reintroduced and recovering predators in Britain, all of which are required to maintain a balanced ecosystem. As quiet regulators of woodlands they would certainly be welcomed by foresters battling the constant destruction of young trees by deer, but sheep farmers see yet another threat and the urbanised public are unsure about a cat the size of an Alsatian stalking the municipal wood where dogs are walked and children play. Our deeply ingrained fear of feline predators makes them a hard sell to the wary.

There are few characterisations of lynx in popular folklore, tales or literary works – they have mostly evaded our make-believe as carefully as they did the early hunters. This is both positive and negative. Positive in that they are not weighed down by our prejudice, but negative in that they are utterly unfamiliar and have no connection to our collective imagination. The likeness of a wildcat to a domestic cat helps us get a handle on their likely presence in the countryside, but a lynx is truly a mystery. Even in Europe, where remnant populations and animals from reintroduction projects still hang on in pockets in several countries, there is precious little folklore or stories to go on.

Lynx appear in medieval bestiaries as strange creatures with the body of a panther and the head of a dog. Stranger still were their behaviours, as they were thought to urinate in a hole in the ground, which then solidified into a gem called Lyngurium, another name for amber. Males were supposed to produce better-quality stones than females, and it was believed that if swallowed with wine these stones would cure kidney stones and jaundice – and could even change a person's sex.[14] They were believed to possess supernatural eyesight, and lynx became creatures that could see through and beyond the ordinary, an ability that struck a chord with seventeenth-century Italian men of science. The Accademia dei Lincei, the 'Academy of Lynx-eyed', of which Galileo was a member, was established in 1603. These far-sighted men identified themselves as discerners of truth among the falsehoods of the world, 'with lynx-like eyes, examining those things which manifest themselves, so that having observed them, he may zealously use them'.

Lynx also captured the heart of a German star-gazer, Johannes Helvelius, in 1687, who named a faint line of stars in the northern hemisphere after them. Barely perceptible, these teasing pin-pricks of light evoked (for Johannes) a lynx rearing on its hind legs, claws extended, scratching at the sky and claiming its territory in the universe. These enigmatic cats were admired as mystical keepers of truth on earth and in the heavens, yet they were still relentlessly persecuted.

In Britain there is virtually nothing to anchor the lynx to our lives; we have a blank canvas upon which to write a new story of relationship. This cultural chain of silence was broken in 1981 by Ted Hughes in his disturbing poem, 'A Lynx'. In just two short verses Hughes paints a word picture of the fragility of the ties that bind us all, the very earth we live on. A sleeping lynx becomes a symbol of our interconnectedness and wholeness. It depicts a cat at peace on the planet, resting safely. If we disturb it, says Hughes, all that is known and supportive of life on earth disintegrates.

Ominous clouds will gather and the world will shift beneath our feet.

> Soundless the forest
> Will fold away all its trees
> And hazy the mountains
> Fade among their stones.[15]

We did destroy its peace, utterly and completely. As its life-blood soaked into forest soils, we erased the lynx from our memory banks and it was no more. The consequences of the destruction of this spirit of the wild and its forest home have been playing out ever since, culminating in the denuded factory floor that constitutes a large proportion of the landscapes of the UK. But whether reintroduced lynx will reinhabit a much different world from the one they had known previously, and whether they will be left to sleep peacefully, is not yet known. In European populations, up to 97 per cent of deaths are related to human activity where lynx is blamed for eating sheep and for depleting the deer stocks that hunters require for themselves. Britain has a lot of deer (near two million of all species), so there are enough to share, but space for forest cats is limited. Depending on the density of prey, each one requires a home range of around 50 to 100 square kilometres. Even in the much greater wilderness areas of the European continent, road collisions are a major threat to their survival, alongside persecution by farmers and hunters.

Studies estimate that Scotland and adjacent areas of northern England could, with the support of locals, host a sustainable population in excess of 250 animals,[16] but it is simply not known how lynx will impact on wildlife or livestock. Comparisons with Europe may be helpful, but are not necessarily translatable to Britain. Lynx

rarely break the cover of trees, so predation of sheep in open countryside is unlikely, but it cannot be ruled out. On the other hand,
it is known that their presence will affect smaller predators such as
foxes, which they will kill (as discussed in Chapter 2). One study
in Sweden showed that lynx predated half of their radio-tagged
foxes[17] (although not all studies have found the same), so their
presence could reduce fox numbers, which will certainly be
welcomed by farmers. As fox numbers fall, then mountain hares,
black grouse, curlew, lapwing and capercaillie may recover. The
rules of the reintroduction game are complex; there will be winners
and losers in a cat's-cradle tug-of-war. Throw in the vagaries of
humanity's varying attitudes to a challenging suite of predators,
and the rules become unfathomable.

Is our heart wild enough to beat alongside that of a lynx? As we
struggle to place them in a modern setting, the eternal, celestial
lynx, barely twinkling in the heavens, is no doubt peering at us
with its far-seeing eyes and watching our machinations with interest, waiting for the next chapter.

*

But if wild cat predators push at the boundaries of our tolerance,
wolves rip them up entirely. The yoik is a traditional form of song
of the Sami reindeer herders of northern Scandinavia. It is performed
by a single voice, often accompanied by a single drum, and is haunting, repetitive, shamanic. A yoik is the sound of yearning to capture
and become one with the essence of wildlife and landscape.
It weaves meaning beyond words and is more akin to musical
method-acting than pure song. A well-known Sami yoik is modelled
on howling wolves chasing down a reindeer, a vocal re-enactment
of the chase and the kill. Rising in drama and changing in form as
the reindeer is brought down, the music is pushed into a particular

tritone, a disturbing, dissonant, chilling series of notes that evokes an inner restlessness that is never resolved in the listener; the music finds no place to settle and has no peace. This Diabolus in Musica or Devil's Tritone, as it was later called by the Christian Church, became the wail of despair of the devil in the face of the goodness of God. Leonard Bernstein uses it multiple times in the music of *West Side Story*, the story of human packs battling for territory in New York City. Wolf howl, devil wail, we tied the wolf to evil through music and story. The electrifying howl of a wolf pack becomes more than a claim on territory. It is a message.

In traditional tales the wolf is always hungry, ravaged and cunning. Few depictions see it as anything other than a terrifying embodiment of forces we cannot control. In our more enlightened age, wolf conservationists have done wonders in shifting these ancient perceptions, but the chill remains. No creature has inhabited our imagination as completely as a wolf. There are far more barriers to bringing them back than worries about sheep, space and compensation schemes.

Wolves are pack-living, pack-hunting predators that live in a variety of landscapes from woodland to open moor. They famously chase their prey to exhaustion before tearing it apart with terrifying savagery. Yet we recognise ourselves in their loyalty to their group and their care of the young and injured. The more we find out about their ecological role in balancing ecosytems, the more their return seems highly desirable. Wolves do not live in a static landscape but one that shifts with the migrations of prey through the seasons. They inject dynamism into a natural system by spreading a 'landscape of fear' and keeping large herbivores constantly on the move. This reduces overgrazing to allow more natural successions of vegetation, with all the benefits that can bring for wildlife. Wolves stir and stimulate; they change the behaviour of smaller predators and reorder the natural hierarchy. There is nothing half-hidden or half-hearted about wolves. They are powerful agents of change.

But the question of how many people want them as neighbours is still very much up for debate. Studies on attitudes to living with predators, such as the Tooth and Claw project,[18] expose our inconsistencies, political affiliation and prejudices. As Marc Baldwin writes in his Wildlife Online blog: 'In general, it seems that the public have a somewhat fickle opinion of wildlife. Most people who completed the survey, for example, agreed that we had a responsibility to reintroduce wolves to the Scottish Highlands; but most of those in favour lived in the south of England and wouldn't be directly affected.'[19]

Very little of our attitude to predators is based purely on science. For now, there are no plans beyond a couple of packs living in a fenced-off area of a large, privately owned estate. The question is, can public consensus allow us to go beyond this to a bigger vision?

Of the three possible carnivores to be brought back to Britain, the wolf is the one that seems most unlikely in the short term. Far more than for wildcats and lynx, we have forgotten the etiquette of living with wolves. Any reintroduction would require landscape-scale agreement, not only from farmers and residents of Scotland, but also from the tourist industry. Attacks on people are rare and almost always associated with wolves that have rabies, feel threatened or are disorientated in urban environments. But a deep-seated, innate fear of packs of carnivores is still part of us, despite the evidence that they pose a minimal threat. Uncontrolled, unwieldy, untameable wolves tear apart logical argument. In his book *Feral*, George Monbiot, using the wolves in America as an example, writes:

Arrange these threats in ascending order of deadliness: wolves, vending machines, cows, domestic dogs and toothpicks. I will save you the trouble: they have been ordered already. The number of deaths known to have been caused by wolves in North America in the twenty-first century is one: if averaged out, that would be 0.08 per year. The average number of people killed in the US by vending machines is 2.2 (people sometimes rock them to try to extract their drinks, with predictable results). Cows kill some twenty people in the US, dogs thirty-one. Over the past century, swallowing toothpicks caused the deaths of around 170 Americans a year. Though there are sixty thousand wolves in North America, the risk of being killed by one is almost non-existent.[20]

Even so, wolves are a far harder sell than solitary, secretive cats.

There is, though, an aspect of reinhabiting our landscapes with carnivores as charismatic and potent as wolves that is rarely discussed or acknowledged. It is the emotional and psychological fallout from dealing with their success. If all hurdles are overcome and wolves once again roam free, they will do more than reinhabit landscapes, they will also recolonise our minds. Their capacity to change our world will go well beyond their ability to control the numbers of deer. The register and the tempo of landscapes will fundamentally alter. A place will become more watchful, more alive. The land will pulsate with a force – a driving life-force. But it won't stop there. Their presence will also transform our perceptions and our imaginings. We will experience emotions that only our long-gone ancestors felt. Both we and the land will change.

We should never underestimate the effect of bringing wolves back to Britain. Aldo Leopold wrote that a land with wolves was fundamentally different to one without them:

… it is felt in all wolf country, and distinguishes that country from all other land. It tingles in the spine of all who hear wolves by night, or who scan their tracks by day. Even without sight or sound of wolf, it is implicit in a hundred small events: the midnight whinny of a pack horse, the rattle of rolling rocks, the bound of a fleeing deer, the way shadows lie under the spruces.[21]

Leopold's conversion from ruthless wolf-hunter to one of the greatest modern conservationists began with his shooting a female wolf and her cubs (described in Chapter 1). His epiphany is recounted in his ground-breaking and deeply moving essay *Thinking like a Mountain*, published in 1949. After shooting down a mother returning to her cubs, he knelt beside the dying female and saw 'a fierce green fire, dying in her eyes'. He realised that some integral, powerful, balancing force had gone from the land.

It is easy to feel passionate about the return of large, charismatic creatures, but to do so successfully we have to plan well. If wolves (or wildcats or lynx) were to thrive and spread to areas where they are not welcome, then we have to have an exit strategy, which may mean culling or removing them from areas where problems arise. Are we prepared to manage them once they begin to claim their lands? There is bitter controversy over the shooting of foxes and badgers; will we allow marksmen to cull wolves when the problems mount? And if we do – what effect will that have on us as individuals and as a society?

In Europe, a quota system is set by a hard-fought agreement between conservationists, hunters and farmers, and any increase above this number is dealt with by government-commissioned culls. A cross-border population of 340 animals live between

Norway and Sweden. The Swedish population is founded on a single pair of wolves that made it there in the 1980s, with only around five more arriving from Finland since 1991. There are very few, if any, fresh genes entering the Scandinavian populations and they are highly inbred. Any wolves trying to migrate from Russia can be legally shot by Sami reindeer herders, but others will hunt them too, and policing is virtually impossible. Hunters dislike them as they compete for deer, but also because they will kill hunting dogs that are often sent ahead into forests to flush out quarry. Even in countries the size of Norway and Sweden, with large forests and low human populations, only a few wolves are tolerated. In the much smaller landmass of Britain, the problems intensify.

Some estimates put the number of wolf packs that could – in theory – live in Scotland at around fifteen, but they will certainly wander and disperse away from the areas where we put them, and they will, if not fenced in, reach towns and cities. If wolf fences are to be erected around parts of Scotland, how will that affect tourism and the right to roam? Will they become a reason to keep people out of estates and restrict our access to the magnificent landscapes of Scotland? There are many problems to solve which go far beyond the basic ecological impact of wolves on sheep and deer. These are questions that must be addressed if wolf reintroduction is to have the support of the public.

On a small island, it is hard to see how we can avoid a European-style quota system, and that will bring to the fore unforeseen issues, both practical and psychological. It has been so long since we have lived with large predators, we are wholly unprepared for the impact they will have on our psyche. Such an exciting, enlivening prospect could transform Britain, but if we get the reintroduction wrong, it will set back the vision for generations.

In 2013, I happened to be in Sweden tracking wolves for a BBC programme when a cull was announced. Numbers had risen beyond the agreed level, and hunters had lobbied for action to be taken immediately, despite fierce opposition from wildlife groups. One of the wolf packs to be targeted for reduction was the pack I was looking for. It was to lose one adult and one juvenile. When we heard the news that confirmed the decision to go ahead with the cull the next day, I was unprepared for the effect it would have on me personally. I was overcome with a tsunami of feelings that ranged from anger to despair. But I was also deeply aware that in Britain we will not, as yet, tolerate even one wild-living pack. Listening to that news, I realised that if wolves ever do make it to Britain, we will have to face the reality of their management, and it is deeply shocking. I can only say that the effect on me was profound.

That evening, after a day in the forest following wolf prints through silent tracts of snowy pines and feeling the animals' invisible presence, I sat in my hotel room in central Sweden as the cold set in and flakes of snow wafted in the street lights by the window, and I wrote a letter to the doomed wolf.

Dear Wolf,

Today I followed you through the forest; it wasn't hard because your tracks were straight down the middle of a road that cut through the pine trees like a scar. You must have passed by early because your prints were clear and sharp; I could see the shape of each pad, each claw pressed into the snow. I put my hand over the top and allowed myself to imagine it was still warm. It stopped snowing at dawn so you must have come by after that. It was thrilling to think you could be so close. I looked and listened hard, but apart from your prints there was no trace.

You knew where you were going, that is for sure. There was no scampering or exploring like my pet dog would do, running here and there, sniffing this and that; your tracks never wavered from the line of the road. You are a wolf and you need to conserve energy; life isn't frivolous. It seems there was nothing for you in this part of the forest, you were just passing through; your sights were set on somewhere distant.

I tried to imagine you, staring ahead, loping, head low, your footfall soft, your breath materialising in the freezing air. From the single line of tracks, I thought there was only one of you, but the tracker told me there were four in your pack; you follow each other's footsteps, like mountaineers do while climbing through snow. It's easier to use the imprint of the one in front, it saves that precious energy, and as you are the strongest, you are the leader. What could you smell? What could you hear? Where were you going with such assuredness? I wish I'd seen you with your pups and partner in tow; a line of wolves padding down an icy forest road. I wonder if the birds go quiet as you pass by? Do you carry a world of silence with you when you travel?

Did you howl in the cold morning light when your sound would have travelled far through the air? Did that disturbing song of the soul ever reach human ears, making them stop and turn? As the biggest wolf, your howl must be deep and throaty and resonate in the depths of the listener, like a Buddhist horn in a monastery. We once lived alongside each other, wolf, your ancestors and mine, and that sound became part of us, instilling dread and thrill in equal measure; we wove it into our tales and imaginings. You are the big, bad wolf, the lone wolf, the wolf in sheep's clothing and it is wise to keep the wolf from the door. We assign you the human characteristic of cunning calculation; I think you would be amazed to know how much we fear you.

Did you hunt today? Did a young moose die violently, taken by surprise by your force and ferocity? Did it collapse in blood and screams while your family moved in? But you are efficient and swift, nothing much is left of flesh and bone, cartilage and sinew. We could learn a lot from you about how to eat to live, not wasting good energy, not wasting a life. The carcass is food for other forest dwellers, the chatty coal tits and the dark ravens, they are waiting nearby to feast from the remnants of your banquet. How long ago was your last meal? Was it good to taste the warm meat and did you feel replenished? I hope you are satisfied; I don't want you to be hungry tonight. Not tonight.

Where are you resting? The Swedish night is so long and cold, but you have each other and that must help. Thick fur against thick fur, warmth seeping through as the temperature plummets. Curl up together, maybe under a rock, fur and snow melding, and the rise and fall of your bodies brings life to a world of ice. The light fades quickly here, it retreats in haste, as though afraid of the cold that sets in so deeply. We too disappear into our buildings; we cannot take these freezing temperatures and we fear the darkness. The blackness obliterates what we know, the once solid trees become ghostly and insubstantial and that is unsettling for creatures of the day. And so, the forest is yours now, you can settle secure, your only known enemy is behind doors, concerned with other things like eating, drinking – finalising plans.

I need to explain some things to you wolf, even though I know you won't understand; this is for my comfort, not yours. You see, we are both similar and different, you and I. The things we share in common are noble. Your kind and mine both care for our own with a passion and nothing is allowed to threaten our young. Our *family bonds are strong within us. You too take care of your injured and bring them food, you won't abandon them; although I never heard you described as compassionate. Caring and wolf don't sit together in our perception of you. I wonder why not. We are both driven by instinct, although we don't like to admit it.*

You are like us in other ways too; you will take the easy way if you can. Why bring down a moose if there is a sheep? Why risk injury from a powerful animal twice your size? Far safer to snatch a benign, domesticated animal. It's an easy meal, a take-away, convenience food. Who can blame you for that? We can, and we do.

But this is where we are so different from you, wolf. You take the unexpected as it comes, you are a chancer. We can't do that; it isn't in us to live for the moment. We plan, manage, devise and organise. We have an overview, a strategy, a policy – a directive, even – and these things give us control. That is how we are seven billion: how many are you?

We also have routines, cultures, traditions and histories. We do things in a certain way and we hold on to our habits as you hold on to the throat of a moose. It is our right, you see, to do things as we have always done them, our rights are assigned by us for us. You don't have rights, especially if you impinge on ours. Sorry.

I can see the moon out of the window, wolf, and I know, somewhere not too far away, you can see it too. I am thinking of you, you are unaware of me. I feel a sadness that is too deep for tears; you … well, I'm not sure what you feel. Contented and peaceful I hope, so gather in that peace and absorb it. Maybe an owl will swoop quietly overhead. In a very few hours it will be different. Tonight, though, dream that there will be many tomorrows. And if by any chance we appear in your thoughts, two-legged ghosts that strut across the forest, rise from your gathering of warmth and togetherness, throw your head back and howl.

There is a weak light now, barely a reality. It seems reluctant to bring the day. What was that? The crack of a twig? An unfamiliar smell in the air? You are alert, watching for signs. Don't wait, wolf, don't let your natural curiosity make you stay a second longer. Start running, all of you.

I hope you pick up speed and feel the forest fly by. I hope you experience that sense of swiftness that only those who are taut and fit can know. Savour the snow under your feet. I want you to fall suddenly, in mid-flight. I want you to be far away from the gun when you crash to the ground so that there is time to feel the cold snow against your muzzle. I want your last picture to be trees framed against a wintry sky, not boots and weapons. See the pines as they tower over you, barely moving in the still air; watch them as your eyes go dim.

Don't think about the panic of your pack; there is nothing you can do for them now. Maybe they will regroup, disorientated and full of fear, or maybe they will disperse for good and try to fend for themselves. That is not for you to know. Just take in the last breaths of clear, cold air and let life fade quickly. Go, please, before they arrive with their mobile phones, their ropes and their data logs. Don't be here when they throw you onto the back of a truck; be long gone, wolf, long gone.

In my mind I am riding with you in the back of that truck and can hear the telephone calls confirming your death. You are no longer a wolf, you have transformed into a number. You are a figure in a column that now has a tick beside it. Job done. You are not alone, wolf, not that it's any comfort. Others await your fate, more lights are fading in other parts of the forest. This is a well-run procedure, wolf, carried out with accuracy.

I don't want to stroke your fur or touch you at all. You are a wild animal and this lump of cooling flesh deserves that dignity. Why now should you be stroked? You have never needed any human, and so my spirit will just sit by you, keeping my arms wrapped around my knees and we will travel this last bit together. Fellow passengers on a cruel planet. The birds may be singing now but there can be no bright melody today as the last vestiges of warmth sink into metal.

Before you are taken away to a laboratory I have to keep explaining, keep trying to help you understand. You see, there is a quota, a set number to be adhered to. That's what we have worked out, taking into account what you are and how you do things. It's a figure that has been carefully calculated. This isn't random, honestly it isn't. It is hard to manage you and your kind; you are too wild, too efficient at killing, and you come into our lives unbidden. We can't tolerate that. There are politicians to appease, lobbyists to listen to, traditions to consider, and today your name appeared on a list. We want to live with you, we really do, but in a controlled way. Please, wolf, don't think we don't care.

As you are dragged out of the back of the truck, red streaking the metal floor, I can't say I know your family will be fine. I'm sorry but I can't guarantee that. But I can say thank you, from the bottom of my heart. For just a few hours I felt tantalisingly close to the wildness of this world, the beating, vibrant heart of this small living planet that lights up the lifeless universe with sound and song and movement. I felt that heartbeat of life through the snow, a beat that has graced this earth for countless generations before anyone devised a management plan. Thank you for giving me a glimpse of that mystery: it sits deep within every soul. Traditionally we say 'rest in peace'. I won't say that today, I'll just sit here and watch you disappear and turn over

the sadness in my heart and try to find the silver lining; the
sensible, ecological reasoning. But no matter how I try to frame it,
you are gone.

Hope in a Time of Extinction

It is an enchanting story. In 1823, an acclaimed young painter fell in love with a duchess twenty years his senior, and they began an adulterous affair. Their hideaway from many judgemental eyes was a small, specially built cottage in a secluded glen in the Cairngorms. Water rippling over rocks and wind playing the branches of Scots pines underscored their days and nights together. Their tryst must have felt as enduring as the mountains that protected them. But when the Duke of Bedford – Georgina's husband – died, she refused Edwin Landseer's proposal of marriage. Landseer's turbulent mind found solace in wandering the places where love had been so freely given. It was in this state of rejection and dejection that he painted his masterpiece, the *Monarch of the Glen* (1851), a portrait of magnificence in isolation. A stag in full prowess stands amidst mountains. His look conveys confidence and self-assurance, but in the background, mist is enveloping the crags. Despite his majesty, he is alone.

Standing at the place where there was once so much passion, cold Highland winds now blow across a changing landscape. Landseer and the duchess are long dead. Their love is but a story and their house reduced to a few bricks. The red deer Landseer so loved to hunt no longer wander the mountain slopes. A few of the grand old Scots pines persist, standing proud above the flood plain of the Feshie River, but today a flush of new growth threatens to subsume them into a new mural. Only the braided rivulets still tumble through the scene.

This is the Glenfeshie, part of a huge area of interlinked estates covering more than 80,000 hectares and owned by the Danish billionaire, Anders Holch Povlsden. He is now the largest land-owner in Scotland. Acquiring so much land is allowing him to realise his long-term vision to make Scotland wild again; to free it from the cut-and-paste management that has dominated Scottish game estates for generations. This is bringing nature back on a vast scale.

Thomas MacDonell is the conservation manager for Wildland Ltd., and architect of this next phase of life for Glenfeshie. An engineer by training, Thomas has a no-nonsense approach to conservation. 'I like to understand how things work so we can fix them.' It was he who told me about Landseer and the duchess on our drive through the glen, relayed as an interesting anecdote, but it is also a metaphor for change. In the throes of Landseer and Georgina's love affair, gamekeepers everywhere were stripping the land of predators to bolster high numbers of game like deer and grouse. Only the richest and most entitled could act out their fantasies in such remote areas of northern Scotland, be that love, game shooting or the wilderness experience. Two hundred years later, the same area is now accessible to the general public and has conservation at its heart. The exclusivity and deer-stalking of old no longer have a place.

'Many deer estates are kudos for the owners, and the gamekeepers are refugees from the Victorian era,' said Thomas. 'We are doing it differently; we have a two-hundred-year vision for the restoration of woodland. We only want as many deer here as would have been present when large predators were still in existence. We are not anti-blood sports; deer stalking is something we still do in Glenfeshie, but the emphasis is on the hunt through a forest, not the shooting of high numbers of animals on a barren hillside.' A stance that hasn't made Glenfeshie popular among more traditional estates.

At present trees are patchily spread over the hillsides, but they are getting more numerous as the years roll by. Some of the new forest is deliberately planted, some is the result of natural regeneration of Scots pine, juniper, alder and birch. 'I have planted four million trees on the open moorland, but not down here by the river. I call this section the 'Mona Lisa', and you wouldn't let your kids draw on the *Mona Lisa*, would you?' Here and there, invasive larch, their seeds blown in from nearby plantations, are beginning to become established. Will the softwoods be removed to retain the original tree assemblage?

'No, this is not about going back to the past, we are building something new, and that includes some non-native trees. I don't like the term rewilding, it can be viewed as a move to go backwards, or to oust communities and to let wildlife take priority over their livelihoods and traditions. This is a landscape for nature and people for the future, which is why I prefer to call it rehabilitation.

We are creating a new landscape out of the ruins of past management. The old mountain bothies have been restored and we may do the same for the old hill farms. Farmers will be custodians of this landscape.'

If you could stand next to what remains of the Landseer love-cottage for the next two hundred years, Glenfeshie would transform in front of your eyes. A mixture of active measures and allowing time to heal is turning this bare glacial valley into a patchwork of forest and more open land. Since 2004, deer have been culled in their thousands, reducing the population from fifty deer per square kilometre to less than one per square kilometre. Relieved of so much grazing pressure, trees that were once eaten as soon as they sprouted can now grow and establish. It is in this emerging mosaic of forest and glade that predators and their prey can thrive once again. Pine martens, capercaillies, red squirrels, even wildcats are found here, and they attract shooters of a different kind to when Landseer stalked the hills.

Peter Cairns is a wildlife photographer, and his super-close images of a wildcat staring into the lens were taken in Glenfeshie. They show the intensity of this animal's existence; pure, focused energy contained in a tabby-cat coat. As he writes:

Despite decades spent photographing and filming in the Scottish Highlands, I can count my own sightings on one hand. So, when I was told of a semi-habituated wildcat, I knew this was a never-to-be-repeated opportunity. Over a whole year I got to know this cat and in a wildcat way, it got to know me. It never allowed me close but in return for a token of food, it allowed me close enough to secure some images that to this day remain my only photographic record of a wild-living Scottish wildcat. And then one day, it failed to turn up at our

regular forest rendezvous and I never saw it again. Did it get
killed? Was it lured away by the prospect of a liaison with a
female cat? Or did it just get bored with me? I will never know,
but what I do know is that to this day, the memory burns
bright.[1]

More wildcats could take up residence as the woodlands expand,
and this may become a release site for the wildcat reintroduction
project discussed in Chapter 8. I asked Thomas if the estate would
also welcome the larger lynx. 'Lynx reintroduction would be
worthwhile considering. If the Scottish people, after an appropri-
ate consultation process, wished to conduct a trial, Wildland
Limited would be delighted to assist with a release site.' The dream
of Glenfeshie as a wildlife hub of the Highlands is taking shape.

The Wildlands project has the audacity, the money and the
space to dream big, but across the country other rewilding/rehabit-
ing projects are making plans to repopulate, recalibrate and re-en-
chant landscapes currently bereft of wildlife. The predator ghosts
of the past are re-forming and lining up to take their place among
the fields and the trees, the villages and the cities, the moors and
the mountains of Britain. Birds of prey, such as white-tailed eagles
and red kites, are at the vanguard, and wildcats are close behind.
Maybe lynx and perhaps, in time, even wolves will follow. We are
looking to the past to move forwards to a richer, wilder world.
People willing, of course.

If these plans do come to fruition, the new ecosystems will need
a hierarchy of predators; the biggest cannot be left out. If the
centuries of eradication of meat-eaters have shown us one thing, it
is that such animals are vital to keeping an ecosystem in balance.
Predators cannot be seen in isolation and simply as dangers to be
removed; they are part and parcel of wholeness.

'A thing is right when it tends to preserve the integrity, stability and beauty of the biotic community. It is wrong when it tends otherwise.'[2] Aldo Leopold's mantra is the founding principle for those working for nature restoration. His words were written in America in the early twentieth century, and with that vast continent in mind. Translating it to modern Britain is the challenge. The predators in this book all live in a working world and interact with real people. They are not 'out there', in some infinite space beyond the city boundary; they move among us and share landscapes that are dominated by human interest. And as the world changes in response to climate change, as species shift in abundance and distribution, and as we struggle with solutions to these crises, the wild ones do what they can to hold on. We are all in this together and share the same changing space.

The rewilding of Glenfeshie is one example of blossoming and sharing, and is not confined to just the trees and mountain slopes; the Feshie River is also benefiting. As the trees establish and fix the substrate, water runoff from the hills is reduced and therefore less likely to sweep away the all-essential gravel beds that are needed by spawning salmon. The shade from the trees along the banks will also help to keep the waters cool. By reducing browsing pressure, many other benefits follow in an intricate display of interconnectedness. Deer stalkers, deer, trees, gravel, water and fish are bound together in an ecological cascade, demonstrating that everybody and everything lives downstream of something else. Scotland is famed for its salmon rivers, and high-quality spawning grounds are vital, because salmon are in serious trouble.

> Merrily swim we, the moon shines bright,
> Both current and ripple are dancing in light.[3]

Further south in Scotland, the River Tweed looked beautiful on a late autumn evening. It was as wide as a motorway, and framed by low-lying, soft green banks. The undulating surface, mercury pure, reflected the grey and pink of the setting sun. I stopped the car to lean over a bridge to watch the water swish strong and steady beneath the arches, a soothing caress against the noise of tyres pounding the wet road behind me. There is nothing that grants more peace to the soul than gently flowing water, and a river's promise to take secrets out to sea. In the distance, the silhouette of a small boat drifted on the flow, its proboscis-like fishing rod probing the depths. It was a scene of tranquillity. Then, as silent as a thought, a large black bird flew downstream and veered across a field, to disappear into distant haze. Its outline was prehistoric – long neck, small head, large bill and long, narrow wings. This cormorant was a reminder that every view of Britain carries shadows.

The great cormorant (*Phalacrocorax carbo*, meaning black, bald raven) is a large, fish-eating bird that weighs up to 3.5 kilograms and is most often found around the coast. They spend much of their day with their bent wings outstretched as if in supplication to the sun god: these are bat-like black-birds. As their feathers are less water-repellent than other seabirds, cormorants need to dry them in the wind and sun. Rocks and buoys are adorned with their characteristic crooked cruciform shape.

For centuries they were thought to be related to ravens. The name cormorant is derived from 'corvus marinus', meaning sea-raven, a common term for them until the seventeenth century. It is an unlikely connection, perhaps simply a reference to their colour and predatory behaviour, but maybe also to the knowing, far-sightedness of the black bird of the fields. As with all predators, we have given them both good and bad associations. In Norwegian mythology, three cormorants were the sons of a wise man who lived on a mythical island of plenty. Even though they purportedly hated the sight of Christians, they guided a devout and destitute young fisherman to a bounty of fish, and then stayed with him to steer his boat to good fortune for the rest of his life. As an antidote, in *Paradise Lost*, John Milton used the sinister image of a cormorant perched on top of the Tree of Life to represent the devil peering down to spy on Adam and Eve in the Garden of Eden below, planning their destruction.

> (Satan) … sits in the shape of a cormorant on the Tree of life,
> as highest in the Garden to look about him. The Garden
> describ'd; Satans first sight of Adam and Eve; his wonder at thir
> excellent form and happy state, but with resolution to work
> thir fall.[4]

But on the River Tweed, poetic tales give way to the reality of fish-eating birds moving in on one of the greatest salmon-fishing rivers in Europe.

'It is *the* hottest topic; tempers get seriously frayed.' Andrew Douglas-Home owns 3 kilometres of the River Tweed, which runs along the border between England and Scotland. He agreed to talk to me about the problem of fish-eating birds, which are increasing in number and expanding their range right along the Tweed's 3,000 kilometres (including tributaries). It isn't just the winter-visiting cormorants that turn up the temperature; a handsome fish-eating duck, the goosander, is also becoming more numerous and has settled in as a resident. These two specialist fish-eaters are an example of how living with predators in Britain is entering a new phase where human interests compete with wildlife in a world in flux.

'Forty years ago, I never saw them. Two reasons. Firstly, they were a lot less common. Secondly, if one did turn up, the river bailiffs were paid a bounty for each one shot – one shilling and sixpence. Seals as well. I have always said the trouble started with the Wildlife and Countryside Act of 1981, when it became illegal to control the birds. They have built up, and during the last five years, winter cormorant numbers in particular have gone through the roof. I have seen roosts of a hundred birds, and they hunt in packs. How can any fish survive that many predators?'

British Trust for Ornithology (BTO) data show that cormorants in the UK increased between 1986 and 2004, but have been slowly declining since then, particularly in Scotland, the northeast and southwest of England. At present it is estimated there are around 9,000 breeding pairs, but that figure has a degree of uncertainty as they are very difficult to count; and fishermen in particular think there are many more. In the winter, an influx of a sub-species from Europe (*Phalacrocorax carbo sinensis*) takes the figure to around 41,000 individuals. European cormorants greatly increased in number after legal protection from intense persecution came into force in the 1960s and in 1981, and many more now spend the winter months in the UK. They are also benefiting from fisheries stocking rivers and lakes (two million fish were released into English rivers in 2015),[5] and from climate change. Warmer winters benefit cormorants as ice cover over lakes, rivers and ponds is reduced or absent.[6] But numbers alone don't tell the whole story; it is the increase in the range of cormorants that causes many problems for commercial and sports fishing. In the UK there has been a 53 per cent range expansion since the 1980s, and they now nest in trees in many lowland and inland areas near lakes and rivers, as well as on cliffs along the coast. These inland breeding birds are mainly, but not exclusively, made up of the European cormorants.

Goosanders have also increased in number, dramatically so. They only began breeding in Scotland in the late nineteenth century, and then, from the 1940s onwards, expanded into northern England and Wales. They are now widely established. Their population is lower than cormorants, only around 3,800 pairs, boosted to 12,000 individuals over winter when continental birds arrive.

Just at the time both cormorant and goosander numbers were expanding, bolstered by an influx of European birds for the winter months, the two fish that are the prize of fly fishermen, trout and salmon, were falling off a cliff. In Scotland alone, both of these have declined by nearly 70 per cent in the last twenty-five years.[7]

Salmon are particularly vulnerable to a whole host of pressures. They spend part of their lives in the ocean, but breed in fresh water, in the upper reaches of rivers where they lay eggs in cold, shallow, gravelly pools. When they return to breed, usually in the river where they were hatched, they create 'salmon runs' where adult fish enter the river from the ocean and swim upstream against the flow. They can (or could) be seen leaping up waterfalls to reach the spawning grounds.

Catching returning salmon has been a sport for fly fishermen for centuries. Gone are the days, however, when there were so many salmon swimming upriver that rod and line fishing had to compete with drift nets placed not only across the mouth of estuaries but also for miles inland. On the River Tweed alone there were thirty drift nets operating all year round between Coldstream and Berwick-on-Tweed. Hundreds of thousands of salmon were caught, both by net and rod, in Britain's once-rich salmon rivers. Today, it is a very different picture; one of empty nets and furrowed brows. The drift-net fisheries have disbanded and over 90 per cent of the rod-caught salmon is mandatory catch-and-release. Every measure is being taken to try to hold on to the fish that still breed.

'We used to get one in three fish that were hatched here back up the river to breed,' said Andrew. 'I used to watch thousands of smolts [salmon turn silver when they are ready to migrate and are called smolts] streaming down river to go out to sea, and knew thirty per cent of them would return. Now there is so much pressure on them, we are lucky if three in a hundred return to spawn.' This catastrophic decline has meant that all the salmon rivers in the UK are emptying. On the River Tweed, the total salmon catch for 2019 was 6,814[8] – less than half of what it was just five years before – and only 47,515 salmon were caught right across Scotland.

No one knows for sure why wild salmon stocks are plummeting, but it almost certainly involves a perfect storm of climate change affecting the oceans, pollution (chemical and plastic), soil runoff into rivers, the building of dams, overfishing, removal of the smaller fish they feed on, changes to riverine spawning areas, warming rivers, disease from salmon farms and interbreeding with escaped farmed salmon. These many complex issues are changing the fortunes of this most famous of fish. The modern world has turned its face against wild salmon, and ordinary citizens feel powerless to help. Sports fishermen, however, see an immediate and tangible way to reduce the pressure on the fish in their own patch – they want to reduce the number of predatory birds.

The sun shone brightly and all seemed well with the world when Andrew and I walked beside his wide and peaceful stretch of the River Tweed. As if to make a point, a cormorant flew overhead as Andrew explained his worries.

'We have almost no cormorants between June and September because they are on the coast breeding. Luckily, we don't get breeding cormorants here, but they pour in during October and stay until the end of March. They are big birds and eat fish up to about two or three pounds in weight, including grayling, brown trout, eels, and of course the young salmon parr, the small salmon that stay in the river to grow before going out to sea. You tend to see cormorants in flocks of between ten and sixty birds. These are pretty devastating and can almost empty a pool of trout by hunting in a pack underwater. I don't think they are the main issue for salmon stocks because cormorants are not here for the run of smolts in the spring and summer, but they are very bad news for brown trout and can wipe them out. The salmon damage is done by the goosanders, which are now resident. They eat lots of smolts as they migrate down the river between March and June. Between goosanders and cormorants, too many small salmon and trout don't stand a chance. We have to do something.'

Given a free rein, the fishermen on the Tweed would like to undertake unlimited scaring (apparently, shining lasers at them works well), and to be able to shoot both species when needed. 'We know shooting isn't the cure; tagged cormorants that have been shot under licence right here have come from as far away as Wales, Scandinavia and the Isle of Man. We will never get rid of them, but we have to give the fish a chance.'

There is a febrile atmosphere in the sports-fishing world. The new phenomenon of proliferating fish-eating birds gives focus to a much broader global angst about the environmental health of the planet. Sports fishing has passionate advocates who see themselves as guardians of the rivers and part of an ancient tradition of skilled hunting. So much history, tourist money, pride in place, reputation, expertise, jobs and enjoyment are on the cusp of disappearing because of human actions changing the functioning of the world. Andrew is sympathetic to the anger directed at cormorants and goosanders: 'I think people are wrong to blame it all on the birds, but I do understand how they feel.'

As an alternative point of view, Tim Martin, a naturalist and keen fly-fishing friend told me, 'I'm anti-culling of cormorants and goosanders, because they are just scapegoats and culling them would have a pretty marginal impact. The real problem is that the whole ecosystem is breaking down – so we need a bigger view than just reaching for a gun. We need to boost young fish recruitment by transforming how we farm the land around rivers and their tributaries – i.e. no maize, which causes soil runoff, no intensive farming at all in fact. We can also make rivers healthier by restoring bogs and planting more trees to hold back runoff, and reintroducing beavers because their dams create more stable flows, and provide shelter and food for young fish. We need more predators that can help control fish-eating birds, like otters and sea eagles and even pine martens (they might predate goosander nests in hollow trees). And finally, we need to end overfishing around our coasts and more widely, so that salmon and sea trout feeding at sea is improved.'

Two different approaches. One short-term, one with a longer, ecological view. At the moment, approach number one has more traction.

In 2019, between 2,000 and 3,000 fish-eating birds were legally shot in the UK to protect rivers and stocked fishing pools, and there are demands for an increase in the number of licences to be made available.[9] The quicker fish stocks disappear, the more anger is directed towards the only thing that seems to be controllable.

As discussed throughout this book, humanity has wrought profound changes on Planet Earth. In the midst of so much transformation, wild things have remained true to themselves but are caught in a kaleidoscopic world that constantly shifts with every turn of progress. They can only do what they know how to do, and that is survive as best they can by exploiting any opportunities that arise. But it is even more challenging still. They must also negotiate the world of the human psyche, especially the complexity of the human psyche under pressure.

So many of us feel a mixture of despair at an increasingly broken world. Huge events pile in like waves crashing down in a storm. Climate change is causing extreme temperatures, storms, floods, wildfires and droughts. At the time of writing, a global pandemic continues to cause illness and death, as well as economic stress. Every day there is more deforestation, destruction, drainage and pollution of wild places. Unsustainable agriculture and development are everywhere. As the human population increases towards ten billion, ever more pressure is being put on already stretched or exhausted resources, and there seems to be no end to the deliberate persecution and elimination of wild creatures that appear to threaten what we want.

It is no wonder that talk of the future is heavily laden with a dangerous combination of anger, fear, guilt, defensiveness, blame and recrimination. A natural human response to threat is to act like pioneers protecting a homestead; erect fences, stockpile resources, man the barricades, and defend what we feel belongs to us. Cormorants, goosanders, hen harriers, foxes, badgers, corvids, buzzards, white-tailed eagles, red kites, grey seals, wildcats – the list goes on – all of these predators seem to breach the walls we build, and they are falling foul of our need to feel safe and to exert control over whatever we hold dear. We all do it, whether it is in a home, a garden, a farm, a moor, a river, a forest or the sea itself.

This mindset profoundly affects British predators. We will only have eagles in the air and wolves in the forests when we all truly and deeply feel secure in their presence. Only when predators are no longer seen as a threat to our lives and livelihoods will they be left in peace. Security is the key to bringing predators back to

Britain, and that comes from learning from past ignorance and superstition, being more environmentally literate and welcoming the enrichment that a wildlife-rich future offers, physically, mentally and spiritually. It depends on us telling different stories about these creatures, releasing them from past prejudice. This is so much easier to say than to put into practice, but many of the answers are already known – what is missing is the confidence to enact change. Only by remembering what it was like to live in a wild, rich world, adapting the lessons learned to the reality of today, and then embracing predators into our designs for the future will we be able to make rewilding/rehabiting a dream everyone can dream. And all of us must want this, not just the rich and privi-leged, otherwise the persecution and the suffering of wild crea-tures will go on and on.

It was the philosopher Søren Kierkegaard who said that life can only be understood by looking backwards at the past, but that it must be lived by going forwards. It is time, then, to face the fact that we are living in an Age of Forgetting. This is not an official term, but it is a fitting one, especially when applied to nature. 'Forget' is derived from the ancient German *getan*, which means to grasp onto or to hold, and *for*, which adds the sense of missing. The Age of Forgetting is, therefore, an era defined by losing our hold over, our collective memory of, life on earth.

There are many, many tales of brutal eradications over the last two hundred years. The last pair of great auks were slaughtered by fishermen in Iceland in 1844, the single egg crushed by their boots. Footage taken in 1936 shows a lone Tasmanian tiger pacing in a cage, the last one alive on earth. It died in a zoo in Hobart, its fellow thylacines shot and trapped by farmers fearful for their sheep. Since 1900, around five hundred species have gone extinct around the world: the Yemen gazelle in 1951, the Japanese sea lion in the 1970s, the Yangtze River dolphin in 2006, the Chinese paddlefish in 2020 … a roll-call of ghosts.

In 2020, the World Wide Fund for Nature (WWF) produced a report that showed just how fast life is disappearing from the planet. The line on the graph showing worldwide species decline plummets ever downwards. Just over the last half-century, two-thirds of the mass of wildlife on earth has gone.[10] Within my lifetime, a host of blooming, singing, buzzing, wailing, growling, croaking, roaring life has thinned out. There is loss and empty space where once there was abundance. Many species now exist in fragmented populations, squeezed out by human demands. Others have literally vanished. In 2014, the journal *Science* published a paper highlighting the worldwide decline of the largest predators, a group especially badly affected:

> They are some of the world's most admired mammals and,
> ironically, some of the most imperilled. Most have experienced
> substantial population declines and range contractions
> throughout the world during the past two centuries … Large
> carnivores face enormous threats that have caused massive
> declines in their populations and geographic ranges, including
> habitat loss and degradation, persecution, utilization, and
> depletion of prey.[11]

If species were not deliberately targeted, they became collateral damage in our schemes and plans for more agriculture, betterment and profits. Snuffed out like candle flames, even the faint wisps of smoke, the memories of the creatures that once lived with us, have dissipated as the last people to encounter them have died too.

The removal of wildlife is accompanied by what author and lepidopterist Robert Pyle termed the 'extinction of experience', a reference to the disappearance of the familiarity of living among wild creatures. Each generation draws a nature-line in the sand which gets washed away, re-formed and reset as wildlife in general becomes less common and with each new wave of extinctions. We believe that the world we see is the world as it should be, the so-called 'shifting baseline syndrome'. We are progressively redefining ourselves as inhabitants of an emptying world. Ross Barnett in his book on the reintroduction of lynx knows this battle: 'Each generation of conservationists must fight against a recalibration of the norm.'[12] Today we think it is normal that no wildcats crouch at the woodland edge, and no lynx stalk in the darkest shadows of the trees. We have forgotten these creatures and how to live with them. We have become apathetic in the face of more loss. In Robert Pyle's words:

> As cities and metastasizing suburbs forsake their natural diversity, and their citizens grow more removed from personal contact with nature, awareness and appreciation retreat. This breeds apathy toward environmental concerns and, inevitably, further degradation of the common habitat … So it goes, on and on, the extinction of experience sucking the life from the land, the intimacy from our connections … people who don't know don't care. What is the extinction of the condor to a child who has never known a wren?[13]

Biologist Edward Wilson defined what he calls the Age of Loneliness, a nightmare vision of the future where the only species left will be domesticated species and scavengers like cockroaches.[14] We will be in control of a bland and empty planet. As wild things physically vanish, they also fade from our imagination as we transition from living with wild abundance to that place of lonely isolation. The colour, form and features of wild creatures, their behaviour and their array of sounds have stirred us at the deepest level, that sacred inner place from which we create beauty and meaning. 'Animals are good to think with' is a sentiment attributed to anthropologist Claude Lévi-Strauss, and so they are; they indulge the exclusively human trait of constant self-analysis. When we no longer have external realities to remind us of our strengths and weaknesses, of both our majesty and baseness, we will become ever more inward-looking and self-regarding. As wildlife dwindles from our memory banks, it slips from our lexicon, our songs, tales, similes and metaphors, those repositories of wisdom about the human condition. The eradication of non-human life can happen so quickly, and in the process we, and the earth, are impoverished.

Arresting the Age of Forgetting and transforming it into the Age of Remembering, and then on to the Age of Abundance, can be done, but only with political will and broad-scale cooperation at every level of society. Conservation in today's world is, in effect, gardening in the ruins of capitalism, but we can garden well to create abundance if we know what we are doing. An understanding of nature must underlie all that we do and influence business, agriculture, industry, education, lifestyle choice and politics. Eco-thinking will transform the world, and wildlife may yet transition from being strangers and commodities to fellow travellers on an exciting and dynamic planet. This nature-rich existence will enable us to make the right choices for the future, decisions that are based on a wise understanding of the interdependence of all life on earth. It is a long journey to embark upon, but it is one we have to begin now.

No one can promise a return to a nature-rich world will be easy, because willing the return of abundance is one thing, while co-existing with it is another – especially if that involves bringing back animals we see as a threat. It may well involve the curtailing of some activities we now take for granted or see as a human right. Personal sacrifices for the greater good may be part and parcel of living with abundance. Restrictions on hunting, shooting, fishing, pet ownership, travel, more limited choices of food and goods, and the establishment of exclusion zones so that wildlife can live unhindered – all may have to come into play. At the moment we seem to be very far away from this vision, but, in agreement with writer Barbara Kingsolver, where else is there to go except to garner the energy of hope and use it to propel us into the future? As she suggests in her book, *Animal Dreams*:

> The very least you can do in your life is to figure out what you
> hope for. And the most you can do is live inside that hope. Not
> admire it from a distance but live right in it, under its roof. What
> I want is so simple I almost can't say it: elementary kindness.
> Enough to eat, enough to go around. The possibility that kids
> might one day grow up to be neither the destroyers nor the
> destroyed. That's about it. Right now, I'm living in that hope,
> running down its hallway and touching the walls on both sides.[15]

Just a short distance away from my city-centre home, a lynx pads down a steep street, heading for the main shopping centre a couple of hundred metres away. It is more than life-size, a powerful strid-ing beast among the close-knit housing and the paving stones of Bristol. I cannot walk past it without my heart beating faster, and I always stop for a while and absorb its company. Even when I'm indoors, I know it is there, day and night. Particularly at night.

Under the never-dark sky its fur glows in the street lamps, a burnished gold and red softened by thick strands of grey. The cat does not look at us; its stare goes beyond the present. It is looking into a future that you and I cannot see.

This lynx, by wildlife street artist, Mark Anthony, is ice-age cave art translated into twenty-first-century Britain. Its presence transforms the street into a thin place, where we walk in two worlds; where the binding between people and the wild is so loosely woven it allows the light to shine through.

I would love to still be on this planet when the first lynx steps from the confinement of a zoo and onto a carpet of soil and leaf on a wildwood floor; into a place of ever-changing light, odours and sounds. Britain will be electrified by its presence. I would like to know that the setting sun will see it stirring from its lair, and dawn bring it back again to rest. To live in a wild world needs a wild heart, and I don't know if we will gather the courage to embrace that. But every day I am grateful that this street-art lynx is in my world, as a reminder of what could be. We have been on a long journey, people and predators, and it still goes on into an uncertain future.

At times when writing this book, I have put my head in my hands and wept at the callous stupidity, self-centredness and short-sightedness of humanity, yet at other moments I have been filled with so much wonder at the magnificence of the earth that nothing but love and hope infuses every fibre of my being. A better world lies in the young dreamers who see beyond the purely human and look outwards to a complete and abundant world. The future does not belong to the defilers, the polluters and the destroyers, but to the young and their hope in a time of extinction.

If wholeness does return, and a richer world does become a reality, then I know it will work its magic on us all. We will be much more human. I don't want to believe that it can't happen and that there will be nothing left of these magnificent predatory creatures but dreams and memories – nothing but paintings on a wall. But that is for all of us to decide. Meanwhile, precious opportunities for renewal slip by with every tick of the clock.

Acknowledgements

Thank you to those who gave me peace and space to write, namely Chris and Sarah Boles in the Highlands and Mary Stevenson and Adrian Drake-Lee in Bedford. Thank you to all the wildlife gurus, readers and commentators who helped in many ways as I struggled with the enormity of it all. Also, to Brian Clarke, Sarah Colwell, Ian Newton, Paul Pettitt, Russell Wynn, Geoff Hilton, Rory Wilson, David Sexton, Patrick Laurie, Tim Guilford, Simon Lester, David Macdonald, Marc Simmonds, John Lister-Kaye, Tim Birkhead, Jeremy Mynott and to all the many generous people who looked at text, answered questions, sent info, corrected errors and showed me around. I am grateful to everyone.

I am very sad to say Robin Prytherch, featured in Chapter 5 on buzzards, died in March 2021. He was a gentle, passionate advocate of birds of prey, and will be so very greatly missed.

Notes

Introduction

1. Homer, *The Iliad* (Penguin, 1990)
2. Ovid, *Metamorphoses* (Oxford University Press, 2008)
3. James Tyrrell, *The General History of England, both Ecclesiastical and Civil*, Vol III (London, 1697)
4. William J. Ripple, et al., 'Status and Ecological Effects of the World's Largest Carnivores', *Science*, Vol. 43, January 2014
5. Birdforum.net, 'How much does a blackbird need to eat daily?': https://www.birdforum.net/showthread.php?t=137159
6. John Stuart Mill, *Nature, The Utility of Religion and Theism* (Watts and Co., 1874)
7. J.A.G. Barnes, *The Titmice of the British Isles* (David & Charles, 1975)
8. Becky Crew, *Zombie Tits, Astronaut Fish, and Other Weird Animals* (New South Books, 2012)
9. Frans de Waal, 'The Evolution of Empathy', *Greater Good* magazine, Greater Good Science Center, University of California, Berkeley (2005)
10. https://www.moorlandforum.org.uk/understanding-predation-report-launch
11. Jefferson McMahan, 'The Moral Problem of Predation': http://jeffersonmcmahan.com/wp-content/uploads/2012/11/The-Moral-Problem-of-Predation.pdf
12. Nick Mayhew-Smith, *The Naked Hermit* (SPCK, 2019)
13. ibid.
14. Isaiah 2:4 and 11: 6–7
15. Jefferson McMahan, 'The Moral Problem of Predation': http://jeffersonmcmahan.com/wp-content/uploads/2012/11/The-Moral-Problem-of-Predation.pdf
16. E.H. Gombrich, *Art and Illusion: A Study in the Psychology of Pictorial Representation* (Phaidon Press, 1977)
17. Graham Greene, *The End of the Affair* (Vintage Classics, 2004)

Chapter 1

1. Joshua New, Leda Cosmides and John Tooby, 'Category-specific attention for animals reflects ancestral priorities, not experise', research paper, Centre for Evolutionary Psychology, University of California, Santa Barbara, August 2007
2. Henry D. Thoreau, *The Maine Woods* (Ticknor and Fields, 1864)
3. J. MacEnery, *Researches, or, Discoveries of Organic Remains, and of British and Roman Reliques, in the Caves of Kent's Hole, Anstis Cove, Chudleigh, and Berry Head* (Marshall Simpkin, 1859)
4. 'The Devonshire Caverns, and Their Contents', *Science*, Vol. 2, No. 38, 1883
5. *Western Morning News*, 8 November, 2011
6. John Berger, *Why Look at Animals* (Penguin, 2009)
7. Meaghan N. Altman, et al., 'Adaptive attention: how preference for animacy impacts change detection', *Evolution and Human Behaviour*, Vol. 37, Issue 4, 2015
8. E.H. Gombrich, 'The Evidence of Images: I The Variability of Vision' in C.S. Singleton (ed.), *Interpretation: Theory and Practice* (Johns Hopkins University Press, 1969)
9. Alain de Botton, *Guardian* column, 28 January 2017
10. A. Larkman, et al., 'Small farmland bird declines, gamebird releases, and changes in seed sources', in *Wildlife Conservation on Farmland*, Vol. 2, ed. D.W. Macdonald and R. E. Feber (Oxford University Press, 2015)
11. John Laundré, Lucina Hernández and William Ripple, 'The Landscape of Fear: Ecological Implications of Being Afraid', *The Open Ecology Journal*, Vol. 3, March 2010
12. Aldo Leopold, *A Sand County Almanac* (Oxford University Press, 1949)
13. Ian Newton, personal communication

Chapter 2

1. Unattributed blog post entry: source unknown
2. Ted Hughes, 'The Thought-Fox', in *The Hawk in the Rain* (Faber and Faber, 1957). Reproduced with permission from the publisher
3. D.W. Macdonald, 'The Red Fox, *Vulpes vulpes*, as a Predator upon Earthworms, *Lumbricus terrestris*', *Ethology* Vol. 52, Issue 2 (1980)
4. Marc Baldwin, Wildlife Online: https://www.wildlifeonline.me.uk/animals/article/red-fox-senses
5. Barbara Kingsolver, *Prodigal Summer* (Faber and Faber, 2013)
6. Aisling Irwin, 'There are five times more urban foxes in England than we thought', *New Scientist*, 4 January 2017
7. C.D. Soulsbury, et al., 'The impact of sarcoptic mange *Sarcoptes scabiei* on the British fox *Vulpes vulpes* population', *Mammal Review*, Vol. 37, No. 4 (2007)

8. Steffan Roos, et al., 'A review of predation as a limiting factor for bird populations in mesopredator-rich landscapes: a case study of the UK', *Biological Reviews* Vol. 93 (2018)

9. 'Remembering keepers', *Shooting Times*, November 2007

10. D.B. Hayhow, et al., 'The State of the UK's Birds 2017', RSPB, BTO, WWT, DAERA, JNCC, NE and NRW (December 2017)

11. National Biodiversity Network, NBN report, 'The State of Nature 2019'

12. Stephen Harris, 'The food of suburban foxes (*Vulpes vulpes*) with special reference to London', *Mammal Review*, December 1981

13. Patrick Barkham, 'Invasion of the urban foxes', *Guardian*, 7 June 2010

14. Carrie Westgarth, Megan Brooke and Robert M. Christley, 'How many people have been bitten by dogs? A cross-sectional survey of prevalence, incidence and factors associated with dog bites in a UK community', *Journal of Epidemiology & Community Health*, Vol. 72, Issue 4 (2017)

15. I. Newton, P.E. Davis and J.E. Davis, 'Ravens and Buzzards in relation to sheep farms and forestry in Wales', *Journal of Applied Ecology*, Vol. 19 (1982)

16. R. Hewson, 'Scavenging and Predation Upon Sheep and Lambs in West Scotland', *Journal of Applied Ecology*, Vol. 21, No. 3 (1984)

17. Heather Pringle, British Trust for Ornithology community blog: https://www.bto.org/community/blog/what-effect-might-annual-releases-non-native-gamebirds-be-having-native-biodiversity

18. Peter Robertson, et al., 'Pheasant release in Great Britain: long-term and large-scale changes in the survival of a managed bird', *European Journal of Wildlife Research*, Vol. 63, No. 6 (2017)

19. T.M. Blackburn and K.J. Gaston, 'Contribution of non-native galliforms to annual variation in biomass of British birds', *Biological Invasions* Vol. 23, Issue 1 (2021)

20. thatsfarming.com, 27 February 2017

21. *Farmers Weekly*, 29 March 2016

22. Farminguk.com, 20 April 2017

23. *Farmers Guardian*, 25 May 2017

24. Improving Lamb Survival', DEFRA booklet PB No.2072 (2004): http://adlib.everysite.co.uk/resources/000/107/984/lambsurvival.pdf

25. Rebecca L. Moberly, et al., 'Factors associated with fox (*Vulpes vulpes*) predation of lambs in Britain', *Wildlife Research* Vol. 30, No.3, July 2003

26. Personal communication

27. ibid.

28. ibid.

29. Curlew Country, 'Project Background': https://curlewcountry.org/project-background/

30. Mid Wales Ringing Group blog, 'Shropshire Curlew Curtain Call?': https://midwalesringers.blogspot.com/2015/11/shropshire-curlew-curtain-call.html

31. Steffan Roos, et al., 'A review of predation as a limiting factor for bird populations in mesopredator-rich landscapes: a case study of the UK', *Biological Reviews*, Vol. 93 (2018)

32. Ian Newton, *Farming and Birds*, New Naturalist series 135 (William Collins, 2018)

33. N. Meyer, et al., 'Gelegeschutzmaßnahmen beim Großen Brachvogel – Bericht 2017', Michael Otto Institute at NABU (2017): http://bit. ly/3bZRtar

34. B.G. O'Donoghue and J.G.J. Carey, 'Curlew Conservation Programme Annual Report 2020', National Parks and Wildlife Service, Killarney (2020)

35. Martin Harper, RSPB Global Conservation Director, blog post: https:// community.rspb.org.uk/ourwork/b/martinharper/posts/the-conservationist-39-s-dilemma-an-update-on-the-science-policy-and-practice-of-the-impact-of-predators-on-wild-birds-5

36. https://www.facebook.com/sheffieldsaboteurs/posts/rspb-employed-fox-shooter-caught-last-nighta-small-team-of-locals-took-to-the-mo/ 919321251571535/

37. Professor Carl Jones, quoted in *The Week*, 25 July 2020

38. Isobel Hutchinson, Animal Aid, June 2020, quoted in: www. thesecretmarketreport.com/2020/06/28/should-we-cull-one-species-to-save-another

39. Professor David Macdonald, Director WildCru, Oxford University, personal communication

40. William Ogilvie, 'Yonder He Goes!' Reproduced with permission from Catherine J. Reid, copyright holder

41. 'Report of Committee of inquiry into Hunting with Dogs in England & Wales': https://assets.publishing.service.gov.uk/government/uploads/ system/uploads/attachment_data/file/265552/4763.pdf

42. Thomas F. Dale, *The Fox* (Longman Green, 1906)

43. Rebecca Hosking, personal communication

44. *Guardian* news item, '400,000 bring rural protest to London', 23 September 2002; and BBC news report, 'Huge turnout for countryside march', 22 September 2002: http://news.bbc.co.uk/1/hi/uk/2274129. stm

45. J-O. Helldin, O. Liberg and G. Glöersen, 'Lynx (*Lynx lynx*) killing red foxes (*Vulpes vulpes*) in boreal Sweden – frequency and population effects', *Journal of Zoology*, Vol. 270 (2006)

46. Marianne Pasanen-Mortensen, et al., 'The changing contribution of top-down and bottom-up limitation of mesopredators during 220 years of land use and climate change', *Journal of Animal Ecology*, Vol. 86, Issue 3, 11 January 2017

Chapter 3

1. Esther Woolfson, *Corvus: A Life with Birds* (Granta, 2009)
2. Seweryn Olkowicz, et al., 'Neuronal density in birds', Proceedings of the National Academy of Sciences, *PNAS*, Vol. 26, No. 3, June 2016
3. Can Kabadayi and Mathias Osvath, 'Ravens parallel great apes in flexible planning for tool-use and bartering', *Science*, Vol. 357, Issue 6347, July 2017
4. Marcus Boeckle and Nicola S. Clayton, 'A raven's memories are for the future', *Science*, Vol. 357, Issue 6347, July 2017
5. Can Kabadayi and Mathias Osvath, 'Ravens parallel great apes in flexible planning for tool-use and bartering', *Science*, Vol. 357, Issue 6347, July 2017
6. Jorg J.M. Massen, et al., 'Ravens Intervene in Others' Bonding Attempts', *Current Biology*, Vol. 24, No. 22, November 2014
7. Orlaith N. Fraser and Thomas Bugnyar, 'Do Ravens Show Consolation? Responses to Distressed Others', *PLoS ONE*, Public Library of Science, 12 May 2010
8. J.J.A. Muller, J.J.M. Massen, T. Bugnyar and M. Osvath, 'Ravens remember the nature of a single reciprocal interaction sequence over 2 days and even after a month', *Animal Behaviour*, Vol. 128 (2017)
9. John Parslow, *Breeding Birds of Britain and Ireland* (T. & A.D. Poyser, 1973)
10. Derek Ratcliffe, *The Raven* (T. & A.D. Poyser, 1997)
11. National Wildlife Crime Unit, 'Bird of the Month – Raven': https://www.nwcu.police.uk/educationmedia/bird-of-the-month/
12. James Rebanks, *The Shepherd's Life: A Tale of the Lake District* (Penguin, 2016)
13. S.T. Campbell, F.G. Hartley and J.C. Reynolds, 'Assessing the nature and use of corvid cage traps in Scotland: Part 4 of 4 – Review and recommendations', *Scottish Natural Heritage* Commissioned Report No. 934 (2016)
14. James Rebanks, *The Shepherd's Life* (Penguin, 2016)
15. Ted Hughes, *Crow: From the Life and Songs of the Crow* (Faber and Faber, 1970). Reproduced with permission from the publisher
16. Mail Online, 'Why We Think Seagulls are Foul': https://www.dailymail.co.uk/news/article-2790229/why-think-seagulls-foul-birds-hated-way-steal-food-cover-cars-mess.html
17. British Trust for Ornithology (BTO) online species entry, 'Carrion Crow': https://app.bto.org/birdtrends/species.jsp?year=2019&s=carcr
18. Craig Ralston, personal communication
19. John Clare, 'The Crow', in *John Clare: Major Works* (Oxford University Press, 2008)

Chapter 4

1. Charles Foster, *Being a Beast* (Profile Books, 2016)
2. H. Kruuk and T. Parish. 'Feeding Specialization of the European Badger *Meles meles* in Scotland', *Journal of Animal Ecology*, Vol. 50, No. 3 (1981)
3. Simon King, *Simon King's Wildguide* (BBC Books, 1994)
4. Wildlife Online YouTube channel, 'Badger worming': https://www.youtube.com/watch?v=5mCGn9EWs8A&feature=youtu.be
5. Ralph Waldo Emerson, *The Journals and Miscellaneous Notebooks of Ralph Waldo Emerson*, 16 vols, eds. William H. Gilman, et al. (Harvard University Press, 1960–1982)
6. Richard Adams, *Watership Down* (Penguin, 1974)
7. Unknown origin, possibly Irish
8. PETA investigation, 'PETA Asia Exposes Extreme Cruelty in the Badger-Brush Industry': https://investigations.peta.org/badger-brush-industry/
9. Edward Thomas, 'The Combe', *Poems* (Selwyn & Blount, 1917)
10. John Clare, 'The Badger', in *John Clare: Major Works* (Oxford University Press, 2008)
11. T.J. Roper, 'Badger Meles meles setts – architecture, internal environment and function', *Mammal Review*, Vol. 22, Issue 1 (March 1992)
12. S. Harris, et al., 'An Integrated Approach to Monitoring Badger (*Meles meles*) Population Changes in Britain', in D.R. McCullough and R.H. Barrett (eds), *Wildlife 2001: Populations* (Springer, 1992)
13. J. Judge, et al., 'Abundance of badgers (*Meles meles*) in England and Wales', *Nature: Scientific Reports* 7, 276 (2017)
14. D.W. Macdonald, et al., 'Population dynamics of badgers (*Meles meles*) in Oxfordshire, U.K.: numbers, density and cohort life histories, and a possible role of climate change in population growth', *Journal of Zoology*, Vol. 256, Issue 1, 2002
15. G.P. Clarke, P.C.L. White and S. Harris, 'Effects of roads on badger *Meles meles* populations in south-west England', *Biological Conservation*, Vol. 86, No. 2, November 1998
16. Emily Wilson and David Wembridge, 'The State of Britain's Hedgehogs', (British Hedgehog Preservation Society and People's Trust for Endangered Species, 2018): https://www.britishhedgehogs.org.uk/pdf/sobh-2018.pdf
17. https://curlewcountry.org/project-background/
18. Marc Baldwin, Wildlife Online, 'European Hedgehog mortality – Predators': https://www.wildlifeonline.me.uk/animals/article/european-hedgehog-predators
19. Iain Trewby, et al., 'Experimental evidence of competitive release in sympatric carnivores', *Biology Letters*, Vol. 4, No. 2 (2008)
20. Iain Trewby, et al., 'Impacts of Removing Badgers on Localised Counts of Hedgehogs', PloS ONE, Vol. 9, No. 4 (Public Library of Science, 2014)
21. TB Hub, 'The Tuberculin Skin Test' (2020): https://tbhub.co.uk/wp-content/uploads/2020/08/AR-factsheet-skin-test-11.08.20.pdf

22. GOV.UK, 'Bovine TB Statistics': https://www.gov.uk/government/statistics/historical-statistics-notices-on-the-incidence-of-tuberculosis-tb-in-cattle-in-great-britain-2020-monthly
23. House of Commons Library, 'Bovine Tuberculosis Statistics: Great Britain (October 2017): https://commonslibrary.parliament.uk/research-briefings/sn06081/
24. Patrick Barkham, *Badgerlands* (Granta, 2013)
25. Angela Cassidy, *Vermin, Victims and Disease: British Debates over Bovine Tuberculosis and Badgers* (Palgrave Macmillan, 2019), Chapter 1, 'Of Badgers, Bovines and Bacteria'.
26. United States Environmental Protection Agency: https://www.epa.gov/ghgemissions/global-greenhouse-gas-emissions-data
27. Veerasamy Sejian, et al., research paper published online on IntechOpen, 30 March 2016: https://www.intechopen.com/books/greenhouse-gases/livestock-as-sources-of-greenhouse-gases-and-its-significance-to-climate-change
28. Waitrose Food and Drink Report 2018–19
29. Dominic Dyer, quoted in 'Out of the woods: why the badger cull is still not a black and white issue', *BBC Wildlife* magazine, Spring 2020
30. United Nations Environment Programme, *UNEP Frontiers 2016 Report: Emerging Issues of Environmental Concern* (UNEP, 2016)
31. Dominic Dyer, former CEO of The Badger Trust, personal communciation

Chapter 5

1. Leslie Brown and Dean Amadon, *Eagles, Hawks and Falcons of the World* (Wellfleet Press, 1986)
2. T. Atkinson Jenkins, 'A French Etymology', *Manly Anniversary Studies*, 1923
3. E.L. Jones, 'The Bird Pests of British Agriculture in Recent Centuries', *The Agricultural History Review*, Vol. 20, No. 2 (1972)
4. R. Smith, *The Universal Directory for Taking Alive and Destroying Rats, and All Other Kinds of Four-Footed and Winged Vermin* (London, 1768)
5. A.G. More, 'On the distribution of birds in Great Britain during the nesting season' Part 1, *Ibis*, Vol. 7, No. 2 (1865)
6. Neil Tranter, *Sport, economy and society in Britain 1750–1914*, New Studies in Economic and Social History series (Cambridge University Press, 1998)
7. Harry V. Thompson and Alastair N. Worden, *The Rabbit*, New Naturalist series 13 (Collins, 1956)
8. N.W. Moore, 'The Past and Present Status of the Buzzard in the British Isles', *British Birds*, May 1957
9. ibid.

10. R.M. Francksen, et al., 'Measures of predator diet alone may underestimate the collective impact on prey: Common buzzard *Buteo buteo* consumption of economically important red grouse *Lagopus lagopus scotica*', *PLoS ONE*, Vol. 14, No. 8 (Public Library of Science, 2019)

11. D. Parrott, 'Impacts and management of common buzzards *Buteo buteo* at pheasant *Phasianus colchicus* release pens in the UK: a review', *European Journal of Wildlife Research*, Vol. 61 (2015)

12. British Association of Shooting and Conservation (BASC), 'Birds of Prey at Pheasant Release Pens: A Practical Guide for Game Managers and Gamekeepers'

13. ibid.

14. Dan Glaister, 'Buzzards back in hunters' crosshairs over threat to UK pheasant shoots', *Observer*, 18 September 2018

15. Natural England news release, 29 July 2016: https://www.gov.uk/government/news/licence-for-buzzard-control

16. Martin Harper, RSPB Global Conservation Director blog post, 23 May 2013: https://community.rspb.org.uk/ourwork/b/martinharper/posts/buzzardgate-2

17. Patrick Barkham, 'Granting this licence to shoot buzzards will unleash a killing spree', *Guardian* online Opinion column, 4 August 2016: https://www.theguardian.com/commentisfree/2016/aug/04/buzzard-licence-kill-slaughter-wildlife-natural-world

18. Joah R. Madden and Sarah E. Perkins, 'Why did the pheasant cross the road? Long-term road mortality patterns in relation to management changes', *Royal Society Open Science* online pub. October 2017: https://www.ncbi.nlm.nih.gov/pmc/articles/PMC5666256/

19. Nicholas Aebischer, 'National gamebag census: released game species', *Review of 2012*, Game and Wildlife Conservation Trust (2013)

20. Peter Robertson, et al., 'Pheasant release in Great Britain: long-term and large-scale changes in the survival of a managed bird', *European Journal of Wildlife Research*, Vol. 63 (2017)

21. British Trust for Ornithology (BTO) 'BirdTrends' online species entry, 'Pheasant': https://app.bto.org/birdtrends/species.jsp?s=pheas&year=2018

22. British Trust for Ornithology (BTO) press release, 'Increases in general predator populations are associated with pheasant releases', 2 July 2019

23. R.B. Sage, et al., 'The flora and structure of farmland hedges and hedgebanks near to pheasant release pens compared to other hedges', *Biological Conservation*, 2009

24. J.H. Neumann, et al., 'Releasing of pheasants for shooting in the UK alters woodland invertebrate communities', *Biological Conservation*, Vol. 191, 2015

25. Game and Wildlife Conservation Trust news item, 21 January 2019: https://www.gwct.org.uk/news/news/2019/january/shoots-urged-to-pay-more-attention-to-release-pen-locations,-says-new-gwct-study/

26. *The Field*, 5 August 2020, 'Churchill's Guns: the personal armoury of Winston Churchill': https://www.thefield.co.uk/shooting/churchills-guns-the-personal-armoury-of-sir-winston-churchill-44492

27. *Shooting Gazette*, 19 June 2007, 'Partridge and Pheasant Shooting in Salisbury': https://www.shootinguk.co.uk/shooting/game-shooting/pheasant-shooting/partridge-and-pheasant-shooting-in-salisbury-13205

28. British Trust for Ornithology press release, July 2019: https://www.bto.org/press-releases/increases-generalist-predator-populations-are-associated-pheasant-releases

29. Roger Draycott, Andrew Hoodless and Rufus Sage (2007), 'Effects of pheasant management on vegetation and birds in lowland woodlands', *Journal of Applied Ecology*, Vol. 45

30. Natural England, 'Environmental impacts of land management' (NERR030, September 2009): http://publications.naturalengland.org.uk/publication/30026

31. http://www.shootingfacts.co.uk/pdf/The-Value-of-Shooting-2014.pdf

32. Megan Murgatroyd, et al., 'Patterns of satellite tagged hen harrier disappearances suggest widespread illegal killing on British grouse moors', *Nature Communications*, March 2019

33. Game and Wildlife Conservation Trust: https://www.gwct.org.uk/wildlife/research/birds/raptors/hen-harrier/hen-harriers-and-grouse/

34. The Langholm Moor Demonstration Project: http://www.langholmproject.com/

35. DEFRA policy paper, 14 January 2016: https://www.gov.uk/government/publications/increasing-hen-harrier-populations-in-england-action-plan

36. Natural England press release: https://www.gov.uk/government/news/innovative-licence-issued-to-help-hen-harrier

37. Mark Avery, personal blog: https://markavery.info/2018/01/17/brood-meddling-mad-muddle/

38. Natural England blog: https://naturalengland.blog.gov.uk/2020/05/22/hen-harrier-brood-management-trial-licence-renewed/

39. Isla Hodgson, 'Raptors and grouse', *BBC Wildlife Magazine*, April 2019

Chapter 6

1. Jon Mooallem, *Wild Ones* (Penguin, 2014)

2. Jon Mooallem podcast, 'Wild Ones': https://earthjustice.org/features/ourwork/down-to-earth-dressing-up-in-bird-costumes

3. William Turner, Avium praecipuarum, quarum apud Plinium et Aristotelem mentio est, brevis et succincta historia (Gymnicus, Cologne, 1544), English translation: A.H. Evans (ed.), *Turner on Birds: A Short and*

Succinct History of the Principal Birds Noticed by Pliny and Aristotle (Cambridge University Press, 2014)

4. George Turberville, *The Booke of Faulconrie or Hauking* for the onely delight and pleasure of all Noblemen & Gentlemen. Collected out of the best Aucthors [sic] as well Italian as Frenchmen and some English practices withall concerning Faulconrie, etc. (London, 1575)
5. Zoological Society of London (ZSL) blog: https://www.zsl.org/blogs/science/red-kite-health-surveillance-in-england-playing-detective
6. Disease Risk Analysis and Health Surveillance (DRAHS) project, ZSL/Natural England: https://www.zsl.org/science/research/drahs
7. RSPB Raptor Persecution Map: https://www.arcgis.com/apps/opsdashboard/index.html#/0f04dd3b78e544d9a6175b7435ba0f8c
8. Fieke Molenaar, et al., 'Poisoning of reintroduced red kites (*Milvus milvus*) in England', *European Journal of Wildlife Research*, Vol. 63, Issue 6, December 2017
9. https://www.shropshirestar.com/news/crime/2020/04/22/investigation-over-red-kite-killings/
10. Melanie Orros, blog post, 'Why are so many red kites visiting our towns?': https://www.bou.org.uk/red-kites-back-in-town/
11. https://www.bucksfreepress.co.uk/news/16149576.pictures-rspb-warns-against-feeding-red-kites-after-toddlers-giulia-and-luca-viarnaud-from-marlow-attacked-in-higginson-park/
12. https://www.oxfordmail.co.uk/news/17564596.oxfordshire-wildlife-trust-warns-people-not-feed-red-kites-attacks/
13. Rachel Taylor, personal communication
14. Mark Anthony, personal communication
15. National Wildlife Crime Unit, 'Animal of the Month: White-tailed Eagle': https://www.nwcu.police.uk/animal-of-the-month/white-tailed-eagle/
16. M. Marquiss, et al, 'The Impact of White-tailed Eagles on Sheep Farming on Mull', Scottish government report, now archived at: https://www.webarchive.org.uk/wayback/archive/3000/https://www.gov.scot/resource/doc/47060/0014566.pdf
17. National Animal Disease Information Service: https://www.nadis.org.uk/
18. Farming UK online article, 23 January 2017: https://www.farminguk.com/news/15-000-sheep-were-killed-by-loose-dogs-in-2016-figures-show_45404.html
19. Adele Waters, 'Helping Prevent Sheep Attacks', *Veterinary Record*, Vol. 180, Issue 13, March 2017
20. Scottish Crofting Federation news item,'Crofting Federation greets SNH admission that sea eagles do kill healthy lambs', 4 June 2019
21. *Herald* Scotland online edition news item, 11 February 2020: https://www.heraldscotland.com/news/18225792.call-protection-livestock-sea-eagles-prey-healthy-lambs/

22. Andrew McCornick, President, National Farmers' Union of Scotland, quoted in an NFU Scotland news article/press release No.79/19, 31 May 2019: https://www.nfus.org.uk/news/news/union-welcomes-plan-for-white-tailed-eagles

23. David Sexton, personal communication

Chapter 7

1. Zoological Society of London (ZSL) presentation, 'What's Killing the Killer Whales', February 2016

2. BBC Radio 4, *A Life With* ... Series 6, Episode 5, 'Seals': https://www.bbc.co.uk/programmes/b01djrph

3. Secretariat of the Convention on Biological Diversity, 'Impacts of Marine Debris on Diversity', CBD Technical Series No. 67

4. United Nations report, 'Abandoned, lost or otherwise discarded fishing gear', FAO Fisheries and Aquaculture Technical Paper 523/UNEP Regional Seas Reports and Studies 185

5. Letter in *Newcastle Evening Chronicle*, November 1964

6. Hansard, 'Conservation of Seals Bill', House of Commons debate, 12 December 1969: https://api.parliament.uk/historic-hansard/commons/1969/dec/12/conservation-of-seals-bill#S5CV0793P0_19691212_HOC_19

7. ibid.

8. ibid.

9. Scottish government, 'Marine Licensing: Seal Licensing': https://www2.gov.scot/Topics/marine/Licensing/SealLicensing/appgraph

10. United Nations Food and Agriculture Organisation (FAO), 'General situation of world fish stocks': http://www.fao.org/newsroom/common/ecg/1000505/en/stocks.pdf

11. Law Society of Scotland, 'The cruel sea: why Scottish salmon farming law must change': https://www.lawscot.org.uk/members/journal/issues/vol-64-issue-08/salmon-farming-law-must-change/

12. Essex Live online news item, 'Two pregnant seals found shot': https://www.essexlive.news/news/essex-news/seals-found-shot-dead-walton-2418928

13. John Vidal, 'Salmon farming in crisis', *Guardian* online, 1 April 2017: https://www.theguardian.com/environment/2017/apr/01/is-farming-salmon-bad-for-the-environment

14. Sea Shepherd YouTube channel: https://www.youtube.com/watch?v=Uk0gC5vtWXg

15. Scottish Wild Salmon Co. video: https://www.youtube.com/watch?v=Pe5vzbSsgeA

16. https://inews.co.uk/news/uk/thousands-of-tonnes-of-fish-still-thrown-away-at-sea-as-britain-fails-to-enforce-ban-to-conserve-stocks-report-255692

17. RTE news item: 'Kerry fishermen renew call for immediate seal cull', 20 January 2020: https://www.rte.ie/news/munster/2020/0127/1111264-seal-cull/
18. Jennifer E. Houle, et al., 'Effects of seal predation on a modelled marine fish community and consequences for a commercial fishery', *Journal of Applied Ecology*, 2015
19. David Thomson, *The People of the Sea* (Turnstile Press, 1954)
20. Sheila S. Anderson, et al., 'Mortality in Grey Seal pups: incidence and causes', *Journal of Zoology*, Vol. 189, No. 3, August 2009
21. E. Bevacqua, et al., 'Higher probability of compound flooding from precipitation and storm surge in Europe under anthropogenic climate change', *Science Advances*, Vol. 5, No. 9, September 2019
22. YouTube footage, 'North Cliffs Failure': https://youtu.be/ZVjr4mii3cE

Chapter 8

1. Portia Simpson, *The Gamekeeper* (Simon & Schuster, 2017)
2. David Stephen, *The World Outside* (Gordon Wright, 1983)
3. Kenneth Richmond, *Highland Gathering* (Bles, 1960)
4. https://clanchattan.org.uk/
5. Benjamin Jones, personal communication
6. L.K. Corbett, 'Feeding ecology and social organisation of wildcats and domestic cats in Scotland', PhD thesis (University of Aberdeen, 1979)
7. Pedro Sarmento, 'Feeding ecology of the European wildcat *Felis silvestris* in Portugal', *Acta Theriologica* 41 (1996)
8. Royal Zoological Society of Scotland, RZSS Conservation Projects, 'Scottish Wildcats': https://www.rzss.org.uk/conservation/our-projects/project-search/zoo-based/scottish-wildcats/, and: F. Mathews, et al., 'A Review of the Population and Conservation Status of British Mammals: Technical Summary. A report by the Mammal Society under contract to Natural England, Natural Resources Wales and Scottish Natural Heritage' (Natural England, 2018)
9. PDSA Animal Wellbeing PAW Report, 2019
10. Roo Campbell, personal communication
11. George Monbiot, personal communication
12. International Union for Conservation of Nature, Peter Jackson and Kristin Nowell, *Wild Cats: status survey and conservation action plan* (IUCN, 1996)
13. Roo Campbell, personal communication
14. S.A. Walton, 'Theophrastus on Lyngurium: medieval and early modern lore from the classical lapidary tradition', *Annals of Science*, Vol. 58 No.4, October 2001
15. Ted Hughes, 'A Lynx', in *Under the North Star* (Faber and Faber, 1981). Reproduced with permission from the publisher

16. Jos M. Milner and R. Justin Irvine, 'The potential for reintroduction of Eurasian lynx to Great Britain: a summary of the evidence' (British Deer Society, 2015)

17. J-O. Helldin et al., 'Lynx (*Lynx lynx*) killing red foxes (*Vulpes vulpes*) in boreal Sweden – Frequency and population effects', *Journal of Zoology*, Vol. 270, No. 4, July 2006

18. https://www.petercairnsphotography.com/conservation-communication/tooth-and-claw

19. Marc Baldwin, Wildlife Online: https://www.wildlifeonline.me.uk/questions/answer/should-we-reintroduce-wolf-and-lynx-to-control-foxes

20. George Monbiot, *Feral: Rewilding the Land, the Sea, and Human Life* (University of Chicago Press, 2014)

21. Aldo Leopold, 'Thinking Like a Mountain – wolves and deforestation': http://www.uky.edu/OtherOrgs/AppalFor/Readings/leopold.pdf

Chapter 9

1. Peter Cairns, personal communication

2. Aldo Leopold, 'The Land Ethic', essay in *A Sand County Almanac* (Oxford University Press, 1949)

3. Walter Scott, 'On Tweed River', in *The Complete Works of Walter Scott* (e-artnow, 2015)

4. John Milton, *Paradise Lost* (Penguin Classics, 2003)

5. Environment Agency press release: https://www.gov.uk/government/news/almost-2-million-fish-released-into-englands-rivers

6. John J. Magnuson, et al., 'Historical Trends in Lake and River Ice Cover in the Northern Hemisphere', *Science*, Vol. 289, 8 September 2000

7. British Ecological Society online, Dr Stuart Middlemass, 'Understanding the decline of Atlantic salmon catches in Scotland', 10 May 2019: https://www.britishecologicalsociety.org/understanding-decline-atlantic-salmon-catches-scotland/

8. Tweed News, 'Official 2019 Tweed catch sees a small improvement on the previous season': https://www.rivertweed.org.uk/news/?p=6658

9. https://www.birdguides.com/news/more-licences-sought-to-shoot-cormorants-and-goosanders/

10. World Wide Fund for Nature, 'Living Planet Report 2020': https://livingplanet.panda.org

11. William J. Ripple, et al., 'Status and Ecological Effects of the World's Largest Carnivores', *Science*, Vol. 343, 10 January 2014

12. Ross Barnett, *The Missing Lynx: The Past and Future of Britain's Lost Mammals* (Bloomsbury, 2019)

13. R.M. Pyle, 'The extinction of experience', *Horticulture*, Vol. 56 (1978)

14. Edward O. Wilson, *A Window on Eternity: A Biologist's Walk Through Gorongosa National Park* (Simon & Schuster, 2014)

15. Barbara Kingsolver, *Animal Dreams* (Harper Perennial, 1990)

Index